PARKS, PRESERVES, AND RIVERS

A Guide to Outdoor Adventures in Virginia's Capital Region

Louise L. Burke and Keith F. Ready
The Metropolitan Foundation

PARKS, PRESERVES, AND RIVERS
A Guide to Outdoor Adventures in Virginia's Capital Region

Copyright © 1985 by The Metropolitan Foundation. All rights reserved.

Co-sponsored by the Department of Recreation, Virginia Commonwealth University

Book designed by Communication Design, Inc./Richmond
Manufactured in the United States of America
The paper in this book is 80 lb. Curtis Brightwater, and has been made available through the generous cooperation of the James River Corporation.

Library of Congress Cataloging in Publication Data
Burke, Louise L., 1921–
   Parks, preserves, and rivers.

   Bibliography: p.
   Includes index.
   1. Outdoor recreation—Virginia—Richmond region—Guide-books. I. Ready, Keith F., 1947–   . II. Title.
GV191.42.V8B87   1985   333.78′025′755   85-13888
ISBN 0-9615016-0-X

Photographs by Louise Burke, unless otherwise noted
Maps supervised by Keith Ready
Drawings by Dick Bernard, unless otherwise noted
Typesetting by William Byrd Press, Inc./Richmond
Printing by Whittet and Shepperson, Printers/Richmond

The Guide is dedicated to all those whose contributions made it possible.

The contributions of the following are gratefully acknowledged. Without their support and encouragement, this Guide would not have been possible.

Bank of Virginia
Best Products Co. Inc.
Chesapeake Corporation
C & P Telephone Company. Inc.
Consolidated Bank and Trust Co.
CSX Corporation
Ethyl Corporation
First and Merchants National Bank
James River Corporation
Media General
Philip Morris USA
Pollard & Bagby, Inc.
Elizabeth Roszell
Safeway Stores, Inc.
Mr. and Mrs. S. Buford Scott
Sovran Bank, N.A.
Mr. and Mrs. Stanley Steelman
Ukrop's Super Markets, Inc.
United Virginia Bank
Virginia Power
Virginia Commonwealth University, Center for Public Affairs
Virginia Commonwealth University, Department of Recreation
Arthur Young & Company

Chesterfield County, Virginia
City of Richmond, Virginia
Henrico County, Virginia (Industrial Development Authority)
Department of Tourism, City of Petersburg, Virginia

Acknowledgements

The authors and The Metropolitan Foundation wish to acknowledge and thank our co-sponsor, the Virginia Commonwealth University, Department of Recreation, and Dr. Charles Hartsoe, Chairman, for continuing support throughout this project. Special mention must be made of the initial research grants made by the Maymont Foundation and the Virginia Commonwealth University Department of Recreation and Center for Public Affairs. The authors are also grateful to those whose contributions to The Metropolitan Foundation made it possible to carry the field guide project to completion, and to Raymond Szabo, whose faith sustained us.

Many agency personnel have given generously of their time and expertise, accompanying us on field trips, furnishing us with information, helping with maps, answering endless questions over the phone, and reviewing submitted text. Our special thanks to those individuals and the administration of the following agencies and institutions.

> Charles City Recreation and Parks Department
> Chesterfield County Parks and Recreation Department
> Colonial Heights Department of Recreation and Parks
> Hanover County Department of Parks and Recreation
> Henrico County Division of Recreation and Parks
> Hopewell Department of Recreation and Parks
> Lewis Ginter Botanical Garden, Inc.
> Maymont Foundation
> City of Petersburg Department of Recreation
> City of Petersburg Department of Tourism
> Prince George Department of Recreation
> City of Richmond Department of Recreation and Parks
> U.S. Department of the Interior
>   Harrison Lake Fish Hatchery
>   Petersburg National Battlefield
>   Presquile National Wildlife Refuge
>   Richmond National Battlefield Park
> Valentine Museum
> Virginia Division of Forestry
> Virginia Commission on Game and Inland Fisheries
> Virginia Division of Parks and Recreation

We are also indebted to Susan McGarry for assisting in the initial Tri-Cities inventory, Dr. William E. Trout, III, for information and verifying text on the James River and Kanawha Canal, Thomas T. Brady, Sergei Troubetskoy, and Dulaney Ward for historical background on several sites, Ann Woodlief for moral support and her patience in editing the last draft of the manuscript, and last, but certainly not least, Frederic A. Fay, Executive Director of The Metropolitan Foundation, without whose faith and continued support in every way the Guide would never have materialized.

Contents

Introduction

Section I - An Introduction to the Natural History of the Region

Chapter 1 - The Changing Landscape	11
Chapter 2 - Plant Communities	20
Chapter 3 - Wildlife	37
Chapter 4 - The Prehistoric Indians of the Region	53

Section II - On and Along the Waterways

Fishing, Boating, and Floating	63
The James River	68
The Appomattox River	78
The Chickahominy River	83
The North and South Anna and Pamunkey Rivers	86
The Lakes	93
Resources	94

Section III - A Directory of the Parks and Preserves

National Preserves

Harrison Lake Fish Hatchery	101
Presquile National Wildlife Refuge	104
(See Also National Battlefield Parks below.)	

State Parks and Preserves

Chickahominy Wildlife Management Area	107
Pocahontas State Park and Forest	111
Powhatan Wildlife Management Area	117

Special Places

The Chesapeake Corporation Nature Trail	120
The Lewis Ginter Botanical Garden	122

Local Parks and Preserves

Richmond Metropolitan Area	
Richmond	124
Chesterfield County	196
Henrico County	218

The Tri-Cities Metropolitan Area
    Petersburg   *237*
    Colonial Heights   *246*
    Hopewell   *248*

Rural Counties
    Hanover   *250*
    Prince George   *253*
    Charles City   *254*

The National Battlefield Parks

Richmond National Battlefield Park   *256*
Petersburg National Battlefield   *273*
City Point Unit   *278*

Index   282

Map Legend
(Inside back cover)

Riverbank

Introduction

Virginia's Capital Region abounds in parks, preserves, and rivers, many of them so little known, they amount to hidden treasures. The *Guide to Outdoor Adventures* was written for those who would like to discover them and enjoy them to the fullest.

In many parks, in all the preserves, and along the waterways, the most outstanding features are their natural environments. These are beautiful, especially in the leafy seasons, but beyond that, to those with some understanding of the region's natural history, they are also extremely interesting to visit and observe.

To enhance the pleasure of exploring the natural areas, Section I provides *An Introduction to the Natural History of the Region*. Chapters written by naturalists interpret the landforms, habitats, plants, and wildlife found in many of the places described in subsequent sections.

Another aspect of the region's natural history has to do with its earliest inhabitants. It is intriguing to realize that Indians inhabited the region for over 13,000 years. As we walk in their footsteps today, in the vestiges of their natural world, we may well wonder how they lived as individuals and societies. Archeological digs are providing fascinating clues to their lifestyles and changing cultures over thousands of years. Chapter 4 of Section I narrates some of these findings.

The rivers and lakes of the region include outstanding fishing and canoeing waters. Section II - *Along the Waterways* - traces and describes the rivers, locates the lakes, pinpoints access areas, and answers some general fishing and boating questions.

Section III - *A Directory of Parks and Preserves* is intended for browsing and choosing, to help visitors find their way around the larger sites (see maps), and to make sure that special attractions will not be overlooked. In our descriptions, we have emphasized the significant preserves, major parks, and unique features worth going out of one's way to find, but neighborhood parks are also included for those who live nearby.

The parks and preserves vary greatly in character. As a whole, they offer something for everyone, and a great deal for those who like variety. Choices include grand old-fashioned landscaped parks; gardens to admire (or cultivate); paths for strolling, jogging, or biking; trails for hiking or horseback riding; places to picnic, play ball, or relax; wonderful places for children, of course; historic sites in the out-of-doors; those natural areas to explore, and much, much more.

Discoveries are one kind of adventure; good times are another. We wish our readers the joy of both in the parks, preserves, and rivers.

L.L.B. and K.F.R. April, 1985.
Richmond, Virginia

Section I

An Introduction to the Natural History of the Region

Bald Eagle

CHAPTER 1

The Changing Landscape

by Marijean H. Hawthorne, PhD

Many of the parks, preserves, and rivers of Capital region offer fascinating glimpses into its geology, particularly if one has a little knowledge to help understand what is seen. Landforms, rivers, and the direction in which they flow, the soils in which the plants grow, and the rocky foundation of the earth's crust, sometimes seen in outcroppings and stones on the surface, are all manifestations of geology, the science of the earth.

We know that life on earth's thin crust within the envelope of air we call atmosphere depends on many natural conditions, including a tolerable climate, soil, water, and interdependent plants and animals, and that the human race thrives best on optimal conditions. The human history of the region, from the Indians to the early colonists and on up to modern times, has been influenced to a great extent by the environment in which ordinary people found themselves, and the natural resources available to them.

As you visit the parks and natural areas, and explore the rivers, consider how the basic structure of the earth's crust and its movements have influenced the development of these landforms, forests, swamps, marshes, and waterways, and how these in turn have influenced history.

Scientists today know a great deal about the geology of the region. To the Indians and the early settlers, however, their discoveries were simpler and mainly geared to the business of living with the land.

When the English first explored west along the James River, less than ten days after they landed at Jamestown Island, they found a land with climate and vegetation very different from those in England. The river flowed through a park-like forest of oak and other hardwood species, interspersed with pine in the sandier soils. Because of the Indian practice of setting fire to the woods at fairly frequent intervals (to improve browse for deer and visibility for the hunter), there was very little underbrush. The trees must have seemed an immensely valuable resource to the English, who had essentially run out of wood for ships, buildings, and industrial processes.

At the falls of the James, the Englishmen were immediately struck by the potential of the rapids to operate water wheels. Grist and flour mills, as well as sawmills, were vital to the economy of the time, and the first report by Captain Newport to King James emphasizes the possibilities of harnessing the power of the rapids.

Captain Newport was also impressed by the suitability of the James for navigation as far west as the falls. The river offered a route into the interior of the new land,

and easy transport for goods produced along the river's edge.

The James River is the most striking feature of the Capital Region. After cutting through the Blue Ridge Mountains, the James flows eastward through the Piedmont "geologic province," a rolling landscape drained by numerous streams, and across the fall zone to the Coastal Plain and the sea. The parks, preserves, and rivers of the Capital Region extend from the Piedmont into the Coastal Plain, and exhibit the characteristics of both provinces, as well as the fall zone. When you visit them with an eye for geology, you will notice many interesting features that might otherwise escape your attention.

Granite Outcroppings - Maymont Park

12

Much of the Piedmont is covered with deep soil from weathered bedrock and sediments carried down from the mountains by streams. Underlying the Piedmont and the fall zone (sometimes called the fall line), exposed in many of the parks and along the falls of the James and Appomattox Rivers, are very old and highly weathered igneous, sedimentary, and metamorphic rocks.

Igneous rocks are those which were once molten, whether they cooled below the earth's surface (for instance, granite), or above ground (lava.) Much of the exposed rock you see along the Falls of the James and Appomattox Rivers, in outcroppings, quarries, and highway cuts is granite. Good examples of exposed granite may be seen in the James River and Appomattox River Parks, Maymont, Forest Hill, Powhite, Rockwood, Point of Rocks, and Pocahontas State Park, among other places. Granite from local quarries can also be seen in many public buildings and in the walls of the old James River and Kanawha Canal.

Sedimentary rocks may be found throughout the Capital Region. These may be defined as everything that washes downhill or settles out of water in rivers, lakes, or oceans, and has over time been consolidated and cemented into rock. Sandstone originates from sand, shale from mud, and limestones from deposits of seashells and microscopic organisms containing calcium carbonate.

Any and all of these igneous and sedimentary rocks can be changed (metamorphosed) into different rock types by time, pressure, and heat, resulting in gneiss or schist from granite, quartzite from sandstone, slate from shale, and (not found in this area) marble from limestone. Quartzite was used by Indians of the region for making arrowheads. Point of Rocks Park, where a great deal of quartzite is lying around on the surface, is known to have been the site of an Indian encampment, and many arrowheads have been found there.

In crossing the Piedmont on their way to the sea, the rivers fall at the slow rate of 1-2 feet per mile, cutting their way to bedrock, occasionally depositing alluvium (sediment), which is washed away by subsequent flooding. Small flood plains have been created along the river banks, with the fertile alluvial soils making the gamble - no flood this year - attractive to farmers planting crops on them. On the ridges between the rivers soils are relatively infertile because the nutrients have been leached out - carried by rain water to lower ground. The early settlers establishing farms in the Piedmont preferred the richer soils of the flood plains, even though they were flooded out some years, and only gradually moved to the ridges when all the preferred land was taken. The houses were built on higher ground than the fields to protect them from flooding.

In the Piedmont just west of Richmond, the James River cuts across what is known as the Richmond Triassic Basin, one of the oldest of a series of elongated basins stretching from Nova Scotia in Canada to South Carolina. This basin, extending some thirty miles in a north-south direction and nine miles wide at its widest point, is located in western Henrico and central Chesterfield County above the fall zone. Recent discoveries confirming the theories of continental drift also explain how these basins were created, and dating of fossil pollens and spores places the

Richmond Basin in a geological period called the Triassic, about 210 million years ago, when the North American and African continents on their separate tectonic plates were welded together and beginning to pull apart, creating the Atlantic Ocean between them. The effect of this pulling apart was experienced not only where the continents separated, but also further inland, creating deep depressions which were then filled with sediments from streams, lakes, and swamps to a depth of 2,500 to 3,000 feet.

Organic materials, mainly dead plants, buried and decaying in oxygen-poor environments, were converted to coal in the lower part of the basin, as much as twelve feet deep in some areas, but more commonly only one to two feet in depth. We know that this happened in the age of dinosaurs, because dinosaur tracks have been found in other Triassic basins, although not in that of the Richmond Basin. Sediments deposited on top of the decaying plants created layers of sandstone, shale, and some limestones.

Coal was little used by the early English settlers, although they recognized its presence as early as 1700, for coal had been mined in England for several hundred years. They knew its value as a fuel, but in the new world wood was both plentiful and easily available, so the first commercial mining did not begin until 1748. By 1750 a combination of declining wood supply in industrial areas and new technologies that could substitute coal for wood or charcoal made commercial coal mining economically attractive, and a new industry was born. By 1800 coal from the Richmond Basin, used for domestic heating and industrial processes, was shipped to New York, Philadephia, Baltimore, New England, and even the West Indies. Several open pit mines, as well as shaft mines, were operated in Henrico and Chesterfield Counties. Deep Run Park is located in the Triassic Basin, and coal was mined there. Where the mines were considerably higher than the river, as in Midlothian, the coal was transported by gravity in carts on rails. An interesting sidelight - Thomas Jefferson allowed only Black Heath coal from Chesterfield County to be used in the White House.

An important and unusual component of this trade was the mining and exporting of natural coke, found only in the Richmond Triassic Basin. Coke is the product of coal which has been intensely heated in an oxygen-poor environment, with the result that the volatile gasses have been driven off. It burns with a very high heat, and for this reason was very valuable in smelting iron, which had also been found in sufficient quantity in the region. Coal could not be used in the iron furnaces of the time because the hot gasses combined with the molten metal and weakened it. Charcoal could be used, but coke was better. Coke was even shipped to England.

Shortly after the English arrived in Virginia they began to mine and smelt a high quality sedimentary iron ore from the swampland clays at Falling Creek. Unfortunately these first furnaces were destroyed and the expert smelters killed in the Indian massacre of 1622. Iron furnaces were among the first important enterprises of the colonists because they made it possible to use the native iron ore to make the implements they needed for farming, wagon and building hardware, and utensils, rather than importing all of these from England. Unfortunately, the Falling

Creek furnace was buried under a construction project in 1963; however, in one of those emergency digs that are undertaken in such instances, its foundations were uncovered, and a number of artifacts were recovered.

The fall zone is a north-south band of resistant bedrock, mainly granite, extending from New Jersey to Georgia, and varying in width from two to fifteen miles. The Petersburg granite, as this bedrock is known in the Capital Region, is about 330 million years old and is believed to be evidence of the collision of two crustal ("tectonic") plates. About 500 million years ago several of these plates, with continents and oceans riding on them, began to drift together, with the oceans diving under them. By 350 million years ago, the North American and African plates had fully collided, with the lighter North American plate riding up over the African crust. The African plate was pushed and pulled down into the earth's mantle underneath, and as the rock heated from the friction and pressure, the sediments of the African crust melted and squeezed upward into the crust of the North American plate through deep faults or cracks. These "intrusions" are called "plutons."

In cutting across the fall zone, the James River drops some 100 feet in seven miles, reaching sea level at the 14th Street Bridge. Both the James and Appomattox Rivers expose the bedrock in their channels in a series of rapids and falls, interrupted by boulders resting on the bedrock. The Falls of the Appomattox are partially concealed in a narrow, natural ravine, but The Falls of the James, readily seen all the way through the City of Richmond, create spectacular scenery and a wonderful

Pluton Along the Falls of the James

opportunity to observe the marvelous phenomenon of African rocks in a setting as American as apple pie. The Chickahominy, a younger river, crosses the fall zone on a more gradual gradient because it has not cut through to bedrock.

Changes in sea level over millions of years have also shaped the land in the Capital Region. The movements of the crustal plates, and later the successive growth and shrinking of the polar ice caps and continental glaciers, caused the sea level to rise and fall several times. As the ocean rose, the Coastal Plain became a shallow sea, and the mouths of the rivers were located as far west as the upper level of the fall zone. During these periods the rivers slowed and spread out as they approached the sea, and in so doing, deposited a great deal of sediment in their flood plains. During the periods when the sea level fell, as much as 300 feet, the Coastal Plain was exposed beyond and below the present coast, and the gradients of the river beds steepened, with the result that they cut deeply into the sediment, creating steep banks, or scarps that can still be seen today. Chimborazo Park is an excellent place from which to see several of these scarps and terraced ancient flood plains south of the James, if you can mentally erase the man-made features covering the land, and recognize the major landforms. (These may best be seen from late fall to early spring when the vegetation doesn't obscure the view.) The physiographic map of Richmond below will help to explain what you are seeing.

As it approaches the fall line, the James River first cuts through an area known as the Midlothian Upland at an elevation of 400 feet to the Chippenham Scarp, an old riverbank, elevation about 300 feet. The step-like series of five terraces are made up of old valley fill deposits. These are the ancient floodplains of the ancestral James,

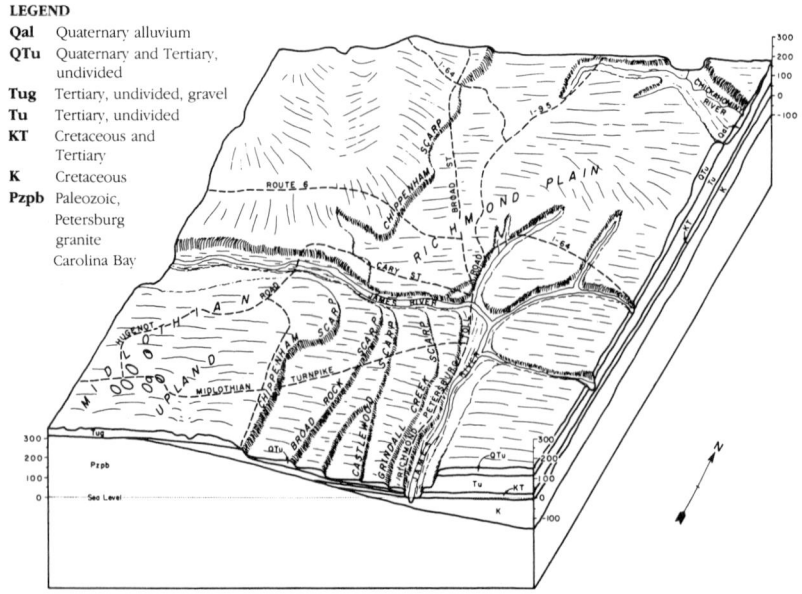

LEGEND
Qal   Quaternary alluvium
QTu   Quaternary and Tertiary, undivided
Tug   Tertiary, undivided, gravel
Tu   Tertiary, undivided
KT   Cretaceous and Tertiary
K   Cretaceous
Pzpb Paleozoic, Petersburg granite
      Carolina Bay

Physiographic Map of Richmond

created during the periods when the ocean advanced. The scarps below each terrace were the banks or shorelines cut by the ancient James when the sea level fell. Several other scarps were cut by the ancestral James and the Appomattox and Chickahominy Rivers as they flowed eastward through old flood plains and ocean sediments. Good examples are Chickahominy Bluff, Drewry's Bluff (both of the Richmond National Battlefield Park) and Point of Rocks Park in Chesterfield County.

From the lower (eastern) end of the fall zone to the ocean stretches the Coastal Plain, a wedge of sediments deposited by the rivers and the ocean during periodic invasions. Among the sediments deposited by the ocean were seashells. Rich deposits of fossil shells are found in many parts of the Coastal Plain in particular. One place to see these is along the Chesapeake Nature Trail in New Kent County. The trail guide pamphlet calls attention to an uprooted tree with seashells adhering to its roots, and comments that the hills of the entire area are underlain with marl (soil containing limestone and shell) deposits, which were mined for fertilizer by farmers in the 1920s and 1930s.

Of great interest to paleontolgists, who study ancient forms of life, are the fossiliferous banks of a little creek called Lieutenant's Run in Petersburg, which are virtually encrusted with shells, including many extinct species, indicating depositions by the sea some fifteen million years ago. (The creek is not within a park, but anyone seriously interested in these fossils can arrange for a tour by calling the Petersburg Department of Recreation and Parks or the Department of Tourism.)

Notice on any map how the Chickahominy, James, and Appomattox Rivers take an abrupt turn southward at the foot of the fall zone. It is believed that they are following a course of weakened rock along a series of faults where the Coastal Plain and fall zone meet. You can see this turn of the James from the hilltop parks in Church Hill - Chimborazo, Libbie, Taylor's, and Powhatan. Drewry's Bluff (See Battlefield Parks) is probably the southern end of the fault along which the James River flows. The fault which causes the Appomattox to turn can be seen at Point of Rocks Park where Ashton Creek flows into the river.

Beginning at the foot of the falls, the rivers become tidal. Flowing slowly from here to the sea, they take on a different character, and you can see several active geological processes going on, as well as the patterns of older changes and manmade alterations. Among the most interesting geological phenomena along the James River are three "oxbows", created by meanders. One of these, a sort of double oxbow at Dutch Gap, can be seen from Fort Brady in Henrico County. In time you will be able to get an even better view of it from a high point in the soon-to-be developed Henrico City Historical Park in Chesterfield County across the way. Another oxbow curls around Jones Neck and may be seen from Deep Bottom Landing in Henrico County. The third nearly surrounds Presquile National Wildlife Refuge on what is now called Turkey Island. Each of these was a hindrance to navigation until the Corps of Engineers cut across the narrow necks of land around which the river flowed, creating the Dutch Gap, Jones Neck, and Turkey Island Cutoffs.

Marshes—wetlands characterized by grasses—(see Chapter 2) are created along the meander necks of the rivers and their tributaries in the Coastal Plain. Among the parks and preserves where marshes may be found are Point of Rocks in Chesterfield County, Vawter Street Park in Henrico County, the Chickahominy Wildlife Management Area (along Morris Creek), and Presquile National Wildlife Management Area. Swamps, characterized by standing water with trees growing in it (mainly Black Gum and Bald Cypress), are found primarily along the Chickahominy River. The closest you can get to one is probably in Vawter Street Park.

Swings of the rivers and creeks cause undercutting of the banks where the water hits with the greatest force, and "point bar deposition" on the opposite banks. Look for these phenomena where ever you see bends. One example on a small scale may be found along Herring Creek on the nature trail at the Lake Harrison Fish Hatchery, interpreted by a charming sign made by a group of Youth Conservation Corps youngsters as a project one summer. Several of the massive point bars along the river have been mined for their sand and gravel deposits, and the ensuing effects of tides and storm wash have partially refilled the excavations with new sediments.

The early English colonists cleared much of the forest for crops, including not only those grown for food, but also for tobacco. Settlement was concentrated along the river banks for the fertile alluvial soil, as well as for ease in transporting the harvest. Each plantation had its own shipping dock, such as Cobb's Wharf at Point of Rocks Park. Several boat landings in the region were once plantation docks. Water transport below the falls was relatively easy. From above the falls, tobacco might also be shipped by batteaux or double canoes. The James River and Kanawha Canal was a heavily used route until the railroads came into their own.

As is well known, the search for a profitable trade relationship with England soon led the settlers into a dependence on tobacco as a staple crop, with significant consequences for the environment. Tobacco turned out to be a greedy crop, robbing the soil of its nutrients. It did best on freshly cleared forest soils, which lost their fertility after three or four years. Planters therefore tried to accumulate large land holdings, and each year cleared a new plot for tobacco, allowing old plots to revert to scrub brush and later to forest. After twenty five or thirty years, a plot could be cleared and planted in tobacco again. Repeated tobacco culture, however, impoverished the soil for long periods of time, and the forests that grew back were not as fine as those that had been there originally. Selective cutting of the most valuable trees for buildings, ships, fences, and firewood also impoverished the forest.

Away from the river, with its easily available transportation of crops and goods, roads followed the ridges, avoiding the swampy bottom lands. Inland, planters rolled their tobacco to markets, turning the hogheads (barrels) on their sides, attaching spikes to the ends, and harnessing oxen or mules to roll them to the markets.

Settlement of the Piedmont replicated the soil-mining practices of the earlier

Coastal Plain plantations, but the falling yield of tobacco, coupled with new demands for wheat and flour for export, led most plantation owners in the Richmond area to switch to wheat as their major cash crop by 1820. Richmond became one of the major flour-milling centers in the country, shipping flour to Brazil and Australia, as well as to other areas of the United States.

In addition to the commercial flour mills, grist mills for grinding corn were closely spaced across the landscape. Because ground meal kept poorly in the hot and humid climate it was necessary to grind small amounts frequently; therefore ownership of a mill was a profitable occupation or sideline for many Virginians. Numerous parks within the region contain mill sites close to falling water; among these are the James River Park (Main Section), the Beaverdam and Gaines Mill units of the Battlefield Parks, Pocahontas State Park, and the Powhatan Wildlife Management Area.

Many modern developments, including roads and railroads, have changed the course of history in the region, but the major landforms and rivers have continued to influence human choices and destinies for many years, including Civil War strategies, victories and defeats, and modern land use planning and industrial decisions and operations. Today planners study the land, and governing bodies direct land use decisions, based on what is considered to be best use. Fortunately sometimes it is determined that the best use of an especially interesting, historical, or beautiful place is to be preserved as a park.

Suggested Reading and other Resources

The Making of a Continent, by Ron Redfern (Times Books) provides an interesting insight into the earth movements now referred to as plate tectonics, with examples in this region.

The Chesterfield County Museum at the County Courthouse has several exhibits relating to the life of the prehistoric Indians and early settlers in the area, and their influence on the changing landscape.

Dr. Hawthorne, is an Associate Professor of Geography at Virginia Commonwealth University, where she teaches courses in Cultural Geography.

CHAPTER 2

The Plant Communities of the Natural Parks and Preserves

with Miles F. Johnson, PhD

To the early English settlers, the landscape of colonial Virginia must have been a marvel to behold. Historians writing about Virginia in the 17th and 18th centuries tell of great forest canopies so dense that light could barely penetrate to the forest floor. Travellers commented on the gloom of the deep woods and their relief on passing out of them into the bright sunlight of clearings again.

They also found other habitats - marshes and swamps along the rivers of the coastal plain, and to the west of Richmond, where the native American Indians had burned some forest areas, newly opened land with reeds and grasses of incredible height. The plants provided shelter and food for flourishing communities of wildlife, and the Indians lived well on both. (See Chapter 4, The Indians of the Capital Region.)

The early settlers also had to live on the land for the most part, and to use existing plants for many of their needs. It has been reported that the region was known in colonial times for its variety of "simples" (medically useful plants) and dyeing-woods, and that the timber trees and fruits and nuts were especially abundant.

Those magnificent forests are long gone, and for centuries few thought to mourn their passing. (See Chapter 1 - *The Changing Landscape*.) Fortunately, however, today's society has begun to treasure our natural heritage. Natural parks and preserves (wildlife sanctuaries and game management areas) have been established to renew and preserve forested areas and marshes and swamps - wildlife habitats that might otherwise have given way to urban sprawl. Thousands of acres in the Capital Region support natural systems with hundreds of species of native plants in several types of habitats, changing with the seasons and the years.

Visiting Natural Areas

Most of the natural parks and preserves have trails which are fine for hiking. Even if you only enjoy the exercise in the fresh air, the beauty of the surroundings, and an occasional glimpse of birds or other wildlife as you go along, a few hours on the trail can be a very pleasant experience.

If, however, you also have an interest in natural history, these are wonderful places to explore as you go along. Taken all together, the natural parks and preserves support five different types of habitats, each with its own special plant community. Notice how they differ, and what happens where they meet, as they do in many of these areas.

Take a stroll through one of the forests. Stop to observe, smell, and listen to the natural world. Reach down and feel the rich humus between your fingers. Plan to return in another season to see the changes that have taken place; woods are a very changing habitat. Each plant species responds to seasonal changes according to its own characteristics and timetable. Visit a tidal marsh and a backwater swamp, and notice how they differ from the forest. Notice how the clearings - meadows and old fields - seem to be returning to forest. If you are not already an amateur naturalist, but you find yourself intrigued, you may be well on the way to becoming one.

Guided walks with naturalists are a very good way to get started. These outings are always informal and companionable, and the naturalist will point out many interesting plants and animals that you might not otherwise notice. Several park agencies and private organizations, including the Richmond Audubon Society, conduct nature walks of general or specific interest. Watch the calendars of events in the newspapers and on library counters and bulletin boards.

If you are on your own, or in charge of others, cultivate the art of observation - of *noticing* what you see. There is much of interest to observe in these natural areas, and the more you observe, the more interesting each object and phenomenon will become, and the more you will want to go on exploring.

Hundreds of native plant species make up the plant communities in the Capital Region. There is only space to mention a few examples here. If you are interested in identifying plants or animals, illustrated field guides are indispensable. Several good native plant guides are listed at the end of this chapter, along with the names of some organizations that may be of interest.

Habitats And Plant Succession

One of the most fascinating aspects of these natural areas is the "whole picture" in any given habitat, what might be called the dynamics of the ecosystems. While ecology is a complex science, anyone with a little understanding can get some idea of what is happening in a forest, old field, marsh, or swamp.

Different kinds of plants growing together in a given habitat or ecosystem constitute a plant community. This community, as a community of people, is a dynamic, continually changing association of plants influencing one another and the animals that use it for food and shelter. (See Chapter 3 - *Wildlife*.) Over a period of time, the kinds of plants in the community will change; some will die out and be replaced by others.

These changes have been studied since the turn of the century, and today we know that the outcome of change is not a matter of guess work, but is indeed predictable. Similar habitats, it can be predicted, will support similar communities.

The concept of a dynamic plant community is summed up in the phrase "plant succession." Plant succession results from changes in the environment brought about by the plants themselves. For example, shade is present under plants, and some plants cannot tolerate shade, and so cannot continue to grow in this habitat. Other more shade-tolerant plants will take the place of the sun-loving plants, and the community will change. Pines, for example, are sun-loving trees that will thrive in an old field, but die out when the returning hardwoods grow taller and cut off much of their sunlight. Also, as plants accumulate on a site, "litter" (dead plant material) will form, affecting soil temperatures and acidity, available soil nutrients will vary, and water run-off will be modified.

It is easy to realize, then, that all organisms in the habitat will be directly or indirectly affected by the plants. Changes in the environment will allow different kinds of plants to become established. Thus succession continues, rapidly in some habitats, and in others more slowly, but predictably producing the climax vegetation. It is nature's way of returning to normal. As the forest succession changes, there is also a predictable change in the species of animals that inhabit it.

As the community ages, the dominant plants start to take over; these can reproduce and establish themselves most successfully and because of competition for open space, prevent other plants from becoming established. Changes are slight, and instead of a dynamic community, the species composition is now more stable. A sort of equilibrium is attained. A climax community may continue indefinitely as individual plants that die are replaced by their own kind. Only natural disasters or drastic man-made alterations may cause enough change so that succession begins again.

Many of the habitats in this region have been severely disturbed in various ways; it may take many years for these to recover. Plant succession, however, will predictably result in climax vegetation in time where appropriate habitats are left undisturbed.

The climax forests of the past developed and stabilized over centuries. In them grew ancient trees of great size, younger trees coming along, and a flourishing "understory" of smaller plants. What we see in our parks and preserves today are mostly younger forests on their way to becoming climax plant communities. Every year brings changes to these forests. As you visit them, you can tell by the size of the largest trees and the preponderant species whether they are young, middle-aged, or old forests. There are even a few stands, for example on the Gaines Mill/Watt House nature trail, which may never have been cut, and are probably vestiges of an ancient forest. (See Section III - *Richmond National Battlefield Park.*) The older the forest, the more beautiful it is apt to be, but areas undergoing plant succession are very interesting.

In the Pony Pasture of the James River Park the meadow, a clearing which presently supports a riotous young plant community of grasses, wildflowers, shrubs, and vines, is rapidly being taken over by young white ash trees and ash-leaved maples, while the old forest east of the meadow changes very little. Controlled clearing is being carried out to maintain the meadow.

In Pocahontas State Park and Forest you can see forest plant succession in many stages, from an area (bordering the Grist Mill Bicycle Trail) that has recently been clear cut, through old fields to woods that have been left undisturbed for many years. The nature trail in the park goes through a forest that is approaching a climax state. Other protected forests in the region that are well on their way to reaching climax conditions include the Chesapeake Nature Trail in New Kent, Lee Park in Petersburg, Poor Farm Park in Hanover, Rockwood and Point of Rocks Parks in Chesterfield, and Powhite and Pocosham Parks in Richmond. Marshes and swamps that have been seriously disturbed also undergo plant succession if protected from further disturbance.

Upland Forests

Although there is no distinct line between upland and lowland forests, - indeed they often merge where wooded slopes meet floodplains or stream banks - upland forests flourish on high ground or well-drained slopes. Their plant communities are suited to this environment.

If succession continues, our geographic area can support a climax upland forest predominantly consisting of beech, tulip tree, oak, and hickory on the uplands. There may be as many as ten oak species and three hickory species making up the primary canopy - the tallest layer. In winter the beech trees are particularly beautiful, with their smooth grey bark and pale gold leaves lingering on the twigs until spring.

The chestnut, once a dominant tree in upland forests, was so afflicted by a bark fungus disease early in this century that it was almost completely wiped out, and today very few specimens may be found. Those that do grow from seeds or stumps that have survived seldom reach maturity before they too are struck by the disease and die. A number of young chestnuts may be seen in Lee Park in Petersburg growing naturally on the slopes above Wilcox Lake. Their prospects are dim, but they are interesting for their rarity. (Chestnuts may be recognized by their large, narrow, sharply toothed leaves, alternately arranged on the twig, upright clusters of tiny flowers appearing after the leaves, and the prickly husks of their nuts.)

In the summer deciduous woods take on a noticeable four-layered pattern, with the tallest trees forming the primary canopy, the sunlight shielding "roof" of the forest. Below is the second tree canopy made up of tall shrubs, saplings and smaller tree species. In the upland forest this canopy may include the sweet gum, (most colorful of all in the fall), persimmon, hop hornbeam, and the familiar flowering dogwood, redbud, and sassafras. (Look for its circlets of yellow flowers in the spring.)

American holly is the only conspicuous evergreen tree in the winter forest. Some wild azalea, rhododendron, and dwarf sumac may also appear in this second upland canopy.

The third layer is made up of short woody shrubs, such as blueberry and huckleberry. (If you have a mind to pick blueberries, visit Lee Park in Petersburg or

Powhite Park in Richmond in August. Look for these plants on high ground.) The shortest plants - wildflowers, grasses, ferns, mosses, and creeping species, such as periwinkle and running cedar, make up the fourth layer.

Poison Ivy

Although poison ivy occurs more abundantly in the lowland forests, it may be found in the upland forest as well. Learn to recognize and avoid it, for contact may result in a very uncomfortable rash beginning a couple of days later and lasting much longer than you would wish. Poison ivy may take the form of a small shrub or high climbing vine. The stems of older plants have aerial roots resembling brown hairs, a characteristic which helps to identify them in winter. These are most conspicuous on the vines that attach themselves to tree trunks. The leaves have three shiny leaflets with coarsely toothed margins. Heed the old saying, "leaflets three, let it be!" Don't pick its lovely white flowers and white berries, though they may dangle temptingly from a vine.

The rich deciduous woods provide habitats for a group of attractive herbaceous (non-woody) plants, the spring "ephemerals," wildflowers which grow, flower, and die back before the leaves on the trees are fully formed. You will notice that the light on the floor of the woods is weak in summer because of the shade of the layers above. The lovely spring ephemerals solve the problem by "fast living" before the canopies above are in full leaf. Among these are spring beauty, dog's tooth violet, and toothwort. Look for these in late March and April. For descriptions, see the calendar of some common wildflowers at the end of this chapter.

Some longer-lived wildflowers of the upland forest floor also bloom early to take advantage of the light before the leaves come out, but their plants remain throughout the growing season, and they produce fruits of various types during the summer and fall. Among these are bloodroot, Jack-in-the-pulpit, wild ginger, and mayapple, which hides its white flowers under large flat leaves like tiny umbrellas. The Indians used all of these plants for food, medicine, or dyes.

Lowland Forest

The plants in lowland forests flourish in the moist soil of floodplains where rivers and streams periodically overflow their banks and the water table is close to the surface. In these habitats organic matter is usually of a higher content than in other habitats, which contributes to a greater diversity of trees than in the upland forests.

The species of herbaceous plants - wildflowers, etc. -, however, may be less diverse, as it is hard to begin growth in the spring if the soil is flooded, as can often happen along the rivers. The floodplain forests of the James River Park are classic examples.

Lowland forests are the favorite habitat of poison ivy, so when you go walking in one it is a good idea to wear long pants, long sleeves, stay on the trails, and keep an eye out, for this is a plant to avoid. (For a description, see The Upland Forest .) Stinging nettles also grow in these woods and should be avoided. These have pairs of sharply toothed leaves and are hairy all over.

Among the common large canopy trees you will see in these moist habitats are the red, silver and ash-leaved maples (also known as box elder), American and winged elm, sycamore, river birch, black walnut, hackberry, black willow, white ash, and eastern cottonwood.The sweet gum may also be present, growing to a larger size than in the uplands.

For a bird's eye view of canopy trees in a floodplain, take a walk along one of the pedestrian bridge-towers in the main section of the James River Park or the sidewalk on the Huguenot Bridge.

The sycamores are among the most conspicuous trees all year round because of their striking white bark with peeling patches of green and brown bark. These and the red or river birches (named for their peeling red bark) and the black willows often grow at the very edge of rivers and streams.

The red and silver maples are sights to behold in early March when their flowers (respectively red and green) appear while the rest of the woods are bare. Within weeks these develop into colorful double-winged fruits (called "keys") that are scattered by the wind before the leaves come out.

A few American elms in the natural areas seem to have escaped the Dutch elm disease, although their fate is uncertain. Of all the trees in the forest, they are the most graceful, with their vaselike shape and arching branches. These are also among the earliest trees to flower and scatter their light, winged fruits to the winds.

Among the medium-size to smaller trees in the second canopy of the lowland forest are the spicebush, pawpaw, sweetbay, common locust, red mulberry, black gum, ironwood, and alder. In mid-March the yellow flowers of the spicebush brighten the lower levels of the otherwise bare forest. By fall they have developed into shiny red berries. Break off a twig and smell it, and you will understand its name.

Several of these trees flower in May and June. The little pawpaw has strange flowers resembling brown tulips, which develop into edible fruits that look like misshapen pears or small eggplants. These taste somewhat like bananas, and are sold as exotic fruits in some markets. Look for a small tree with huge simple leaves in any floodplain in September, and you may find ripe pawpaws, if the animals have not already eaten them.

The sweetbay is a small evergreen magnolia with shiny dark leaves, white on the underside, and fragrant cup-shaped white flowers in early summer. The more common locust tree bears clusters of fragrant flowers in May. The red mulberry produces fuzzy flowers followed by delicious berries in late June. For a mulberry treat, take the westward trail in the James River North Bank Park around that time of year.

The pink swamp rose is one of the prettiest shrubs in the lowland forest. Its fruits are encased in "hips," from which jelly can be made. Other shrubs include blackberry. and (less commonly) raspberry, the buttonbush, with flowers like little rounded pincushions, bladdernut, its seed capsules resembling golden Japanese lanterns, and elderberry, with its frond-like leaves and clusters of white flowers developing into purple berries in the fall.

Many vines grow in these habitats, among them honeysuckle and two species of grape. The delicious muscadines ripen in October. The fox grapevines are especially interesting because they grow to a very old age, and having climbed and fallen with several generations of trees that are not as long lived, become contorted into strange convoluted shapes. You will see many of these in the Huguenot Woods and North Bank Park in Richmond, and the Henrico City Park nature trail at Dutch Gap.

Wildflowers of the lowland forest include violets, which may carpet the ground early in the spring, and patches of jewel weed, a tall plant with small orange flowers and translucent stems. This common herb was used by the American Indians, who rubbed the leaves and stems on their poison ivy and nettle rashes. (Some people today make a brew of the leaves and stems, freeze it, and rub the ice cubes on the afflicted skin; it does seem to help.) Less common, but not too difficult to find, is the striking great Solomon's seal with its dangling pairs of white flowers.

The strangest of all plants in lowland thickets is a parasite called dodder, which lives on other plants because it has no chlorophyll. It resembles nothing so much as a tangle of orange string winding itself around the green herbaceous plants, like a fisherman's broken line. Still it bears flowers (white), like any herbaceous plant.

One area of low-lying Presquile National Wildlife Refuge supports an uncommon assemblage of plants where the horsetail or scouring rush *Equisetum hyemale*, is very abundant. These strange, primitive plants are tall, thin, straight, and lack any branches, although many other varieties of horsetail are profusely branched. They almost seem to lean against each other for support. The tip of the plant bears the spores, the reproductive parts of these primitive plants. The stems contain the element silicon, which is also found in sand and glass and makes them hard and somewhat durable. The early settlers used them for scouring pots and pans, hence the name, scouring rush. The stems are hollow internally, and the wind rustling through them produces an interesting sound. Although they sound most unappetizing, deer eat these plants, and seem in fact to favor them. Perhaps they enjoy their crunchy texture.

Old Field

Take a path through one of the meadows in the parks or preserves. These are old fields and pastures, cleared and planted years ago for their rich soil and moisture holding conditions. They are being allowed to return to nature, and sun-loving wild plant communities have taken over the habitats. You will find especially fine meadows in Crump Park and the James River Park (Main Section and the Pony Pasture).

Grasses predominate, but other herbaceous plants have invaded these old fields showy wildflowers and herbs we tend to call weeds because they are less attractive. These are colorful places during the growing season. Many wildlife species depend on these plants for food. If the meadows are at the edge of a forest, deer will come out to browse, and smaller animals - rabbits, chipmunks, snakes, lizards, etc. - may also live in the tall grass. In the growing season the meadows are alive with bees and butterflies and other insect pollinators. At all times of the year certain species of birds inhabit or visit these old fields, feeding on their favorite seeds and using plant material for their nests.

Some of the many species of wildflowers you will see in most old fields during the growing season are violets, bluets, blue asters, buttercup, the common milkweed, blue chickory, pink bouncing Bet, black-eyed Susan, ox-eye daisy, morning glory, golden rod, Queen Anne's Lace, thistles, and several clovers and other legumes, (sweet peas and their relatives.) Interestingly, many of our common wildflowers originally escaped from gardens planted by the early settlers from seeds carried with them from England - or arrived as stowaway seeds adhering to their clothing from having brushed against them on walks in the fields back home!

Other wildflowers grow best in the open along the edge of the forest, especially in moist areas. Some of these are also garden varieties, but must not, of course, be picked or dug. (All park agencies prohibit picking or digging plants.) Spectacular displays of blue and lavender spiderworts and orange day lilies grow near the river in the Pony Pasture in mid-May. (These could have been carried downstream from gardens during floods.) The most spectacular of all are the enormous pink and white hibiscus blooming in August along the edge of the Huguenot Woods and the river bank, among other places where we have seen them.(Anyone who breaks the rules to pick these will be disappointed; they last for only one day, and less if picked.)

In the game management areas (Powhatan, Chickahominy, and Pocahontas State Forest) clearings are specially created and planted to attract and sustain wildlife. In

Point of Rocks Park an old field has recently been planted to attract songbirds and small mammals, which in turn attract foxes, and a permanent bird blind has been constructed so that visitors may watch them.

Old fields are temporary habitats undergoing rapid plant succession. The sun-loving pines are the pioneer trees - the tall loblollies, scrubby Virginia pine, and the in-between shortleaf pine. As the field gets older, deciduous tree saplings will appear, and the competition for sunlight begins. In time, the canopy trees will take over, and a hardwood forest will once again be established. If an old field or other clearing is to be maintained as such, it must be judiciously mowed or burned every year or so, well before the growing season. This practice will not harm the herbaceous plants, as they will grow anew in the spring.

Marshes and Swamps

Marshes and swamps are wet places where plants grow. They may be found at the edges or backwaters of lakes or streams, or in depressions where the water table is at or above ground level. Except where walkways extend into them, the best way to explore the larger ones is in a canoe.

Swamps are forests standing in water much of the time, and are populated by species that flourish in very wet habitats. The dominant plants are certain woody trees. In this region you would expect to see an abundance of black gum, sweetbay magnolia, and red maple in fresh water swamps. Bald cypress grows in certain tidal swamps along the lower reaches of the Chickahominy River, and may be easily recognized by its knobby "knees" projecting out of the water.

Woody shrubs, such as buttonbush, alder, and silky dogwood (*Cornus amomum*) make up the understory, and thorny greenbrier vines often form an impenetrable growth where water has receded. Sphagnum moss may be found as a ground cover. Larger than the tiny mosses on higher ground, sphagnum is a spongey greenish yellow plant almost saturated with water. You can pick up handfuls and squeeze out the water, leaving a very absorbent substance. (This plant has been used by primitive peoples as diapers are used today - the first disposables.) Today in its dried and crumbled form it is known as peat moss, a useful soil conditioner in gardens. Look for sphagnum growing along the edge of the marsh in Vawter Street Park in Henrico County.

Herbaceous plants are also found along the edges of swamps, among them skunk cabbage, Jack-in-the-pulpit, the blue monkey flowers of the snapdragon family, and several of the broadleaved species that grow in marshes. As might be expected, swamps and marshes may merge in transitional areas. A good example is Morris Creek in the Chickahominy Wildlife Management Area, where marshes line the creek, with swamps behind them.

Marshes are characterized by herbaceous plants, including grasses, cattails, bul-rushes, wild rice, and several broadleaved species peculiar to these habitats. Freshwater marshes are found in the piedmont province above the fall line. Below

Wild Rice - Ashton Marsh, Point of Rocks Park

the fall line along the rivers they may be subject to tidal movements carrying salt water upstream.

Not all marshes are alike. The vegetation may vary according to the salinity of the water and the duration of the wet period in the habitat. Sometimes after a prolonged dry spell exposes the surface, plants dependent on a constant supply of water will die for a season and grow again from seed or roots the following year. In tidal marshes along small streams, a dry spell may also increase the salinity of the water, as a greater proportion of salty water enters the marsh, and this may influence the mix of plants.

Many of the marsh plants are eaten by wildlife. The Indians of the region also used parts of several of these plants for food, including wild rice and the flowers and underground stems of cattails. Wild rice is prominent in many marshes, including one along Ashton Creek in Point of Rocks Park, where a wooden marsh walk makes it possible to come very close to the plants. It is a tall grass growing as high as nine feet, with leaves that may be more than a yard long and two inches wide. The rice kernels are present in the upward pointing branches at the top of the stout stem. Wild rice was and still is a source of food. In some parts of the midwest gathering it is a privilege restricted to the native Indians, who have done this from canoes for thousands of years.

Most people recognize cattails. There is a well developed display visible from the overlook at Beaver Dam Creek Battlefield Park. Some of the other marsh plants, however, may need to be pointed out or identified with the use of a field guide. Except for the grasses, many of them bear conspicuous flowers and are included in wildflower guides.

Three interesting plants with large arrow-shaped leaves grow in several of the marshes. Arrow arum, also known as Tuckahoe, has large pointed leaves with prominant veins and tiny green flowers borne in an egg-shaped cluster concealed by a modified leaf, the spathe. Broadleafed or aquatic arrowhead is similar in leaf shape, but without the sharp tip and prominent veins. Its lovely three-petalled white flowers are conspicuous during its blooming period. Most noticeable of all is the pickerel weed, which carries its striking blue flowers clustered on a club-like spike.

Water willow, named for the shape of its leaves, also grows in the water. Its loose clusters of blue flowers are a common sight in summer along the shallow edges of the river in the James River Park. Many other swamp and marsh plants are interesting and worthy of investigation.

Seasonal changes in marshes are dramatic and also worth following. Swamps and marshes may be found in several of the region's parks and preserves. Good examples of swamps along the Chickahominy River may be seen in the Vawter Street Park in Henrico County and in the Chickahominy Wildlife Management Area, particularly where Morris Creek approaches the Chickahominy and becomes tidal. Here you will see fine specimens of bald cypress growing in the water. Other swamps occur at the upper end of Harrison Lake in the National Fish Hatchery, on Presquile National Wildlife Refuge, and in Henrico City Park, (in Chesterfield County), where the nature trail will cross one on a wooden walkway.

Especially interesting marshes may be seen along Ashton Creek in Point of Rocks Park, along Swift Creek just above its confluence with the Appomattox River, (accessible from White Bank Park in Colonial Heights), along the Appomattox at the edge of Fort Clifton (also in Colonial Heights), and on Presquile, as well as Morris Creek. Many other streams and lakes have small marshes associated with them, generally along their shallow edges.

References for Vegetation

Audubon Society Field Guide to North American Trees - Eastern Region

Audubon Society Field Guide to North American Wildflowers

Brockman, C.F. 1968. *Trees of North America - A Field Guide to the Major Native and Introduced Species North of Mexico.*
Golden Press, New York.

Gupton, O.W. and F.C. Swope. 1979. *Wildflowers of the Shenandoah Valley and Blue Ridge Mountains.*
University of Virginia Press, Charlottesville.

Gupton, O.W. and F.C. Swope. 1982. *Wildflowers of Tidewater Virginia.*
University of Virginia Press, Charlottesville.

Gupton, O.W. and F.C. Swope. *Trees and Shrubs of Virginia.*
University of Virginia Press, Charlottesville.

Justice, W.S. and C.R. Bell. 1968. *Wild Flowers of North Carolina and Surrounding Areas.* Univeristy of North Carolina Press.

Peterson, L.A. *Field Guide to Edible Wild Plants.*
National Audubon Society. Houghton Mifflin Co., Boston.

Peterson, R.T. and M. McKenny. 1968. *A Field Guide to Wildflowers of Northeastern and Northcentral North America.*
Houghton Mifflin Co., Boston.

Petrides, G. *Field Guide to Trees and Shrubs.*
Peterson Field Guide Series. Houghton Mifflin Co.

Organizations

Richmond Audubon Society - P.O. Box 804, Richmond, Va. 23207.

Lewis Ginter Botanical Garden - 7000 Lakeside Avenue, Richmond, Virginia 23228 - 804/262-9887.

Virginia Wildflower Preservation Society, Richmond Chapter
Ms. Sarah Richardson, President
P.O. Box 14646, Richmond, Va. 23221 - 804/358-7504.

Dr. Johnson is a Professor of Biology and Curator of the Herbarium at Virginia Commonwealth University, where he teaches courses in Biology and Botany.

Muscadine Grape

Herbs Beginning to Bloom in March

Scientific Name Common Name Habitat	Distinguishing Characteristics
Stellaria media Common Chickweed Everywhere	5 petals so deeply lobed that they appear as 10, short oval leaves bear long petioles
Taraxacum officinale Dandelion Everywhere	Jagged leaves, lobes point back, cluster of small yellow flowers crowded into a head, fruits have white fluff

Herbs Beginning to Bloom in April

Scientific Name Common Name Habitat	Distinguishing Characteristics
Alliaria officinalis Garlic Mustard Roadsides, waste places	Triangular heart shaped leaves, odor of garlic, flowers small, white, clustered at top of stem, 4 petals.
Anemonella thalictroides Rue Anemone Woods	Whorl of 3 lobed leaves, white flowers in loose cluster above; delicate aspect to plant.
Antennaria plantaginifolia Plantain-leaved Pussytoes Woods, disturbed areas	Stem and lower surface of basal spoon-shaped leaves white woolly; flowers appear as masses of white fluff.
Aquilegia canadensis Columbine Woods	Leaves divided into 3's; flowers red and yellow, seem to hang upside down.
Arisaema triphyllum Jack-in-the-Pulpit Wet woods	Flap-like leaf (spathe) encloses club like spadix; flowers tiny, at base of spadix; leaves 3-parted; spathe variously colored from pale green to deep purple.
Asarum canadense Wild Ginger Woods	Leaves heart shaped, stalk soft hairy; flower red-brown, 3-parted, in crotch beteen 2 leaves. You may have to remove forest litter to see flower. Odor of ginger when stem broken.
Claytonia virginica Spring Beauty Woods	Petals white or pink with darker pink veins, a pair of smooth leaves midway up the stem.
Dentaria laciniata Cut-leaved Tooth-Wort Woods	4-petaled flowers on a slender stalk above 3 deeply divided leaves with sharply toothed margins.
Duchesnea indica Indian Strawberry Waste areas	Trailing, 3 toothed leaflets, 5 petaled yellow flower, conspicuous 3 toothed bracts beneath each flower; fruit resembles strawberry.

Erythronium americanum Trout Lily Woods	Yellow petals bent back and two brown mottled leaves.
Geranium maculatum Wild Geranium Woods	5 parted hairy leaves, 5 petaled pink flowers, fruit resembles a crane's bill.
Glechoma hederacea Gill Over the Ground; Ground Ivy; Creeping Charlie Lawns, roadsides	Plant creeping, 2-lipped flowers in leaf axils, strong odor of mint when crushed.
Hepatica americana Round-lobed Hepatica Woods	Reddish 3-lobed leaves, flowers white to blue, 3 bracts beneath each flower.
Houstonia caerulea Bluets Woods, grassy areas	Small plants often in colonies, flowers pale blue with yellow center.
Lychnis alba Evening Lychnis Waste areas	5 lobed white petals, 5 styles, opposite leaves; plants male or female.
Podophyllum peltatum May-Apple Woods	Single white flowers attached in the angle between 2 deeply divided leaves.
Sanguinaria canadensis Bloodroot Woods	Showy 8–10 petaled flower, lobed, pale green leaf, orange juice seen when stem broken.
Saxifraga virginiensis Early Saxifrage Woods, fields	Leaves in basal rosette; flowers white, 5 petals, 10 yellow stamens, borne on hairy stem above leaves.
Silene caroliniana Wild Pink Woods	Flowers pink, 5 petals, calyx and upper stem sticky, leaves clustered at base.
Smilacina racemosa False Solomon's Seal Woods	Oval shaped leaves arranged alternately, cluster of yellow-white flowers at the tip of the stem. In flower near end of April.
Uvularia grandiflora Large Flowered Bellwort Woods	Leaves clasp stem, yellow flower relatively large at tip of branched stem.
Viola papilionacea Common Blue Violet Woods, yards	Leaves heart-shaped, 5 violet-blue petals, darker toward the center, side petals with noticeable veins.

Herbs Beginning to Bloom in May

Scientific Name Common Name Habitat	Distinguishing Characteristics
Cyprepedium acaule Pink Lady's Slipper; Moccasin Flower Woods	Flowers have noticeable pink pouch-like petal, 2 basal leaves.
Dianthus arnoria Deptford Pink Fields, roadsides	Stem stiff, very narrow opposite leaves; flowers small, clustered, 5 pink petals with white spots.
Fragaria Wild Strawberry Fields, open areas	Leaflets with 3 teeth, flowers white, 5 petals, fruit a strawberry.
Hypochaeris radicata Cat's Ear Lawns, fields	Hairy leaves form basal rosette; yellow flowers clustered into dandelion-like head, upper stem may be branched.
Polygonatum biflorum Solomon's Seal Woods	Yellow or whitish flowers in pairs beneath alternate leaves.
Prunella vulgaris Heal All Roadsides, lawns	Leaves opposite, rectangular cluster of violet, 2-lipped flowers among bracts; plant may creep or be upright.
Ranunculus bulbosus Bulbous Buttercup Fields, roadsides	Flowers with 5 bright yellow shiny petals; expanded, bulblike stem base underground.
Rhododendron nudiflorum Pink Azalea Woods	Small tree with pink flowers appearing before leaves; stamens and pistils elongate and conspicuous.
Tradescantia virginiana Spiderwort Woods	Flowers clustered, with 3 purple petals, leaves long, grasslike.
Uvularia perfoliata Perfoliate Bellwort Woods	Stems seem to grow through leaves, single yellow, drooping flower at tip of leafy stem.
Uvularia sessilifolia Wild Oats Woods	Leaves attached directly to stem, creamy-yellow drooping flower.

Herbs Beginning to Bloom in June

Scientific Name Common Name Habitat	Distinguishing Characteristics
Achillea millefolium Yarrow Waste areas	Leaves finely cut, flat-topped flower cluster; flowers usually white, rarely pink; pleasant odor when crushed.
Asclepias syriaca Common Milkweed Roadsides, fields	Coarse, downy plant, sap milky; flower clusters near top of plant, petals pink to lavender; fruit warty.
Chimaphila maculata Spotted Wintergreen Pine Woods	Midrib of leaf white, leaves in whorls; flowers pink to white; very sweet odor.
Chrysanthemum leucanthemum Ox Eye Daisy Fields, roadsides	Common white daisy with yellow center; leaves lobed.
Cichorium intybus Chickory; Blue Sailors Roadsides, waste areas	Dandelion-like basal leaves, upper stem stiff, naked; stalkless flower clusters, flowers usually blue, at times pink or white; close by noon.
Cirsium vulgare Bull Thistle Waste areas	Prickly leaves and stems, with a "wing" on stem between leaves; flower cluster with stiff spines, flowers reddish-purple; fruits with white fluff.
Commelina communis Asiatic Dayflower Roadsides, wet areas	3 petaled flower, 2 upper petals large and blue; single lower one small and white; plant often reclining.
Daucus carota Queen-Anne's-Lace; Wild Carrot Fields	Large flat clusters of small white flowers; leaves finely divided, odor of carrots.
Galium Bedstraw, Cleavers Woods	Leaves in clusters of four or six, flowers very small, white.
Ipomoea pandurata Wild Morning Glory Fields, Roadsides	Vine with heart shaped leaves, flowers white with red center.
Nymphaea odorata Fragrant water lily Ponds	Large dinner-plate like leaves floating, large flowers with many pink to white petals; sweet odor.
Pontederia cordata Pickerel Weed Ponds	Blue spikes, large arrow-shaped leaves.
Rosa Wild Rose Roadsides, fields	Shrubs or vines with thorns and showy pink 5-petaled flowers.

Herbs Beginning to Bloom in July

Scientific Name Common Name Habitat	Distinguishing Characteristics
Asclepias tuberosa Butterfly Weed Fields, roadsides	Stems hairy, leaves numerous, crowded; flowers orange; a milkweed without milky sap.
Chimaphila umbellata Pipsissewa Woods	Dark green, shiny whorled leaves; flowers white to pink, anthers reddish.
Coreopsis verticillata Whorled Coreopsis Roadsides, fields	Daisy-like flowers with 8 petal-like yellow rays; leaves whorled, divided into filament-like segments.
Goodyera repens Dwarf Rattlesnake-Plantain Woods	Checkered pattern of white veins on green leaf, leaves in rosette; flowers white, in tight spike.
Impatiens capensis Spotted Touch-Me-Not; Jewel Weed Wet, shady areas	Orange flowers hang pendant-like; soft stems, fruit explodes when touched.
Phytolacca americana Poke Weed Damp woods, roadsides	Red stems, white flowers in elongate drooping clusters; fruits blue-black.
Rhexia Meadow Beauty Wet soil, roadside ditches	4 pink petals, yellow curved stamens; leaves opposite; 3 prominent veins.
Rudbeckia hirta Black-Eyed-Susan Roadsides, fields	Large yellow daisy with brown center; leaves and stems bristly.
Saponaria officinalis Bouncing Bet; Soapwort Roadsides, waste places	Clusters of pink or white flowers, stems and leaves smooth; often in large colonies.
Silene stellata Starry Campion Woods	Leaves in group of 4; 5 white petals fringed.
Verbascum blattaria Moth Mullein Roadsides, fields	White or yellow 5 parted flowers in loose elongate cluster, anthers orange with purple hairs; leaves and stem free of hairs.
Verbascum thapsus Common Mullein Roadsides, waste areas	2–6 feet tall, flannel textured leaves; club-like, elongate cluster of yellow 5 parted flowers.

CHAPTER 3

Wildlife of the Natural Parks and Preserves

by Charles R. Blem, Ph.D.

Before the European colonists arrived in Virginia, animal life abounded. Tales of great numbers of turkeys, deer and bear, often repeated, are nevertheless probably true. The American Indian, even in his heyday in Virginia, had only a slight impact on wildlife, particularly in comparison with the later effect of modern man. We have little idea of the occurrence and real numbers of large animals, but anecdotal accounts describe flocks of waterfowl that "darkened the sky" and there are stories of passenger pigeons in migratory flocks that were tens of miles in length (the species is now *extinct!*). Black bears, timber wolves and mountain lions once occurred in our area, but the presence of any of these animals today would be surprising.

Our streams were full of fish when the colonists arrived. Spring runs of shad, herring, striped bass and other species were spectacular. Sturgeon, five feet or more in length, were sometimes plentiful. Now abundant, carp were not present in our waters then, but were later introduced by Europeans. The smallmouth bass, now a major gamefish in the James River and other nearby streams, was likewise not part of the native fish community but was introduced near the beginning of the 20th century.

Records and identification of smaller animals by the settlers were none too precise, partly because few of these organisms had been described by zoologists and partly because colonists paid little attention to anything they couldn't eat (or which couldn't eat them!). However, reference has been made to great clouds of insects that sometimes filled the air. Mosquitoes and other pests plagued the colonists, and malaria apparently was soon present.

As the land was cleared and game animals were harvested in ever greater numbers, the original forest community disappeared and can no longer be seen in our region. Some older patches are available which give an impression of the early vegetation (e.g. the forest in the ravine near Watt House), but virtually all of the biological communities present today are highly modified from that of pre-colonial times.

Although the activities of modern man are viewed as generally detrimental to the wilderness, his impact has not been all bad. For example, the original Virginia wilderness was largely unbroken, mature forest. As such, it was beneficial to deciduous forest animals, but did not encourage species that preferred successional communities or less mature habitats. The disturbance begun by the colonists and continued by modern man has encouraged successional stages at the expense of mature forest organisms. Deer, preferring forest edge, are probably more abundant today than in early colonial times, while the turkey, a forest species, is less abundant. Many songbirds and some gamebirds probably were rare in Virginia several centuries ago. Blue grosbeaks, prairie warblers, northern bobwhite and even the cardinal, our state bird, were scarce or unknown in colonial times. Now they are most abundant around early successional communities.

It should also be recognized that animal distributions are not static, but change through time. These changes may be due to habitat changes or variations in climate, or may occur for reasons that we do not entirely understand. In the past few decades, the cotton rat, barking treefrog, and house finch have invaded our region and now breed and live here permanently.

The parks included within this book contain a very large number of animal species. This high diversity is because: (1) the region straddles the fall line and consequently incorporates sections of both the coastal plain and eastern piedmont, (2) a variety of habitats are available in these parks and (3) many southeastern species reach the northern limits of their distribution in this area (because of zoogeographic phenomena too complex to be addressed here). Field guides are useful aids in learning to identify many of these animals. (Several of these books are referenced at the end of this chapter.)

Because of space limitations, little detail can be provided here. Invertebrates are neglected totally, but many thousands of species occur within these parks. I must warn that two potentially dangerous invertebrates are fairly common: the black widow spider, a poisonous species that is capable of taking a human life, and "lone star" ticks capable of communicating Rocky Mountain spotted fever. A comprehensive fish list is likewise not included, but would have to incorporate a very large number of species. The major tributaries of the region (the James, Appomattox and Chickahominy Rivers) contain a wide variety of resident sport fishes including largemouth and smallmouth basses, crappie, several species of smaller sunfishes, chain pickerel, yellow perch, walleye, white perch, channel catfish, and rough fishes such as carp, bowfin, and longnose gar. Striking migrations of fish occur in the major tidal tributaries. These include two species of shad, plus other herring and striped bass. Atlantic white sturgeon, while rare, still occur in the James River and may reach sizes in excess of 100 lbs.

Amphibians and reptiles

Amphibians and reptiles include a variety of animals considered by many to be undesirable—the frogs, toads, salamanders, turtles, snakes and lizards. In fact, nearly all of these animals are beneficial to us in one way or another and deserve protection in our parks. We should view the casual killing of one of these animals as an act of vandalism, not very unlike cutting down a tree or pulling up a flower. A majority of Virginia's species of amphibians and reptiles are found in the area described by this book. It is probable that Chesterfield County alone has more species of reptiles and amphibians than any other county in the state (or did before urban development began). There is not enough space here to begin to discuss all of these animals, but several items may be of interest.

The amphibians, including frogs, toads, salamanders and sirens, mostly include small secretive forms found only during the milder weather of the annual cycle. For example, there are many species of frogs and toads in the region which, while they may not be highly visible, are among the more vocal members of most biological communities. There is a pronounced seasonal cycle in the vocalization of frogs and toads. In breeding season, males migrate to aquatic sites where they call in order to attract mates. These calls may be quite loud; male barking treefrogs, for example, can be heard over a mile from their call sites. Frogs may first be heard with late winter thaws and the first "warm" rains of spring. This may occur as early as mid-February, but often happens later. The order of appearance of common species of frogs is as follows: upland chorus frog and spring peeper (February); American toad, green frog, pickerel frog (April); Fowler's toad, narrow-mouthed frog, gray treefrog and leopard frog (May); and green treefrog, barking treefrog and pine woods treefrog (June). For those interested in learning frog vocalizations, there are recordings available that illustrate our local species (see references). Grab your flashlight on the next warm, rainy night in the spring and visit the local pond or puddle. You may be amazed by the activity and noise there.

Salamanders, while not vocal, may be locally abundant also. They must be near moisture, as water is required for reproduction, and without moist soil most species quickly dry up and die. Although salamanders superficially look like lizards, they always have a moist, scaleless skin and are not capable of as much prolonged activity as a lizard. Local species are never larger than about 6 inches in length and most are much smaller. Turn over a few rocks or logs and look closely. You may be rewarded by seeing one of these animals. However, be sure to return the log or rock to its original state; a lot of this activity will severely disturb a forest.

The reptiles—snakes, lizards and turtles—may be slightly more visible than amphibians. For example, there are at least 24 species of snakes that occur in our parks. Most of these are harmless, and none should be bothered. They will usually threaten if cornered. This may include striking and biting, and most species will shake their tails much like a rattlesnake to signal that they are disturbed. They almost always prefer escaping to fighting.

Perhaps no other members of the reptile group excite more interest than the two species of poisonous snakes that are found in the parks and surroundings of central Virginia. These are the copperhead and the eastern cottonmouth. The former is fairly common and the latter has only a restricted distribution in our area. Both of these snakes are shy and nonaggressive (despite stories to the contrary). They are the subject of many myths and legends and, as a result, are poorly understood. For example, cottonmouths are often called "water moccasins," thus causing confusion with the several species of harmless water snakes in our region. Poisonous cottonmouths do *not* occur in most of Virginia, but we encounter many people who refuse to accept this fact. The lower Appomattox River and the lower reaches of Swift Creek, Newport News City Park, and the southeastern corner of Virginia include most known Virginia records for the cottonmouth. The similar, nonpoisonous water snakes will sometimes appear to have white mouths, triangular heads, and will strike fiercely. They are capable of drawing blood with their bite, but are not particularly dangerous. Those who plan to spend time in the field locally should always be aware of identification characters of poisonous snakes when near the range of these reptiles, but should also learn to recognize and protect the harmless species.

Note: Although poisonous snakes are present in the parks of central Virginia, we do not wish to alarm those visitors who may not be familiar with reptiles. The chance of encountering a poisonous species is very low. For example, we have seen two live copperheads in hundreds of field trips. This does not mean that you should not be careful. Watch where you step, particularly along woodland trails, and never turn over boards, logs, and other debris without care. Copperheads prefer to hide under materials that protect them from the sun's heat and from harm by humans. Woodpiles are often choice sites. Cottonmouths are almost always found deep in thickets along the water's edge, or swimming along such areas. Neither species is likely to bite unless you step near them or attempt to handle them.

If you have the misfortune of being bitten by a poisonous snake and you are near medical help, you probably should not attempt to do anything about the wound. Professional care, administered within less than an hour after the bite, may be better than amateur efforts to cut and suck the poison from the wound. Of course, this depends upon the location of the bite on the body, the size of the snake and the general health of the victim. Bites on the face or directly on major blood vessels are potentially life-threatening. Large snakes usually have more venom than small ones. Small children and the elderly are usually less tolerant of the bite of venomous snakes.

Lizards frequently are encountered in our parks. The commonest species include several species of skinks that have blue tails and conspicuous stripes when young and are a more cryptic brown as adults. Fence lizards are gray or brown lizards often seen on pine trees or stumps. All of these species readily climb trees. They are all fairly small, never exceeding 8 or 9 inches in total length. They can bite, but often are not capable of breaking human skin. They are beneficial as they eat many insects.

More than a dozen species of turtles are present in our area. Most of these are pond-dwelling species that are difficult to see well. The commonest of these is the eastern painted turtle, but spotted turtles, river cooters and red-bellied turtles may be locally common as well. On land, the only terrestrial species is the eastern box turtle. Temptation to remove these reptiles from the local parks is great as they are easy to catch. However, they are not very exciting pets and require special care during the winter. Leave them in their native habitat. The largest reptile in our area is the common snapping turtle, and this may well be the most dangerous of this group. A large snapper is capable of inflicting damage on fingers and toes. You may encounter one of the females of this species laying eggs far from the nearest water. Look, but don't touch!

Birds

The Capital region has an impressive diversity of bird life; at least 271 species of birds have been identified locally (see Appendix). Identifying most of these birds requires some practice and a bit of study of the available field guides (see references at the end of this section). Those who are interested in improving their skills in identifying birds should consider keeping a list of the species they see and can identify. Lists compiled with care for many years in the same region are valuable in that they reflect changes in the birds of that area and may provide clues as to when and where to expect certain species. Lists kept of all birds one has seen anywhere are called *life lists* and indicate the relative skill and experience of the birdwatcher. The list in the appendix can be useful in beginning such a list locally, and part of the excitement in listing may be realized if you discover a species in the area that is not now on the list. If you are a novice birdwatcher and would like help in improving your skills, you may wish to go on one of the many bird walks offered by both Chesterfield and Henrico Departments of Parks and Recreation or by the local Audubon chapter. These are usually announced in the local newspapers well beforehand.

A beginning bird student should recognize that birds belong to one of several residency categories. Some species are present in our area all of the time and, as such, are called *permanent residents*. Permanent species may range in abundance from common to rare. For example, among the more important, but less common, species in our region is the bald eagle. This magnificent bird is slowly increasing in numbers, and few people realize that there are several nests within the area of this book. In fact, one roost on the lower James River has included nearly 50 eagles at times.

The great blue heron is a more common permanent resident in the area and can routinely be seen on the James River as well as on lesser creeks and streams. Some people call them "cranes," but they are not closely related to cranes and their allies. Herons fly with their necks crooked in an "S" shape, while cranes fly with their necks outstretched. Several breeding colonies of great blue herons are present in the general area, including one on Tuckahoe Creek in western Henrico County and one on the Chickahominy River near Mechanicsville, in the vicinity of Vawter Street Park and Chickahominy Bluff of the Richmond National Battlefield Park.

Species that are present only in summer breeding season are known as *summer residents*. Many of these tend to be visitors from the tropics (orioles, hummingbirds, tanagers). Birds present only in the winter are called *winter visitors*, and their presence varies from year to year. For example, red crossbills, evening grosbeaks, and pine siskins may be abundant one year and nearly absent the next, depending upon food supplies and the severity of the winter. Additionally, Richmond hosts thousands of gulls during most winters. The majority of these are ring-billed gulls with a few herring gulls and occasional rarities such as the Iceland gull thrown in. The main attraction holding these flocks in the area are the landfills. Gulls have a great fondness for garbage; they are accomplished scavengers (they

Great Blue Herons

almost never catch live food). As a result, the landfills provide an almost inexhaustible source of nourishment. Most of the gulls spend their nights on the James River, and fan out to the various dumps each morning. They manage to stop off at many other locations where a handout may be available. They therefore also appear at many shopping centers, parks and schoolyards.

Many species of birds are *transients* in our region. That is, they are seen generally only during migration. Although one species or another is migrating nearly every month of the year, the major migratory times are late April and May (warblers, vireos and shorebirds) and late August through November (warblers, flycatchers, waterfowl, shorebirds).

The remainder of the avian species found in our region may be classified as *accidentals*. These are usually uncommon or rare vagrants who simply wander into our region and vanish later. This category is most interesting to the advanced birdwatcher since it is this group that one encounters less frequently.

The beginning birdwatcher should not restrict his activities to daylight hours. Several species of owls, including great horned owls, barred owls and eastern screech owls, are commonly heard after dark. Whip-poor-wills and (rarely) chuck-will's-widows loudly advertise their presence in the spring. Common nighthawks may be seen at twilight times or around lights.

To find some species of birds in our parks, one must realize how specifically birds may choose their habitat. For example, few grasshopper sparrows are seen outside of grassy fields (and in our region they can only be seen in summer). Yellow-

dense understory, and the insect pests can be oppressive. In late autumn, winter visitors such as the American woodcock appear, and white-tailed deer may retreat here to avoid hunters. In spring, wood ducks may be seen flying among the trees, and the abundant dead trees of the bottomland may house their nests as well as those of common flickers, red-bellied woodpeckers, pileated woodpeckers and eastern screech owls. Some of the best developed floodplain forest in the region may be found along the James River in Richmond's James River Park.

Swamps

Two kinds of swamps may be encountered in our region. *Freshwater swamps* consisting mostly of cypress or black gum trees in standing water or slowly flowing creeks may be found throughout the coastal plain. These sites have a diversity of animals. Many species of birds breed in these swamps, including American redstarts, prothonotary warblers, Louisiana waterthrushes, parula warblers, yellow-throated vireos and (rarely) Swainson's warblers. Muskrats, mink, beavers and deer are common mammals. Insects are sometimes a problem in such swamps, particularly mosquitoes.

Areas near Chickahominy Lake and on lower sections of almost all of the coastal plain streams present some of the better examples of these swamps. In the lower coastal plain near major rivers, *tidal swamps* may be found. Bald cypress, black gum and red maple are common trees at such sites, but the habitat is characterized by fluctuating water levels due to tidal action. At high tide, these swamps may be fully covered by water. At low tides, the swamp may be dry.

Bird species in these swamps are similar to those of freshwater swamps, but may be dominated by more large species. Barred owls are common in such habitats. Duck populations may be relatively large in the fall. Herons, bald eagles, ospreys and other species may visit such sites to nest or to feed. Insects are seldom a problem, since the small fish coming in with each high tide eat most of the larvae of mosquitos and other pests. Mammal populations are not as great as in freshwater swamps, but beavers, muskrats, raccoon and others are present. A rare rodent, the cotton mouse, may occur in Virginia only in a few of these swamps.

Marshes

Like swamps, marshes in our region are of two general varieties. *Freshwater marshes* may form where static waters collect or where slow-moving streams flow through treeless areas. *Tidal marshes* form in areas around major rivers where siltation forms large shallow bays; the water is at least a bit salty. Sophisticated students of marshes actually recognize more than two dozen kinds of marshes, so this presentation is a bit simplistic. Examples of freshwater marshes may be found along Chickahominy Lake or the shallow ends of most large inland lakes. Marshes such as those on Presquile National Wildlife Refuge, or at other sites on the lower James River, are tidal.

The freshwater marshes are generally lively habitats including a diversity of aquatic and semi-aquatic organisms. In our region, these marshes usually have breeding populations of red-winged blackbirds, several species of ducks, including mallards and black ducks, and less commonly, water birds such as the least bittern. Egrets and other herons, gulls, and a variety of other avian species visit these areas for food. A variety of snakes and turtles may be present. Insects are often abundant enough to discourage the summer visitor. Muskrats usually are the only obvious mammal, and their mounds usually are visible in the middle of the best marshes.

Tidal marshes tend to be harsh habitats and in this region include very few breeding species of birds. The reason for this is not known. Rails and marsh wrens, both typical of tidal marshes and common around the tidal marshes of Chesapeake Bay, are conspicuously absent. Red-winged blackbirds and a few ducks constitute the majority of the breeding bird populations. Brown water snakes are often abundant, particularly in areas where tidal marsh and swamp are in contact. Turtles include only large species such as the common snapping turtle, river cooter, or red-bellied turtle. Several fish species use the marsh at high tide for breeding activities. During the spring, the numbers of carp and their splashing may be spectacular.

The primary production of the marsh itself may be important to the overall richness of the surrounding river. Seasonal changes in such marshes illustrate this: in summer the upper marsh is an impenetrable jungle, while by mid-winter it looks as if someone had mowed it. The tremendous turnover of vegetation washes out with each outgoing tide and feeds the food chains of the lower river.

References

Borror, D. J. (no date) *Songs of Eastern Birds.*
Dover Pub. Co.

Burt, W. H. and R. P. Grossenheider. 1952. *A Field Guide to the Mammals.*
Houghton Mifflin Co., Boston.

Conant, R. 1975. *A Field Guide to Reptiles and Amphibians of Eastern and Central North America.*
Houghton Mifflin Co., Boston.

Kellogg, P. P. and A. A. Allen (no date) *Voices of the Night:* A recording of the calls of 34 frogs and toads of the United States and Canada.
Houghton Mifflin Co., Boston.

Kellogg, P. P. and A. A. Allen (no date) *A Field Guide to Bird: Songs of Eastern and Central North America.*
Houghton Mifflin Co., Boston.

Larner, Y. R. 1979. *Virginia's Birdlife An Annotated Checklist.*
Virginia Society of Ornithology. No. 2.

Martof, B. S., W. M. Palmer, J. R. Bailey and J. R. Harrison III. 1980. *Amphibians and Reptiles of the Carolinas and Virginia.*
Univ. North Carolina Press, Chapel Hill.

National Geographic Society. 1983. *Field Guide to the Birds of North America.*
Nat. Geo. Soc.

Peterson, R. T. 1980. *A Field Guide to the Birds East of the Rockies.*
Houghton Mifflin Co., Boston.

Robbins, C. S., B. Bruun, and H. S. Zim. 1966. *A Guide to Field Identification: Birds of North America.*
Golden Press, New York.

Dr. Blem, a vertebrate ecologist and Professor of Biology at Virginia Commonwealth University, teaches courses in Ecology, Ornithology, and Herpetology.

Copperhead Snake

Eastern Cottonmouth Snake

Ned Smith
Reprinted from Virginia Wildlife

Birds of the Capital Region

This list summarizes the birds known to occur within the scope of this book. The order in which they are listed conforms to that of the American Ornithologists Union Checklist, the standard used by all scientific ornithologists. The list reflects the evolutionary relationships of the birds in it rather than their appearance, habitat or size.

It is impossible to indicate the full range of abundance of each species with respect to season, local habitat and geography, but this list attempts to indicate the probability of encountering each species. Abbreviations used in the list include:

- **C** Common; found most of the time in proper habitat
- **U** Uncommon; infrequently found, restricted habitat or relatively low abundance
- **R** Rare; infrequently found, recorded more than a few times over the past ten years
- ***** Species breeding in the area
- **F** Autumn; 15 September-15 November
- **W** Winter; 16 November-15 March
- **Sp** Spring; 16 March-30 May
- **S** Summer; 1 June-14 September

Very rare species that have been detected only a few times or less are included at the end of this list under "accidentals." Transient individuals and residents (e.g. breeding birds) are difficult to separate by season. Early migrants often appear out of season (e.g. shorebirds in summer), stragglers from the deep south and southwest appear often in summer, and late spring migrants may still be present in "summer" (e.g. some passerines). The list is based upon records published in THE RAVEN, the journal of the Virginia Society of Ornithology, on the publication: *Virginia's Birdlife: An Annotated Checklist* (also by the VSO) and on more than 16 years of personal observation.

Species	SP	S	F	W
Common Loon	U	R	U	U
Red-throated Loon	—	—	—	R
Horned Grebe	C	R	C	C
Red-necked Grebe	R	—	—	R
Pied-billed Grebe*	C	R	C	C
Double-crested Cormorant*	U	U	U	—
Great Blue Heron*	C	C	C	C
Green-backed Heron*	C	C	C	—
Little Blue Heron*	R	U	U	—
Cattle Egret*	C	U	U	—
Great Egret*	U	U	C	R
Snowy Egret*	U	U	R	—
Tricolored Heron	R	R	R	—
Black-crowned Night-Heron*	R	R	R	R
Yellow-crowned Night-Heron	R	R	—	—
Least Bittern	R	R	R	—
American Bittern	U	—	U	—
Glossy Ibis	R	—	R	—
White Ibis	—	R	R	—
Tundra Swan	U	—	U	U
Canada Goose	C	R	C	C
Snow Goose	U	—	U	U
Mallard*	C	U	C	C
American Black Duck*	C	U	C	C
Gadwall	U	—	U	U
Northern Pintail	U	—	U	U
Green-winged Teal	U	—	U	U
Blue-winged Teal	C	R	C	R
Eurasian Wigeon	R	—	—	R
American Wigeon	U	—	U	U
Northern Shoveler	U	—	R	R
Wood Duck*	C	C	C	C
Redhead	U	—	U	U
Ring-necked Duck	C	—	C	C
Canvasback	U	—	U	U
Greater Scaup	R	—	R	R
Lesser Scaup	C	R	C	C
Common Goldeneye	U	—	U	U
Bufflehead	C	—	C	C
Oldsquaw	R	—	R	R
White-winged Scoter	R	—	R	R
Surf Scoter	—	—	R	R
Black Scoter	R	—	R	—
Ruddy Duck	U	R	U	U

Species	SP	S	F	W
Hooded Merganser	C	—	C	U
Common Merganser	C	—	U	C
Red-breasted Merganser	U	R	R	U
Turkey Vulture*	C	C	C	C
Black Vulture*	C	C	C	C
Sharp-shinned Hawk*	U	R	U	U
Cooper's Hawk*	R	R	R	R
Red-tailed Hawk*	C	C	C	C
Red-shouldered Hawk*	U	U	U	U
Broad-winged Hawk*	C	U	C	—
Rough-legged Hawk	R	—	R	R
Bald Eagle*	U	U	U	U
Northern Harrier	U	—	U	U
Osprey*	C	U	C	R
Peregrine Falcon	R	—	R	R
Merlin	R	—	R	R
American Kestrel*	C	U	C	C
Northern Bobwhite*	C	C	C	C
Ring-necked Pheasant*	R	R	R	R
Turkey*	U	U	U	U
King Rail	R	R	R	—
Clapper Rail	R	—	R	—
Virginia Rail*	R	R	R	R
Sora	R	—	U	—
Common Gallinule*	R	—	R	R
American Coot*	C	R	C	U
Semipalmated Plover	U	—	R	—
Killdeer*	C	C	C	C
Lesser Golden-Plover	—	—	R	—
Black-bellied Plover	R	—	R	R
Greater Yellowlegs	C	—	C	R
Lesser Yellowleggs	C	—	C	—
Solitary Sandpiper	C	—	C	—
Spotted Sandpiper	C	R	C	—
American Woodcock*	C	U	C	U
Common Snipe	C	—	C	C
Short-billed Dowitcher	R	—	R	—
Semipalmated Sandpiper	U	—	U	—
Western Sandpiper	R	—	R	—
Least Sandpiper	C	—	C	—
White-rumped Sandpiper	R	—	R	—
Pectoral Sandpiper	U	—	U	—
Dunlin	R	—	R	R
Upland Sandpiper	R	—	U	—

49

Species	SP	S	F	W
Sanderling	R	—	R	—
Great Black-backed Gull	C	R	C	C
Herring Gull	C	R	U	C
Ring-billed Gull	C	R	U	C
Laughing Gull	U	C	C	—
Bonaparte's Gull	C	—	U	U
Forster's Tern	R	R	R	—
Common Tern	R	R	R	—
Caspian Tern	C	U	C	—
Black Tern	R	—	R	—
Rock Dove*	C	C	C	C
Mourning Dove*	C	C	C	C
Yellow-billed Cuckoo*	C	C	C	—
Black-billed Cuckoo*	R	R	R	—
Barn Owl*	R	R	R	R
Eastern Screech-Owl*	C	C	C	C
Great Horned Owl*	U	U	U	U
Barred Owl*	C	C	C	C
Short-eared Owl	R	—	R	R
Chuck-will's-widow*	U	U	—	—
Whip-poor-will*	C	C	U	—
Common Nighthawk*	C	U	C	—
Chimney Swift*	C	C	C	—
Ruby-throated Hummingbird*	C	C	C	—
Belted Kingfisher*	C	C	C	C
Northern Flicker*	C	C	C	C
Pileated Woodpecker*	C	C	C	C
Red-bellied Woodpecker*	C	C	C	C
Red-headed Woodpecker*	U	U	U	U
Yellow-bellied Sapsucker	C	—	C	C
Hairy Woodpecker*	U	U	U	U
Downy Woodpecker*	C	C	C	C
Eastern Kingbird*	C	C	C	—
Great Crested Flycatcher*	C	C	C	—
Eastern Phoebe*	C	C	C	U
Acadian Flycatcher*	C	C	C	—
Least Flycatcher	R	—	—	—
Eastern Wood Pewee*	C	C	C	—
Olive-sided Flycatcher	R	—	R	—
Horned Lark*	C	U	U	C
Tree Swallow	C	—	C	—
Bank Swallow*	U	U	U	—
Rough-winged Swallow*	C	C	U	—
Barn Swallow*	C	C	C	—

Species	SP	S	F	W
Cliff Swallow*	U	U	R	—
Purple Martin*	U	U	C	—
Blue Jay*	C	C	C	C
American Crow*	C	C	C	C
Fish Crow*	C	C	C	U
Carolina Chickadee*	C	C	C	C
Tufted Titmouse*	C	C	C	C
White-breasted Nuthatch*	U	U	U	U
Red-breasted Nuthatch	U	—	U	U
Brown-headed Nuthatch*	U	R	U	U
Brown Creeper	C	—	C	C
House Wren*	C	C	C	R
Winter Wren	U	—	U	U
Carolina Wren*	C	C	C	C
Marsh Wren	U	—	U	—
Sedge Wren	R	—	R	—
Northern Mockingbird*	C	C	C	C
Gray Catbird*	C	C	C	R
Brown Thrasher*	C	C	C	U
American Robin*	C	C	C	U
Wood Thrush*	C	C	C	R
Hermit Thrush	C	—	C	U
Swainson's Thrush	C	—	C	—
Gray-cheeked Thrush	R	—	R	—
Veery	U	—	U	—
Eastern Bluebird*	C	C	C	C
Blue-gray Gnatcatcher*	C	C	C	R
Golden-crowned Kinglet	C	—	C	C
Ruby-crowned Kinglet	C	—	C	C
Water Pipit	U	—	U	U
Cedar Waxwing*	C	R	C	C
Loggerhead Shrike*	U	U	U	U
European Starling*	C	C	C	C
White-eyed Vireo*	C	C	C	—
Yellow-throated Vireo*	C	C	C	—
Solitary Vireo	U	—	U	—
Red-eyed Vireo*	C	C	C	—
Philadelphia Vireo	R	—	R	—
Black-and-white Warbler	C	U	C	R
Prothonotary Warbler*	C	C	C	—
Worm-eating Warbler*	U	U	U	—
Golden-winged Warbler	R	—	R	—
Blue-winged Warbler	U	—	U	—
Tennessee Warbler	R	—	U	—

Species	SP	S	F	W
Nashville Warbler	R	—	R	—
Northern Parula Warbler*	C	C	C	—
Yellow Warbler*	C	U	U	—
Magnolia Warbler	U	—	C	—
Cape May Warbler	U	—	U	R
Black-throated Blue Warbler	C	—	C	—
Yellow-rumped Warbler	C	—	C	C
Black-throated Green Warbler	U	—	U	—
Cerulean Warbler*	R	R	R	—
Blackburnian Warbler	R	—	R	—
Yellow-throated Warbler*	C	C	C	—
Chestnut-sided Warbler	U	—	U	—
Bay-breasted Warbler	U	—	U	—
Blackpoll Warbler	C	R	C	—
Pine Warbler*	C	C	C	U
Prairie Warbler*	C	C	C	—
Palm Warbler	U	—	U	R
Ovenbird*	C	C	C	—
Northern Waterthrush	C	—	U	—
Louisiana Waterthrush*	C	C	U	—
Kentucky Warbler*	U	U	U	—
Connecticut Warbler	—	—	R	—
Mourning Warbler	R	—	—	—
Common Yellowthroat*	C	C	C	R
Yellow-breasted Chat*	C	C	C	—
Hooded Warbler*	C	C	C	—
Wilson's Warbler	U	—	U	—
Canada Warbler	U	—	U	—
American Redstart*	C	C	C	—
House Sparrow*	C	C	C	C
Bobolink	C	R	C	—
Eastern Meadowlark*	C	C	C	C
Red-winged Blackbird*	C	C	C	C

Species	SP	S	F	W
Orchard Oriole*	C	C	C	—
Northern Oriole*	C	R	C	U
Rusty Blackbird	U	—	U	U
Common Grackle*	C	C	C	C
Brown-headed Cowbird*	C	C	C	U
Scarlet Tanager*	C	C	C	—
Summer Tanager*	C	C	C	—
Cardinal*	C	C	C	C
Rose-breasted Grosbeak	U	—	U	—
Blue Grosbeak*	C	C	C	—
Indigo Bunting*	C	C	C	—
Dickcissel*	R	R	R	R
Evening Grosbeak	C	—	U	C
Purple Finch	C	—	C	C
House Finch*	C	C	C	C
Pine Siskin	U	—	U	U
American Goldfinch*	C	C	C	C
Red Crossbill	R	—	R	R
Rufous-sided Towhee*	C	C	C	C
Savannah Sparrow	C	—	C	U
Grasshopper Sparrow*	U	U	U	—
Vesper Sparrow	R	R	R	—
Dark-eyed Junco	C	—	C	C
American Tree Sparrow	R	—	R	R
Chipping Sparrow*	C	C	C	R
Field Sparrow*	C	C	C	C
White-crowned Sparrow	U	—	U	U
White-throated Sparrow	C	R	C	C
Fox Sparrow	U	—	U	U
Lincoln's Sparrow	—	—	R	R
Swamp Sparrow	C	—	C	U
Song Sparrow*	C	C	C	C
Snow Bunting	—	—	—	R

Accidentals:

Anhinga, Brant, White-fronted Goose, Paint-billed Crake, Purple Gallinule, Whimbrel, Buff-breasted Sandpiper, Royal Tern, Iceland Gull, Least Tern, Sooty Tern, Long-eared Owl, Saw-whet Owl, Golden Eagle, Red-cockaded Woodpecker, Common Raven, Western Kingbird, Yellow-headed Blackbird, Warbling Vireo, Bell's Vireo, Orange-crowned Warbler, Western Tanager, Bell's Vireo, Orange-crowned Warbler, Western Tanager, Black-headed Grosbeak, White-winged Crossbill, Lark Sparrow, Black-throated Sparrow, Common Redpoll, Henslow's Sparrow, Bachman's Sparrow.

Chronology of Indian History in the Capital Region

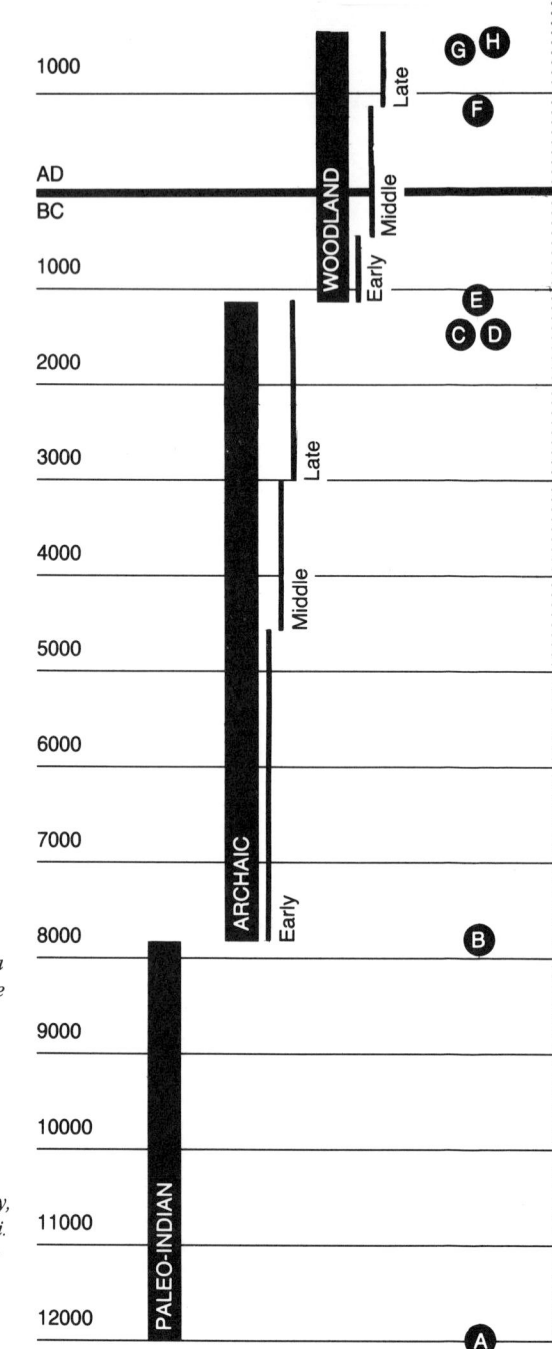

A Approximate arrival of man

B Extinction of large mammals

C Beginnings of settlement

D Introduction of stone bowls

E Introduction of pottery

F Introduction of beans and squash

G Beginnings of tribal confederations

H Arrival of Europeans

The two great tribal confederations in this area were the Monacan and the Powhatan Indians. Monacan tribal villages included Rassawek, Mowhemcho, and Massinicack. Powhatan tribal villages included Powhatan, Arrohattock, Appomattoc, Chickahominy, Pamunkey, and Mattoponi. The Monacans lived in the area to the west of the fall line, and the Powhatan in the area to the east.

52

CHAPTER 4

The Prehistoric Indians of the Capital Region

by Frederic W. Gleach

The history of Virginia as taught in our schools generally begins with the arrival of the colonists at Jamestown in 1607. The story of the Indians who met them when they arrived is seldom told, except as they related to the early settlers. Yet these first inhabitants of the region are thought to have arrived as long ago as 12,000 B.C., and their history, as revealed through archeology, is very interesting, particularly as one visits the natural parks and preserves which constitute the remnants of the natural world they lived in.

Many archeological sites excavated in this region have yielded (and continue to yield) artifacts from Indian encampments and settlements.

These provide information about the lifestyles of Indians at different times in the past, allowing their history to be deciphered, so that now we can begin to speak with confidence on the progressive changes in Indian cultures over that enormous time period (as shown in the time chart.)

The Paleo-Indian Period

The earliest period of prehistory in this region is known to archeologists as the Paleo-Indian period, and includes the time from the first arrival of man to approximately 8000 B.C.. During this period, animals living in the area included several species of very large mammals which are now extinct, such as the mastodon and large forms of bison, beaver, and caribou. The people of this time are generally thought of as hunters of these big game species, which indeed provided for a large part of their needs, but they also hunted smaller animals and collected nuts, berries, and other plants in season.

The Paleo Indians made tools of wood, bone, and stone, although the stone tools are the only ones to survive in any quantity. Housing for the most part consisted of tents made from the skins of the animals they hunted for food. The region was a land of plenty, providing a wide variety of resources to meet every need.

The population spent most of the year in small groups, basically in extended families, roaming a large area of the countryside in pursuit of game and other food. Periodically these small groups, called micro-bands, would come together at a central location to form a larger group known as a macro-band. This central location was often chosen because some relatively scarce resource was located there, such as the fine-grained chert and jasper rocks they favored for making tools. While assembled as a macro-band, the group's activities included trading, marrying between families, meetings, and celebrations. At the end of this time together, the macro-band again split into the smaller micro-bands, which went on their way as before.

This pattern of isolated groups periodically coming together created two main types of Paleo-Indian archeological sites - those where the smaller bands camped, and those of the large, collected macro-bands. Because the macro-bands tended to meet at the same location repeatedly and remained there longer than at the smaller sites, these are usually larger and, to the archeologist, more complex to excavate.

The Archaic Period

The next period defined by archeologists is known as the Archaic, and lasted approximately from 8000 to 1000 B.C. In terms of artifacts that are commonly found, this period is differentiated from the Paleo-Indian period in the shape and composition of stone tools used, owing to changing environmental conditions.

By this time the climate was warming as it recovered from an earlier glacial period. As a result, over a period of several thousand years changes took place in the plant and animal species available to the Indians. Also, the very large mammal species that had been hunted in earlier times had become extinct, and the Indians were forced to adapt from their specialized hunting of these animals to a more generalized and diversified selection of prey.

Deer and turkeys came to be staple foods in this region, with bear, waterfowl, turtles, and fish also contributing to the Indian diet. There was an increased emphasis on plants as a food source, including the nuts, fruits, and seeds of many different species.

This generalized approach made it easier for each group to find what it needed as its members foraged in smaller areas. If one resource was not available, another could be substituted for it. The same flexibility applied to material for tools. Owing to a scarcity of the fine-grained chert and jasper that had been favored for tools in the Paleo-Indian period, the much coarser but more common quartzite was more widely used.

In order to find all of the resources needed, the groups remained mobile, but each roamed a smaller territory than in the Paleo-Indian period. Because the population was steadily growing, the individual groups were larger. They no longer periodically formed macro-groups, and were relatively independent of the others.

Each group had a slightly different mix of resources on hand in the area occupied. For instance, groups in the coastal plain, to the east of the fall line, had plants and animals available to them which were different from those available to the groups in the piedmont. Over a period of thousands of years, each group gradually adapted to its own particular situation, using specialized tools and practices that met its needs.

Certain environments were rich enough to support settlements for much of the year without the need to move. These areas were mostly along the rivers, especially in the piedmont floodplains, where rich, fertile soil supported an abundance of plant foods. If the vegetation is cleared from such an area, the plants that grow up immediately afterward consist largely of grasses and shrubs, many of which have edible and wholesome parts. That deer and turkey were attracted to these habitats was an added advantage of clearing.

The high grounds above these floodplains were covered with various nut-producing trees, and the rivers were full of fish, particularly in the spring with shad, herring, striped bass, and sturgeon coming upstream to spawn. In the coastal plain, areas around swamps provided a similar variety of resources. In areas such as these, semi-permanent settlements began to appear toward the end of the Archaic period, around 1500 B.C.

These sites mark the beginnings of a settled way of life, a shift from moving to find the resources needed by a group to producing them within the settlement area. Some groups settled in before others; some had to move at certain times of the year when resources became scarce in their settlements; others continued to wander for a long period of time.

Settling in one place created a great many complications, and more complex societies evolved to support this new way of life. People in a group maintaining semi-permanent residence at a specific location are less likely to tolerate encroachment on what they begin to see as "their" territory; the concept of territoriality began to develop. A social hierarchy also evolved. In earlier stages there was little need for any one person to have higher status than any other, but with semi-permanent residence, a ranked system became useful in maintaining order and defending territory.

Because some needed resources were not available in given settlements, trade networks arose. In addition, trade in exotic goods and materials supported the newly developing hierarchical system because possession of exotic goods conferred a certain prestige on the possessor. The excavation of a limited number of these artifacts on a site provides clues to the structure of the society which inhabited it.

The establishment of a semi-permanent place of residence also created the need for certain types of tools, such as stone axes for clearing forested areas. Other tools that would have been difficult to carry on the move could be developed and used. A mobile population must carry all of its tools along with it. In this situation, it helps if none of these are excessively heavy or fragile. The implements most used for carrying gathered nuts or fruits were therefore baskets, light and durable - but a basket cannot be used for cooking. The beginnings of permanence meant that weight and fragility were no longer of much concern; Bowls carved from soapstone, a very soft stone, began to be used for cooking and food preparation, and were among the items carried by trade networks.

The Woodland Period

At its beginning, the Woodland period, which extended approximately from 1000 B.C. to the arrival of the European colonists, was marked by no major changes other than the use of pottery - pots made from readily available clay instead of stone bowls. Many of these have been excavated in the region.

The slow process of settling in, begun in the Archaic period, continued. Some groups were still living in ways virtually identical to those of the earlier period, hunting and gathering as they moved within a relatively large territory. This pattern was common in the uplands of the piedmont. Others lived in semi-permanent settlements, particularly in areas rich in resources, such as the margins of swamplands. Yet others, commonly those settled along the floodplains of the piedmont rivers, were clearing fields and selectively allowing new growth to come in, then harvesting the grains and fruits thus produced.

The hierarchies and trade networks that had begun to develop flourished and became more complex. The Woodland period was to see these carried to great heights before the coming of the colonists forced great changes on the Indian culture from outside.

The Beginnings of Agriculture

The groups who were already cultivating the land in a basic fashion were responsible for the next great innovation in the region - agriculture.

Clearing the land to allow new growth to come in and be harvested is a simple method of selecting the plants that you want to have growing because certain plants will naturally flourish on cleared land. A better method is to sow the seeds of the plants you want to produce. The Indians first planted the seeds of the locally available plants, such as wild mustard, lamb's quarters, and pigweed, which provide either edible greens or seeds that can be ground to produce flour. Later, plants which were not native to this region were introduced from other areas. Among these were beans, peas, squash, pumpkins, and corn.

The diet of the Indians was a healthy mix provided from many sources. (See also Chapters 2 and 3 - *Plant Communities and Wildlife.*) Meat included venison, turkeys, and fish. Plants furnished meal for bread, greens, and other vegetables. Nuts could be eaten raw or cooked, or boiled to produce oil. One method used to prepare food was to cook everything together - meat, fish, vegetables, and nuts - as a stew in a big pot. Fish were often smoked so that a large supply could be laid in during the annual fish runs, to be used in other seasons.

The use of planted species allowed a larger population to be supported by a given plot of land, and the need to cultivate these plants, to encourage them to grow to their fullest potential, tended to further stablize settlements in a permanent location, at least for the duration of the growing season.

A Late Woodland Village

The village of Secotan in North Carolina, as engraved by Thomas de Bries, based on a watercolor by John White painted in 1585, showing Indian houses and fields.

Villages

The larger of these agricultural settlements, by the Late Woodland period, can be classified as villages. We have descriptions and drawings of these made by the early colonists. They consisted of a cluster of houses with garden plots and often fruit trees nearby. The houses were made of saplings set in the ground and bent over to form an oval to rectangular framework with an arched roof. Bunches of grass were then woven in to form thatched walls, or mats woven of grasses were lain over the framework like the skin of a tent. By the Late Woodland period, warfare was enough of a threat that many of the larger villages were also fortified by a palisade for defense. The tools and supplies needed by the villagers were either produced there or obtained by trade.

Confederations

By the time the Europeans arrived, the individual villages of the Indians had been joined in networks, forming confederations of different groups. This further increase in the complexity of the social organization allowed easier control of the flow of resources through trade from one group to another. In the hands of wise leaders, this kind of control provided security for all groups. If crops failed in one area, food could be supplied from other areas where they had been successful. Thus all members of the confederation had an equal chance to survive.

In order to support this system, a complex mechanism had to be developed to insure close ties between the member groups of the confederation. This was accomplished largely through intermarriage between the families of the chiefs of the different villages. In this way, the heads of all groups were related by marriage, and each had an interest in the survival of the others. Redistribution was accomplished by gifts given by the chiefs of the villages that were doing well to the chiefs of the villages in need, for distribution to their members.

Impact of the European Settlers

Had they been left to themselves, the Indians' culture would have continued to develop. What forms it would have taken cannot be known. What happened when the Europeans arrived has happened where ever a highly developed group settles in an area populated by a primitive group; the more highly developed group displaces the other.

On first arrival, the Europeans began to make friends with the Indians in order to help assure their own survival in the new land, and to defend themselves in case friendship could not be maintained. Jamestown was established at a position that offered great potential for defense, but the location was a breeding ground for many diseases and a poor choice for farming. By 1611 the colonists were spreading out throughout the region. The most common approach was to seize an Indian village, killing or running off the inhabitants. This offered the advantage (to the colonists) of providing them with already cleared fields, saving them a great deal of effort in the heavily wooded territory. The Indians began to fight back; thus began several decades of intermittent warfare between the Indians and the colonists.

Although fewer in number at first, the colonists were much more heavily armed than the Indians, and were led by military men with experience in the wars of Europe. Given this situation, plus the steady influx of more colonists, the outcome was inevitable. Most of the Indians were pushed further west or south, into territory not yet claimed by the colonists, to compete for their survival with other Indian groups already established in those areas. Many died of diseases brought by the Europeans; others were killed outright; yet others were pushed onto land of marginal use to the colonists. Some of these areas were later established as reservations.

A few made the great cultural leap to assimilation at the time. Pocahontas, daughter of Chief Powhatan, is a famous example. Most of the descendents of the survivors were also assimilated over the years. A few live on the Pamunkey and Mattaponi Reservations in King William County just outside the Capital Region. In a few short decades, however, a culture which had been developing for millenia was essentially eradicated from the region, preserved only in tales handed down from generation to generation, and in the remains left in the ground, to be excavated, studied, and interpreted by archeologists.

As you walk through the natural parks and preserves of this region, realize that the entire area was once a wilderness that supported a people for thousands of years. For information about archeological discoveries, colonial accounts, and natural resources available to the Indians, see *References* below.

Postscript

While archeology is essential to an understanding of Indian history in the region, it is also very useful in discovering the history of the early colonists of the region. History is generally written about the important and influential figures of the past; little has been recorded about the lives of the ordinary people who settled the area and kept society running for many generations. There are now several archeologists specializing in the excavation of early colonial sites in this region, and in the interpretation of artifacts and other information gathered. Their findings will add greatly to our knowledge of the early history of the region and of particular sites, some of which are located in the parks and preserves.

Frederic W. Gleach holds a degree in Anthropology from Virginia Commonwealth University and is presently employed by the University as an archeologist.

References

Hume, Ivor Noel 1969. *Historical Archeology*. Alfred A. Knopf. (Tells how to lay out and excavate an historic archeological site and what is done with artifacts after they have been removed from the ground.)

Jennings, Jesse D. 1968. *Prehistory of North America*. McGraw Hill. (Gives a good overview of the prehistory of all of North America.)

MacCord, Howard A., Sr. and Wm. Jack Hranicky (no date) *A Basic Guide to Virginia Prehistoric Projectile Points*. Published by the Archeological Society of Virginia. Available from the Archeologial Society of Virginia, Dr. Theodore R. Reinhart, Department of Anthropology, College of William and Mary, Williamsburg, Va. 23185, at a cost of $3.75.

McCary, Ben C. 1957. *Indians in Seventeenth-Century Virginia*. Pamphlet published by the Anniversary Celebration Corporation on the occasion of the 350th Anniversary of the settling of Jamestown. Available in most libraries or from the Jamestown Visitor Center.

Smith, Capt. John (sic) 1970 reprint of 1624 edition. *The General Historie of Virginia, New England, and the Summer Isles*. Published by Walter J. Johnson. (Written in 17th century prose, Smith's account provides a good description of the lifestyles of the Indians met by Smith in his travels, as well as of the early colonies.)

Smith, Captain J. (sic) 1968 reprint of 1630 edition. *True Travels, Adventures, and Observations of Captain J. Smith*. Published by Walter J. Johnson.

Peterson, Lee Allen 1977. *A Field Guide to Edible Wild Plants, Eastern/Central North America*. Houghton Mifflin Company. (A handbook identifying the wild edible plants of the region, the Guide helps to explain the variety of food sources available to the Indians.)

Young Red Foxes

Section II

On and Along The Waterways

Spectators - On and Along the Waterways

On and Along the Waterways

by the Authors and Rose W. Deane

The rivers and lakes of the Capital Region are among the finest fishing and boating waters in the country. Even city dwellers and travelers staying in downtown hotels are as close to good fishing as the proverbial barefoot country boy. (More citation size smallmouth bass are caught in the Richmond James than anywhere else in the state!) Bank fishing spots are numerous, and boat landings and canoe launches provide access to boat fishing on many rivers and several lakes.

Fishing in General

According to the Virginia Commission of Game and Inland fisheries (Game Commission), species caught in the rivers and lakes of the region include largemouth and smallmouth bass, channel catfish, crappie, pickerel, white and yellow perch, walleye, bream, eel, and the introduced carp (good for catching, not so good for eating). In addition, striped bass and herring (including shad) run upstream during the spring spawning season. For more information and illustrations that will help you identify your catch, we recommend purchasing a copy of *Freshwater Fishing in Virginia*, published by the Alexandria Drafting Company and available in most sporting goods and 7-11 stores.

Freshwater fishing in Virginia is regulated and managed by the Game Commission. Virginia residents between the ages of 16-65 are required to purchase a fishing license and carry it while fishing in fresh waters. Licenses are sold in most stores that carry fishing tackle, and are valid for the calendar year. Current cost is $7.50 for Virginia residents and $15 for non-residents. Virginia senior citizens may obtain lifetime fishing (and hunting) licenses for a one-time cost of $5. Temporary fishing licenses and dipnet permits may also be purchased.

The Commission publishes booklets on fish and game species and regulations, wildlife management areas, and boating access, any of which may be obtained by dropping by or writing to the Virginia Game Commission, 4010 West Broad Street, Richmond, Va. 23230 - or telephoning 804/257-1000.

For up-to-date information about where the fish are biting, we recommend reading Max Ailor's column in the Sports Section of the Richmond Times Dispatch. For boating information, read on. For bank and lake fishing, see the end of this section.

Boating and Floating

The tidal rivers and major impoundments are fine for motorboating, and a great deal of fishing is done in these areas. Several landings for trailered boats provide access to these waters. (See *Rivers* below.)

The rapids along the fall zone and the shallow stretches above are best suited for canoeing, kayaking, rafting, and "tubing," for obvious reasons. A few small tidal streams and backwaters are also canoeable. These craft will take one through beautiful natural areas not usually seen otherwise, and (with the exception of inner tubes) through some of the best white water rapids in the country. Canoes are also perfect for fishing in flat waters where the current is not too swift.

Canoes are rapidly becoming the most popular craft in the region for upstream exploring and fishing, as well as for running the rapids. Several canoeing clubs are active in the region. (See *Resources* at the end of this section.) Experts have explored and mapped ideal canoeing waters, even to the extent of identifying put in and take out areas a suitable distance apart for a run of several hours and describing the character of each river segment. Two new canoe launches have been constructed in response to the frequent use of popular stretches, and it is likely the future will bring more.

H. Roger Corbett's excellent canoeing guide, *Virginia White Water*, published by the Seneca Press in 1977, is indispensable to any canoeist considering trips in this region (or, for that matter, in the state). His detailed descriptions of every stretch of river that can conceivably be canoed are about the best source of information around, with the possible exception of the new river rapids maps prepared for the falls of the James and Appomattox Rivers. An added feature in Corbett's book is historical background on the rivers and their environments, lending even more interest to many of the trips described.

For those who would like to try canoeing for the first time, several private liveries and organizations conduct easy trips, as does the Chesterfield County Parks and Recreation Department. Canoeing and kayaking lessons and rentals are also available. (See *Resources* at the end of this section.) Lessons are very important because canoeing and kayaking require skill and the knowledge of special safety practices. White water canoeing in particular requires a high degree of skill that must be learned and practiced.

We are indebted to Larry Hart, John Heerwald, Emily Kimball, Ralph White, and Chuck Wyatt for much of the information provided in this section. The numeric classifications used to describe rapids refer to the *International Scale of River Difficulty*, a rating system used and understood by canoeists everywhere.

Under this system, rapids are rated on a scale from I-VI, beginning with easy riffles and ending with challenging, even dangerous waters for teams of experts only, and even then under the best and most carefully controlled conditions. In general, Class I and II rapids are the only ones relatively safe for beginning white water canoeists with novice skills. Class III rapids are considered to require some complex maneuvering. Beginning with Class IV rapids, real expertise and all sorts of precautions are necessary. Our descriptions, however, are only intended to give a general indication of the characteristics of any given river segment. Canoeists and kayakers planning trips through rapids should consult river maps, Corbett's guide, and, if possible, expert canoeists who have experienced the contemplated trip.

Any listing of craft used above the falls would be incomplete without mentioning the truck-sized inner tubes rigged out for one or more lazy passengers and an ice chest for refreshments. These floating "craft" are popular during hot weather and low flow periods, especially on the upper James. On hot summer weekends whole flotillas float downstream between the Huguenot Bridge and Williams Dam, with passengers draped over their tubes, relaxing and socializing as they effortlessly drift along.

Like so many other popular pastimes, tubing is on its way to becoming an institution and a commercial enterprise. Several liveries are now renting inner tubes specially constructed for added safety, and requiring that life preservers be worn - an excellent idea.

Concession-operated trips are a wonderful way to experience the James River without risk or the need for equipment or experience. We have already mentioned canoe trips, most of which are on flat water. Undoubtedly the most thrilling rides are the James River Experiences white water rafting trips. (See also the description below under the *James River - Pony Pasture Take Out and Launching Area*.) The most sedate trips are cruises of the lower James on comfortable boats operated by Richmond-on-the-James. Concessionaires are listed under *Resources*.

James River Experiences - Richmond Times Dispatch/Rich Crawford

The Rivers

The James River flows through the heart of the Capital Region, crossing the fall zone in Richmond. (See Section II - *The Changing Landscape*.) The Chickahominy and Appomattox Rivers are major tributaries. All of these waters are superb for fishing and boating and fascinating to explore. Fortunately, several boat landings, canoe launches, and riverside parks provide access to these waterways.

To the north, the Pamunkey River and its three tributaries in the region - the North and South Anna and the Little River - are also fine recreational waters, although at this time access to these is mostly limited to public easements at bridge crossings. In carrying down canoes and parking along the shoulders of the bridge approaches, one must be very careful to avoid trespassing on adjacent property.

As they enter the Capital Region from the west, these rivers wind gently through the rolling piedmont countryside. In crossing the fall zone, the James, Appomattox, and the Pamunkey tributaries drop through a series of rapids (known in some instances as the falls) several miles in length, to reach the coastal plain below. (In contrast, the Chickahominy, a younger river which has not cut deeply through its channel, flows over the fall zone on a gentle gradient, lacking rapids.) In the coastal plain they slow, widen, and become tidal. The differences among the rivers, and their changing characteristics as they flow through the region, create interesting choices and challenges for fishermen and boating enthusiasts who enjoy a variety of experiences.

Boating in the tidal rivers may be strongly influenced by the tides; this should be taken into consideration in planning excursions. Tide charts for the day are published in most newspapers on Fridays and Sundays. To obtain a long-range daily tide chart, send a request and a stamped, self-addressed envelope to Tide Charts, Richmond Times Dispatch, Box C-32333, Richmond, Va. 23293, or drop by the lobby at 222 East Grace Street in Richmond.

In tracing the rivers below, we begin as they enter the region, and follow their courses to its eastern limits.

Rose Deane, a graduate student in the Virginia Commonwealth University Department of Recreation, carried out much of the research, and assisted in writing this section of the Guide. Before returning to graduate school, Ms. Deane was Environmental Education Coordinator for the Maymont Foundation.

The James River

The James is a superlative river, deserving of more than regional treatment, and important for more than its recreational value, though this is the focus here. Two excellent books have done its greater aspects justice—the recently published *In River Time—The Way of the James*, by Ann Woodlief, and *The Falls of the James*, by David Ryan (unfortunately now out of print.) Both are worth reading, owning, and cherishing by anyone who appreciates the James for its magnificence, the richness of its heritage, and its meaning to the people who live alongside it.

West of Richmond, Above the Falls

To explore the James in the Capital Region west of Richmond, start at Columbia Landing, across from the small town of Columbia in Goochland County. From Columbia to Beaumont Landing downstream the river flows quietly through rolling farm and forest land, interrupted only by little country towns. This is a beautiful stretch of the river. Too shallow most of the way for anything but canoes, kayaks, rafts, and tubes, ever since the canal boats faded away,—and what a sight they must have been!—the river now belongs to these. Exploring in downstream runs is a joy, and fishing is excellent all the way.

Five boat landings owned and maintained by the Virginia Game Commission make it possible to canoe this stretch of the river in short downstream segments, or explore and fish in the immediate vicinity, without having to shuttle cars. These are all simple affairs, strictly utilitarian, with one ramp (no piers) and parking for several cars. Bank fishing is possible at each of these, but the shore may be slippery when wet.

Columbia Landing

> Located on the south bank in Cumberland County where Route 690 crosses the river to intersect with State Route 6 at Columbia in Goochland County.

This landing also provides a take out for trips on the Rivanna River, which flows into the James immediately upstream. The entire area is delightful for fishing and paddling. The distance to Cartersville Landing downstream is approximately nine miles, an easy four–five hour trip under normal flow conditions; however, more time should be allowed if you intend to fish.

Cartersville Landing

> Also located on the south bank in Cumberland County, on Route 45 where it crosses the river to intersect with State Route 6 at George's Tavern in Goochland County.

The river here is similar to the area above and below Columbia. The run downstream to Westview Landing is a short one, only five miles that should not take more than three hours to paddle. Westview Landing is on river left behind an island. Watch for the island and try to approach it from upstream.

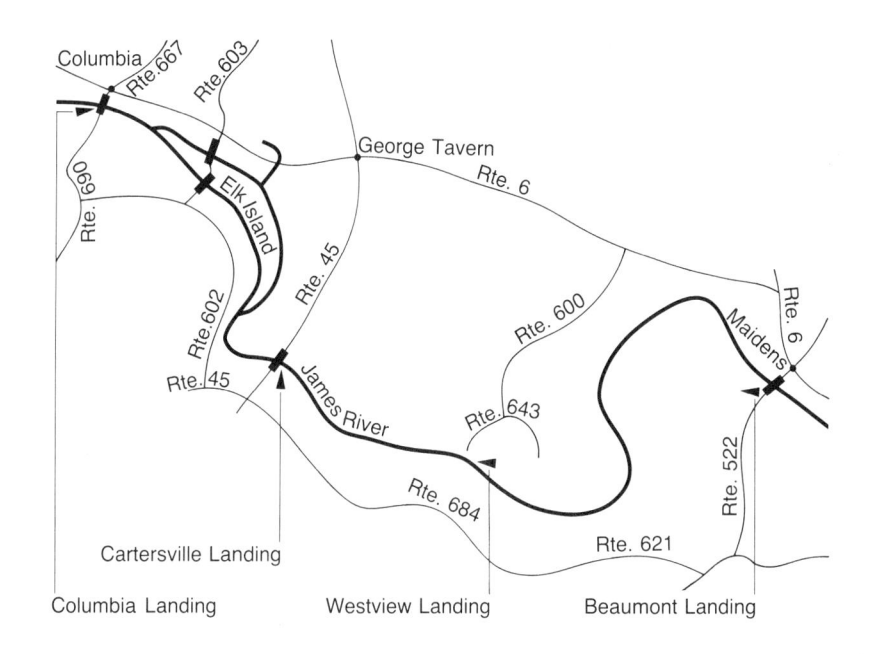

Westview Landing

>Located on the north bank in Goochland County at the end of Route 643. (There is no bridge crossing here. Westview can only be approached from the north.) From State Route 6 take Route 600 south to Route 643 and follow the signs to the landing, a distance of about five miles. The last few hundred feet are on a dirt road which is rutted but passable.

This landing is at the edge of a cowpasture, in a lovely bucolic setting with trees overhanging the bank. (But watch your step!) An island separates the landing from the main channel, which can be entered downstream. The distance to Beaumont/

Maidens Landing is 12.5 miles, a long paddle which may take up to seven hours. This stretch has a few riffles and more islands than the area upstream. Beaumont/ Maidens Landing is on river right.

Beaumont/Maidens Landing

> Located in Powhatan County on Route 522 along the south bank, across the bridge from Maidens.

The fishing is said to be exceptionally good here, particularly for smallmouth bass and bluegill. The distance downstream to Watkins Landing is another 12.5 miles, another long paddle of up to seven hours through occasional riffles and past several islands. The river is approaching Bosher Dam, and the last 1½ miles may be slowed by backwaters from the dam; paddling is no longer assisted by the current. Upriver traffic may be a problem here. Take out on river right at Watkins Landing.

Watkins Landing

> Also in Powhatan County, accessed from Route 711 via Route 642, seven miles west of State Route 147 and fifteen miles east of State Route 522. Route 642 is not on State Highway maps and rather unobtrusive. Watch for the Game Commission Landing sign.

This is a favorite launching area for fishermen with motor boats because Bosher Dam approximately nine miles downstream has a reservoir effect, deepening and widening the river. There being no other public landing between Watkins and the dam, boats must return to Watkins. The river is suitable for water skiing a short distance below where the river widens, but the traffic precludes comfortable canoeing.

Bosher Dam

(No public access here)

> Crosses the James from western Richmond to Henrico County, just east of the mouth of Tuckahoe Creek on the north bank.

Boaters in the area should anticipate the dam and be careful to avoid it. Watch for the warning signs. An interesting feature north of the river here is Tuckahoe Creek, which marks the western extent of the James River and Kanawha Canal in the Capital Region. The canal followed the creek almost to its mouth before cutting over to join the river above the fall zone. Canal boats entered the river here going upstream and entered the canal going downstream.

The Richmond James—Along the Falls

Below Bosher Dam the river starts on its journey over the fall zone; however, the rapids do not begin until it has flowed over Williams Dam. The flat water stretch of

71

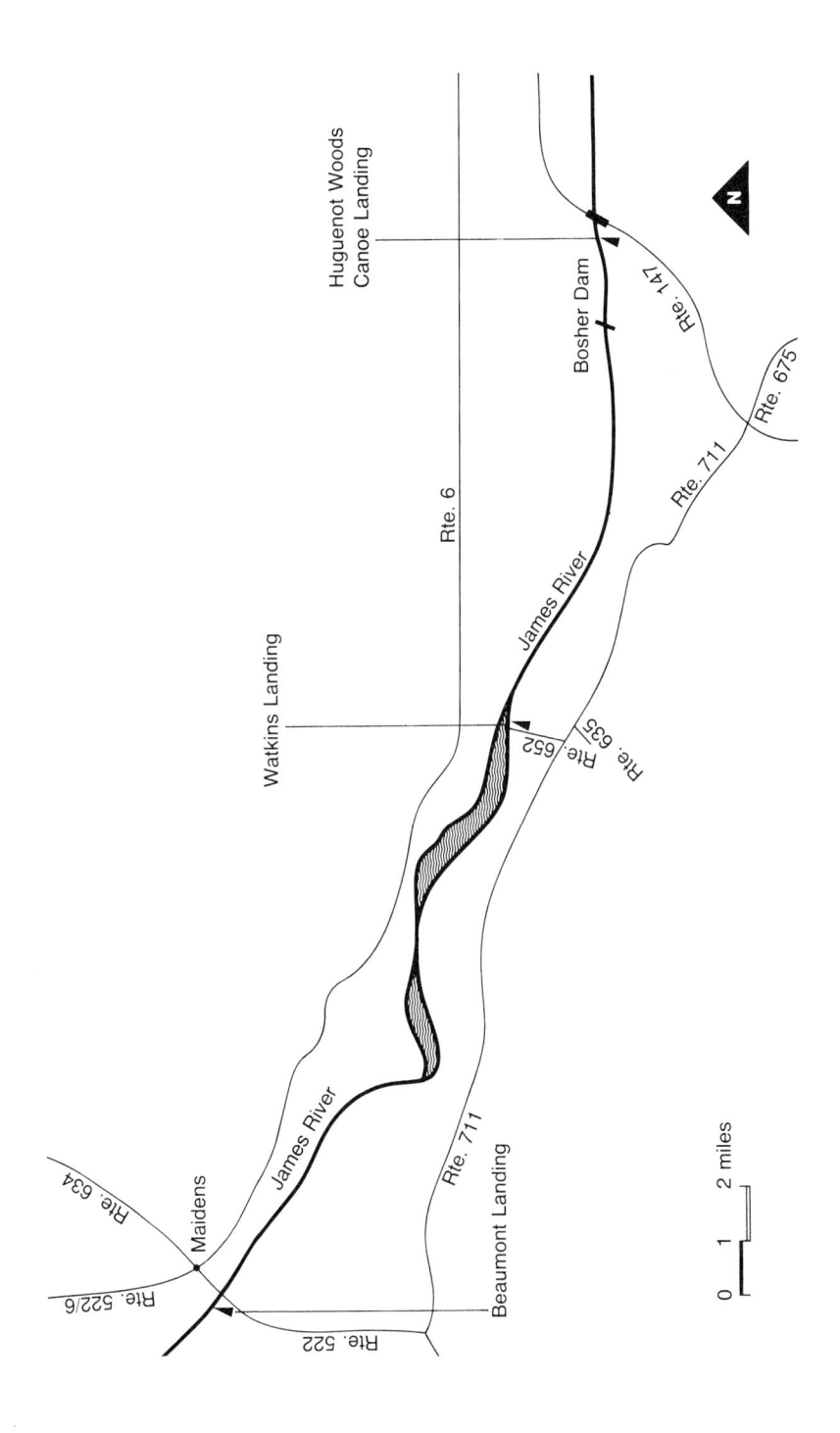

river between Bosher and Williams Dams is among the most beautiful of all, and the first upstream to be accessible from a park. Here under normal to low flow conditions the river flows so serenely between wooded banks and islands that reflections are almost perfect on sunny days. Fishing is excellent. Grassy shallows and little coves among the islands make it possible to linger in a canoe to cast. The Huguenot Woods Park provides good access for bank fishing.

Note that the City River Safety Ordinance requires that U.S. Coast Guard approved life jackets be worn if the river level is above five feet. When the level is above nine feet no one may enter the water without a special permit from the Department of Public Safety—telephone 804/780-8621.

Huguenot Bridge Canoe Launching Area

Located in the Huguenot Woods of the James River Park on the south bank just upriver of the bridge. Canoes may be unloaded from a new parking lot accessible from Southampton Road, off Riverside Drive west of the bridge.

This is a regular canoe launching facility, with steps down which canoes, kayaks, and similar craft (rubber rafts, inner tubes, etc.) must be carried. It is also possible to carry down johnboats, the shallowest draft motorboats practical for these waters. A James River Rapids map with information about the rapids and the city ordinance is posted here, and a river level gauge is being installed. From this launching area it is possible to canoe (or carefully motor) upstream as far as Bosher Dam and downstream to Williams Dam, altogether a very pleasant river environment, and to go island exploring as well. Williams Island is well worth a visit—a virtual wilderness in the river, except for a sandy beach along its south shore. (See Section III—Richmond—*James River Park*.)

The river in this area is shallow, with many submerged rocks. Even in a canoe it is a good idea to have a lookout in the bow. Both dams should be avoided; above all, Williams Dam should not be run. Watch for warning signs calling attention to it.

Most canoeists return to the launching area, but it is possible to portage around Williams Dam by taking out on Williams Island. Look for the portage signs, and be sure to put in well below the dam, as the hydraulic effect of the water immediately below it has caused several drownings. The downriver take out is on the bank of the Pony Pasture.

Pony Pasture Park Canoe Launching And Take Out Area

Situated in the Pony Pasture of the James River Park along Riverside Drive (south bank) 1½ miles downstream from the Huguenot Bridge Canoe Launch. Carry canoes from the parking lot.

An informal launching area (one simply shoves off from a rock-strewn shore), this is nevertheless a very important access to good canoeing on the river. Class I and II

Kayaking the Hollywood Rapids

rapids begin a short distance above the launching area and continue intermittently all the way to the Main Section of the James River Park downstream. In the vinicity of the Pony Pasture the rapids flow among rock outcroppings and boulders (a "rock garden" in canoeing language), creating a very beautiful environment of sparkling, churning water. Yet the shallowness of the river and the close proximity of the shore provide a great degree of safety. This area is frequently used for canoeing and kayaking lessons and practice, as well as for recreational canoeing.

Under normal to low-flow conditions, the three mile run downstream to the take out at the Visitor Center in the James River Park Main Section is classified as a novice or beginner's white water run. (Beginner in this context means a novice who has mastered certain skills and safety practices.) The Annual Urban Whitewater Races on the Falls of the James during Richmond's June Jubilee start with this run—the Downriver Race.

Novices should *not* go beyond the take-out at the Visitor Center in the Main Section, as the next stretch requires a great deal of white water experience and skill. The take-out area is on river right a short distance downstream from the Boulevard Bridge (see map). To reach the take-out area it is necessary to navigate between Archer and Bohannon Islands. The channel is marked with a blue sign.

The rafting trips of the James River Experiences also begin at the Pony Pasture launching area and travel all the way downstream to Great Shiplock Park, through rapids that only the most experienced canoeists should undertake. These strong inflatable rafts make the trip safely because of the way they are constructed and air cushioned, and because an expert guide in each raft directs the passengers how to paddle and maneuver. Anyone wishing to travel the length of these exciting falls without worry should consider one of these trips. For information call 804/323-0062.

James River Park Main Section Put-In to Great Shiplock Park Take-Out

This stretch of the James is for expert whitewater canoeists only. Class III-V rapids occur in several areas; when the river level is high, the Class V rapids become Class VI—very dangerous! (See map.) Boulders, rock outcroppings, old dams, bridge abutments, and log jams create obstructions that have to be avoided. Even experts planning to run this stretch study the map, scout the route, pick a team, check river levels, and take all possible safety precautions. (See also the City River Safety Ordinance under *The Richmond James—Along the Falls.*)

To see teams of experts run this stretch, watch the annual Championship Wildwater Race in June. For information on the date and time of the race and spectator access, check the newspapers.

Two informal take-outs on the north bank provide opportunities to shorten the run—one opposite the northeast shore of Belle Isle just below Tredegar Iron Works, another at Reynold's Metals a short distance downstream. Both have James River Park signs facing the river. In addition, a regular boat landing is planned for Brown's Island about midway between Tredegar and Reynolds. This will also have a river facing sign.

Canoeists with time to enjoy the scenery from the river will get a close look at Belle Isle and interesting views of Hollywood Cemetery, the Virginia War Memorial, Gamble's Hill, several bridges, Mayo's and Brown's Islands, the Richmond city skyline, Church Hill, and old Tobacco Row.

The informal take-out at Great Shiplock Park on the north bank is apt to be a muddy ending to a glorious run, but the historic lock is worth taking a look at on the way out. (See Section III—Richmond Parks.) Ancarrow Boat Landing a short distance below on river right is an alternative take out spot. (See *The James Below Richmond.*)

The James Below Richmond

Beginning at the 14th Street Bridge, the river slows, widens, and becomes tidal, as it flows into the coastal plain. Characteristic of a meandering coastal river, the James over millenia has created three large oxbows in its upper tidal area. These big swings in the river used to require boats travelling between Hampton Roads and Richmond to follow a long, tortuous navigation route, until cuts were made to straighten the river channel. The oxbows and the cuts across them may easily be seen on maps of the area.

The cutoffs, combined with natural changes in the course of the river and earth-moving gravel operations, have resulted in the creation of Hatcher, Farrar, Jones

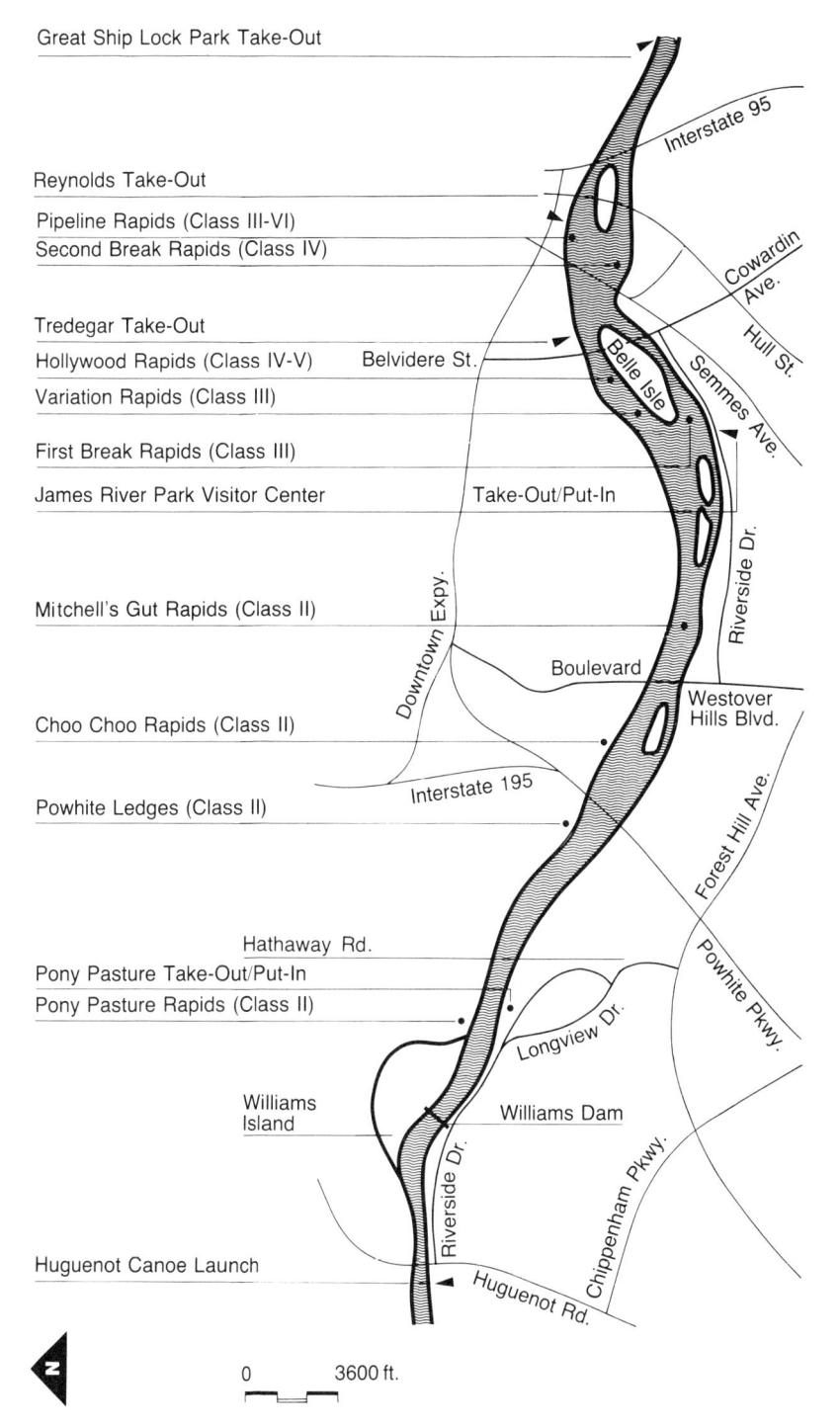

Great Ship Lock Park Take-Out

Reynolds Take-Out
Pipeline Rapids (Class III-VI)
Second Break Rapids (Class IV)

Tredegar Take-Out
Hollywood Rapids (Class IV-V) — Belvidere St.
Variation Rapids (Class III)

First Break Rapids (Class III)
James River Park Visitor Center — Take-Out/Put-In

Mitchell's Gut Rapids (Class II)

Choo Choo Rapids (Class II)

Powhite Ledges (Class II)

Hathaway Rd.
Pony Pasture Take-Out/Put-In
Pony Pasture Rapids (Class II)

Williams Island — Williams Dam

Huguenot Canoe Launch

Interstate 95
Cowardin Ave.
Hull St.
Belle Isle
Semmes Ave.
Riverside Dr.
Downtown Expy.
Boulevard
Westover Hills Blvd.
Interstate 195
Forest Hill Ave.
Powhite Pkwy.
Longview Dr.
Riverside Dr.
Chippenham Pkwy.
Huguenot Rd.

N   0   3600 ft.

75

Neck, and Turkey Islands. The same changes have created large placid backwaters where canoes may safely navigate without entering the main channel.

At one time when ships were smaller, the James was navigable to Shockoe Slip and Great Shiplock Park in Richmond. As ships became larger with deeper drafts, they loaded and unloaded at the old intermediate terminal along Dock Street at the end of Water Street. Today this is a favorite pier fishing spot. The terminal is also the embarkation point for the Richmond-on-the-James cruises of the lower James River.

The Deepwater Terminal further downstream on the south bank now marks the westernmost point of navigation for large ships travelling between Hampton Roads and Richmond. A strictly commercial operation, this is not a recreation area. Small boats travelling below the Deepwater Terminal should watch out for larger vessels passing.

Except for the backwaters mentioned above, the river below the 14th Street Bridge should only be travelled in motorboats because the current is strong and swift on the outgoing tide, and the incoming tide is also a force to be reckoned with. The wakes from larger vessels even create problems for small motorboats.

Unfortunately, water quality for some distance below the 14th Street Bridge is affected by effluent from the secondary sewage treatment plant and several industries discharging wastewater into the river along the route. Although the wastewater is treated and the State Water Control Board monitors water quality, the area is not as clean as that above the falls. (Contact recreation is not recommended.)

Cruising the lower James gives one an unusually interesting view of the natural and historic features of the river. From this perspective it is possible to see Drewry's Bluff (Fort Darling) as the crews of the Union gunboats saw it in 1862. (See Section III - *Battlefield Parks.*) Below the Turkey Island cut the Appomattox River flows into the James, cutting around City Point, the high bluff in Hopewell on which historic Appomattox Manor is visible. Seeing the bluff from the river, one realizes why General Grant chose to establish his logistical headquarters here during the Campaign for Petersburg. (See Section III - *City Point Unit.*)

At the confluence, the river widens considerably, and three famous colonial plantations come into view - Shirley above, Berkeley, and Westover downstream. From this perspective it is easy to understand the intimate relationship between the plantations and the river, which served as their main transporation corridor for travel, shipping, and supplies for many years.

Boat Landings on the Lower James

Only three public boat landings provide access to the lower James in the Capital Region.

Ancarrow Landing

>Along the south bank below the 14th Street Bridge in Richmond where the river turns south. To reach the landing, take Maury Street east to the entrance of the City Sewage Treatment Plant. Go through the gates to the landing site. At this writing the landing is only open between March 15 and June 15; at other times the gate is locked.

This landing provides the only access to the Richmond James for trailered boats. During the spring spawning runs upstream, rockfish (striped bass), shad, and herring are particularly abundant. This is a favorite spot for fishermen with small boats and a liking for striped bass.

Be sure to schedule launchings and take-outs during high tide periods, as the ramp is heavily silted and difficult to use at other times.

Dutch Gap Landing

>Located on the south bank in Chesterfield County on the Dutch Gap cutoff in the great double oxbow south of Richmond. To reach the landing from U.S. Route 301, take Osborne Road east to its junction with Coxendale, and continue on Coxendale to the end. From Interstate 95, take either Osborne or Coxendale east and continue as above.

Dutch Gap is a favorite launching area for trailered boats and is heavily used by fishermen and recreational boaters. The landing features a long wooden pier used for tying up boats and fishing. This is also the starting point for the planned trail to Henrico City Park downstream.

Deep Bottom Landing

>Located on the north bank of the river in Eastern Henrico County on the Jones Neck oxbow. Four Mile Creek enters the old channel just east of the ramp. From State Scenic Route 5 about eleven miles south of Richmond take Kingsland Road to Deep Bottom Road (about one mile). Turn left on Deep Bottom Road and travel about 1.4 miles to the landing.

This landing, which is owned and operated cooperatively by Henrico County and the Virginia Game Commission, features a few more facilities than most - a pier, restrooms, picnic tables, water fountain, and pay phone. Note that the county has a no-wake ordinance in effect here to prevent power boats from swamping smaller craft. In order to prevent interference with boat launching, pier fishing is prohibited on weekends and holidays.

Appomattox River

The Appomattox River, a major tributary of the James, originates in Appomattox County and continues as a small stream, though with several canoeable stretches, until it approaches Lake Chesdin, where it backs up behind Brasfield Dam. (See Lakes at the end of this section.) Within the region, the stretch of river between U.S. Route 360 and Route 602 downstream makes a good, short (5-1/2 mile) flat water trip for canoes. Canoeing below Route 602 is impractical because of the distance to the first take-out on the lake (27 miles) and traffic from motorboats and water skiing.

Below Brasfield Dam the river begins its journey across the fall zone, to enter the James at City Point. Throughout its course the river affords excellent fishing. The Falls of the Appomattox from an abutment dam downstream to Campbell's Bridge has been designated by the General Assembly as a State Scenic River for its spectacular scenery, rich history, and ecological diversity, as well as for its superb recreational qualities. This stretch of the river is known for its exceptional white water canoeing.

In many respects the Appomattox Scenic River is similar to the Scenic and Historic Falls of the James; however, access to and views of the Appomattox are more limited. The only good vantage points for overlooking the river are the Matoaca and Campbell's Bridges and the bluffs at Point of Rocks Park. (See map.) Three areas afford river level viewing and access to the rapids - the Appomattox River Boat Launch, the Matoaca Bridge (canoe) put-in and take-out area, and the Fleet Street area along the south bank above and below Campbell's Bridge.

The only way to see the entire stretch of the river along the falls is by canoeing it. Beside impressions of the river itself, canoeists will be fascinated by the remnants of the Upper Appomattox River Canal system, which ran from Petersburg to Farmville, and the ruins of several old mills that at one time lined the banks. (See Section III, Petersburg - *Appomattox Riverside Park*.)

To begin a canoe trip down the rapids, put in at the Appomattox River Boat Launch at the south end of State Route 669 (Chesdin Road) in Chesterfield County. A map of the rapids is posted near the launching area, with detailed descriptions and other information important to canoeists.

Also posted is information on river levels, which is keyed to a color-coded gauge attached to the dock. The lower the river level, the safer the trip and the less skill is required; conversely, the higher the river, the more skill is needed, and more potentially dangerous the run becomes, particularly at the end. Experienced canoeists will appreciate the care that has gone into this public information effort. Novices should be especially attentive.

The *Appomattox River Canoe Guide: White Water and History*, a pamphlet published by the Chesterfield County Parks and Recreation Department and the

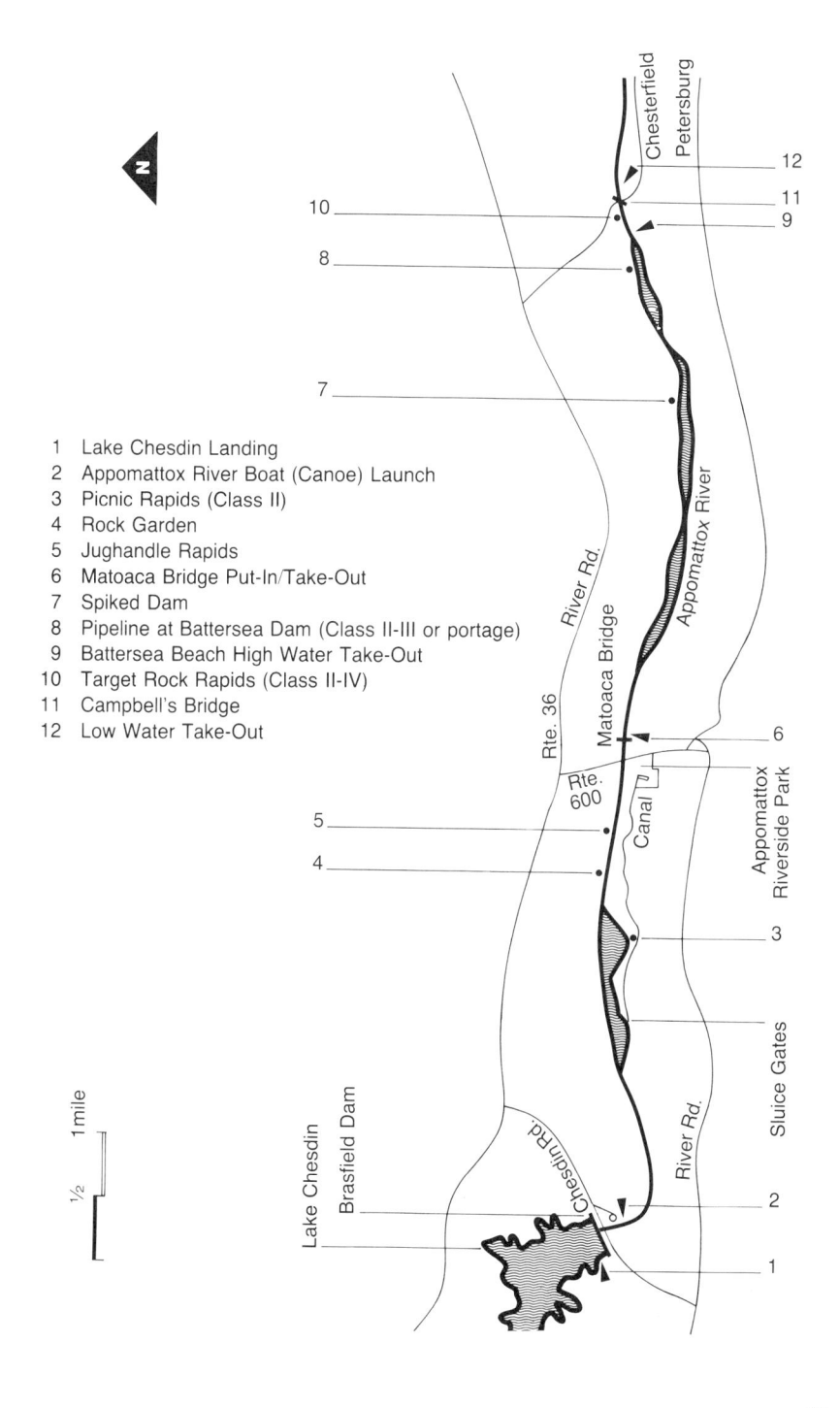

1 Lake Chesdin Landing
2 Appomattox River Boat (Canoe) Launch
3 Picnic Rapids (Class II)
4 Rock Garden
5 Jughandle Rapids
6 Matoaca Bridge Put-In/Take-Out
7 Spiked Dam
8 Pipeline at Battersea Dam (Class II-III or portage)
9 Battersea Beach High Water Take-Out
10 Target Rock Rapids (Class II-IV)
11 Campbell's Bridge
12 Low Water Take-Out

Appomattox River Rapids - Near Fleet Street Peninsula

Virginia Game Commission, furnishes much of this information and is highly recommended for trip planning. Copies may be obtained from the Department at the County Courthouse, (P.O. Box 40, Chesterfield, Va. 23832), the Virginia Game Commission in Richmond, and at several canoeing outfitters in the area. We are indebted to both agencies for the following information, which is amplified both in the pamphlet and the postings.

Under low to normal flow conditions, the first mile and a half downstream is an easy flat water run; however, it does require a portage around an abutment dam where part of the river is still diverted into the old Upper Appomattox River Canal, (and where the State Scenic River begins). Below the dam the river map shows Class II-III rapids, numerous islands, and "rock gardens", where the water flows around boulders and exposed bedrock. Canoeists planning a short (three mile) trip can take out on river right just downstream of the Matoaca Bridge.

The Matoaca Bridge take-out area can also be used to put in for the run down to Battersea Beach or Campbell's Bridge, (depending on river conditions). (Cars can be left in the parking lot of the adjacent Appomattox Riverside park.) The Class II-IV rapids and several obstacles along this downstream run require foreknowledge and careful maneuvering, including a possible portage.

Both take-out areas are on river right. A river map is also posted at Battersea Beach (the upstream tip of the Fleet Street peninsula) for canoeists scouting the problematic area between Battersea and the Bridge. At high river levels a dangerous whirlpool forms under the bridge, and taking out at Battersea Beach is recommended.

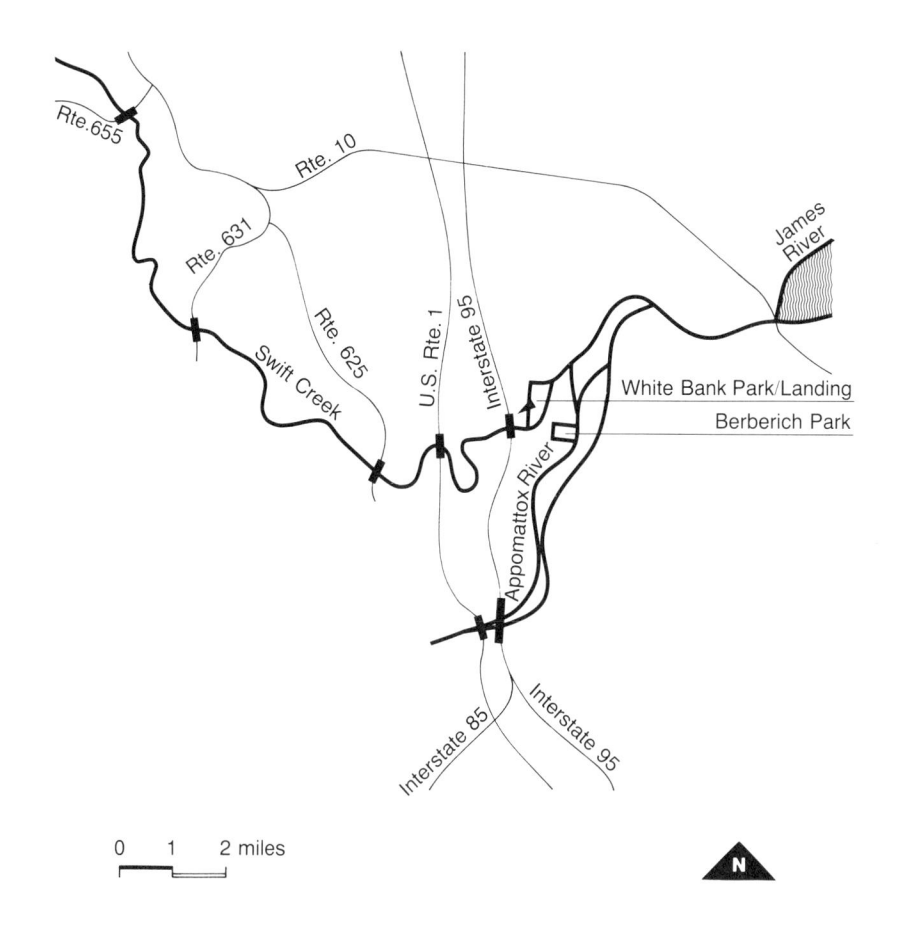

Below Campbell's Bridge a dam impedes navigation, and the river enters the coastal plain, flattening as it does so. After flowing through an urbanized area of Petersburg, the river turns abruptly northeast to enter the James. Water quality becomes somewhat degraded and brackish, owing to urban development and tidal influences.

Between Petersburg and Hopewell the banks become more natural, and a number of islands appear in the river. Public boat access in this area is, however, limited, to say the least. The only public area suitable for launching a canoe on the lower Appomattox is at Berberich Park in Colonial Heights. (See Section III, Colonial Heights - *Berberich Park/Fort Clifton*.) A regular boat landing on Swift Creek at White Bank Park (also in Colonial Heights), just above its confluence with the Appomattox River, also provides access to the Appomattox via an easy run downstream. The two parks are only a short distance apart, affording an easy shuttle.

An extensive tidal marsh spreads out in the area of the confluence, with numerous channels and low-lying islands which are fascinating to explore. Needless to say, bird watching is excellent. Fish are abundant, as the marsh is rich in food. Watch out for the poisonous eastern cottonmouth snake (sometimes erroneously called water moccasin), as this is the northernmost range of its habitat.

For the most part, boating is localized around the area just above and below the confluence of the two rivers. Of far more important consideration is the tidal action. At low tide the water may become so shallow in some areas as to make navigation difficult, especially for boats with outboard motors. Even with canoes, care must be taken not to run aground. In addition, the outgoing tide, added to the river currents, can make it difficult to return from a downstream trip. Trips should be planned with tides in mind.

The adventuresome may wish to paddle downstream as far as Point of Rocks Park - about a two hour trip, planning around the tide. It is possible to take out along the bank in the park for a rest, lunch, or look around, but parking is a long way off, so a regular take-out, shuttling cars, is impractical.

To explore the marsh with an experienced guide, join a field trip sponsored by the Chesterfield County Parks and Recreation Department. For information, check the published program schedules, or call 804/748-1623.

Marsh on Lower Appomattox

The Chickahominy River

The Chickahominy differs in character from the James and Appomattox Rivers, in that it has not cut deeply through its channel and therefore follows a gentle gradient, even across the fall zone, spreading over its indistinct banks to create a swampy environment for much of its length. West of State Route 360 the river channel is ill defined, meandering, and not recommended for boating. To get a good look at this part of the Chickahominy, visit Vawter Street Park in Henrico County or the Chickahominy Bluff Unit of the Richmond National Battlefield Park. (See Section III.)

Below State Route 360 to State Route 155 at Providence Forge, a distance of 27 miles, the channel widens, and the river becomes navigable, although fallen trees and thick vegetation create formidable obstructions. Explorers and naturalists who don't mind occasionally portaging here and there will be rewarded by the interesting flora and glimpses of wildlife along the way. Canoeing is the most practical way to travel this stretch, but johnboats may work in certain areas.

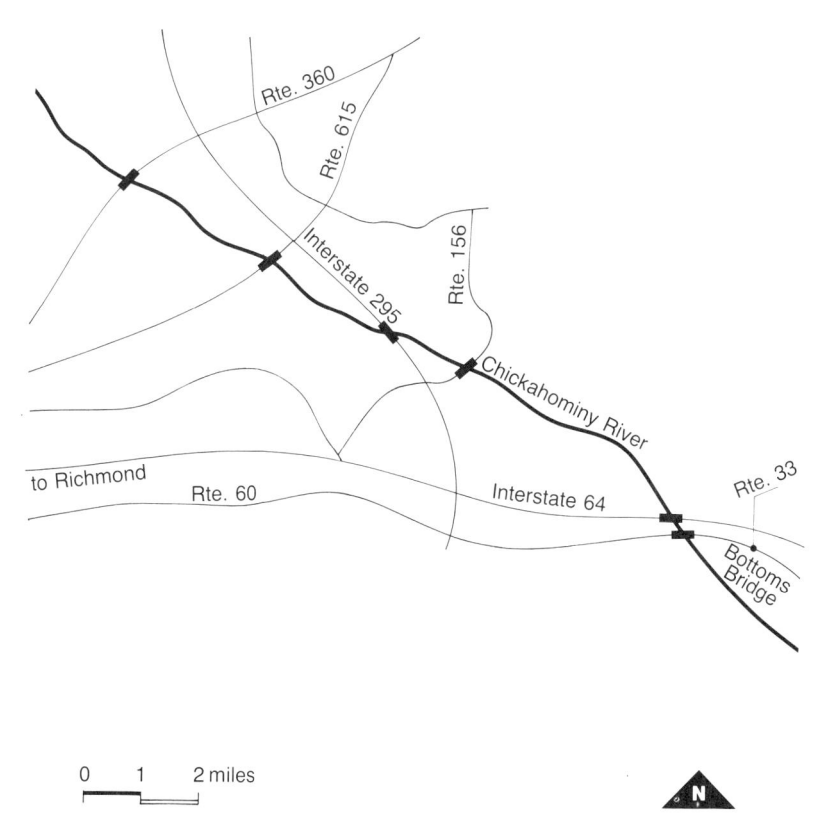

Highway bridges provide the only access - albeit informal - to this stretch of the river. Three crossings - at Routes 615 and 156 and U.S. Route 60 - allow it to be travelled in short segments. Be careful to park well off the road and away from private property.

Below Providence Forge in New Kent County, Walker's Dam impounds the river, creating the 2,000-acre (more or less) Chickahominy Reservoir, sometimes called Chickahominy Lake, and preventing tidal waters from intruding upstream beyond this point. The reservoir is used as a water supply by the City of Newport News, but fishing and boating are allowed and excellent. Approximately half the reservoir is swamp and a rich habitat for fish and wildlife.

Several private boat landings provide access to the reservoir, and either canoes or johnboats are suitable for getting around. Bank fishing may be difficult because of the swampy edges. Many citation size largemouth bass are caught here. Other plentiful fish include crappie, pickerel, and sunfish. Fishermen and other visitors wanting to stay awhile have their choice of three campgrounds located near the shore.

Naturalists will enjoy canoeing this beautiful swampy area for its interesting plant communities, including the magnificent bald cypress trees, and wildlife, especially the birds. Sightings of bald eagles and egrets are not unusual, and great blue herons are common.

A short distance below the dam the Chickahominy widens tremendously, typical of coastal streams, meandering through swampland and lowland forests. For some distance above its confluence with the James River it flows past the 5,300-acre Chickahominy Wildlife Management Area, operated by the Virginia Game Commission.

A boat landing on Morris Creek in the Wildlife Mangement Area affords good access to the Chickahominy a mile or so downstream. A motorboat is best for travelling in this direction, because of the current in the river. Morris Creek, however, is a beautiful tidal stream, which may be canoed by putting in where Route 623 crosses the creek outside the WMA and taking out at the landing. Parking is available at the Route 623 bridge.

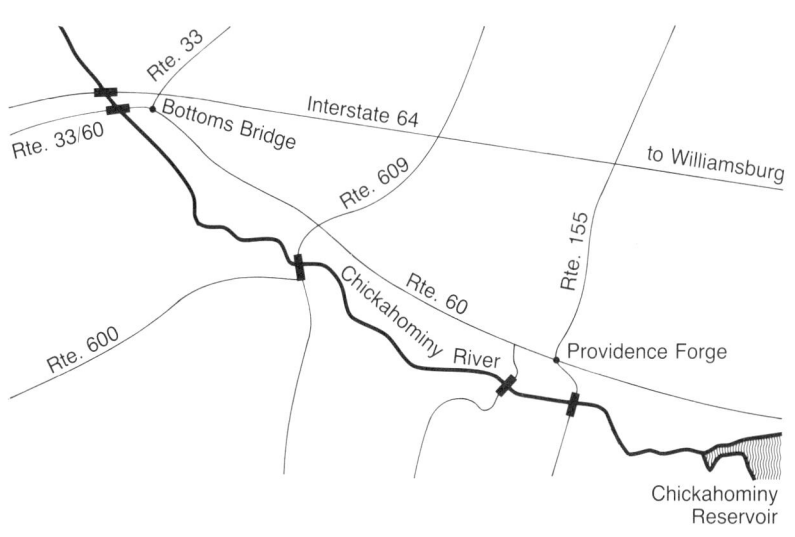

The North and South Anna and Pamunkey Rivers

Rivers in the northernmost part of the Capital Region drain into the York River basin. On entering Hanover County, The North and South Anna Rivers flow eastward across the fall zone, joining to form the Pamunkey River in the coastal plain. The Pamunkey, continuing in a southeast direction, meets the Mattaponi at West Point to create the York River, which flows into the Chesapeake Bay north of the mouth of the James.

The North and South Anna Rivers and the Little River, a tributary of the North Anna, flow through beautiful environs, and afford good fishing and excellent whitewater canoeing where they cross the fall zone. Unfortunately, access to these rivers is very limited.

At this writing, the only access areas are under the bridges mentioned below; however, the situation could change for better or worse. The area underneath bridges is always a state (public) easement. The problem in some places that might otherwise be accessible is that private property - often fenced and posted - directly abuts the bridge approaches, making it difficult to carry canoes beneath them without trespassing. It is important to recognize and respect private property, even if it means having no access. In some areas although there is room to carry down canoes, parking may not be permitted, even on the shoulders of the road. These conditions should be investigated before planning to put in.

The North Anna River

Before entering the Capital Region the North Anna is impounded in Louisa County for a Virginia Power Company nuclear power plant. Recently an area on the north side of the lake has been developed as Lake Anna State Park (one of the amenities on the periphery of this region).

As the river leaves Lake Anna it enters Hanover County, crossing the fall zone through a series of rapids into the coastal plain. Although several bridges cross the river, only the section between State Route 601 and Route 1 is accessible to the public because the other bridge crossings present access problems.

Route 601 to Route 1

The most beautiful section of the river, this stretch is said to contain Class II, III, and IV rapids (requiring some scouting) and several "rock gardens" as it tumbles over the fall zone. Water levels are generally suitable for canoeing except during late summer low flow periods. The water distance between bridges is approximately 9-1/2 miles; normally a canoe trip takes a minimum of 3-4 hours. The take-out is on river right after passing under the Route 1 bridge.

87

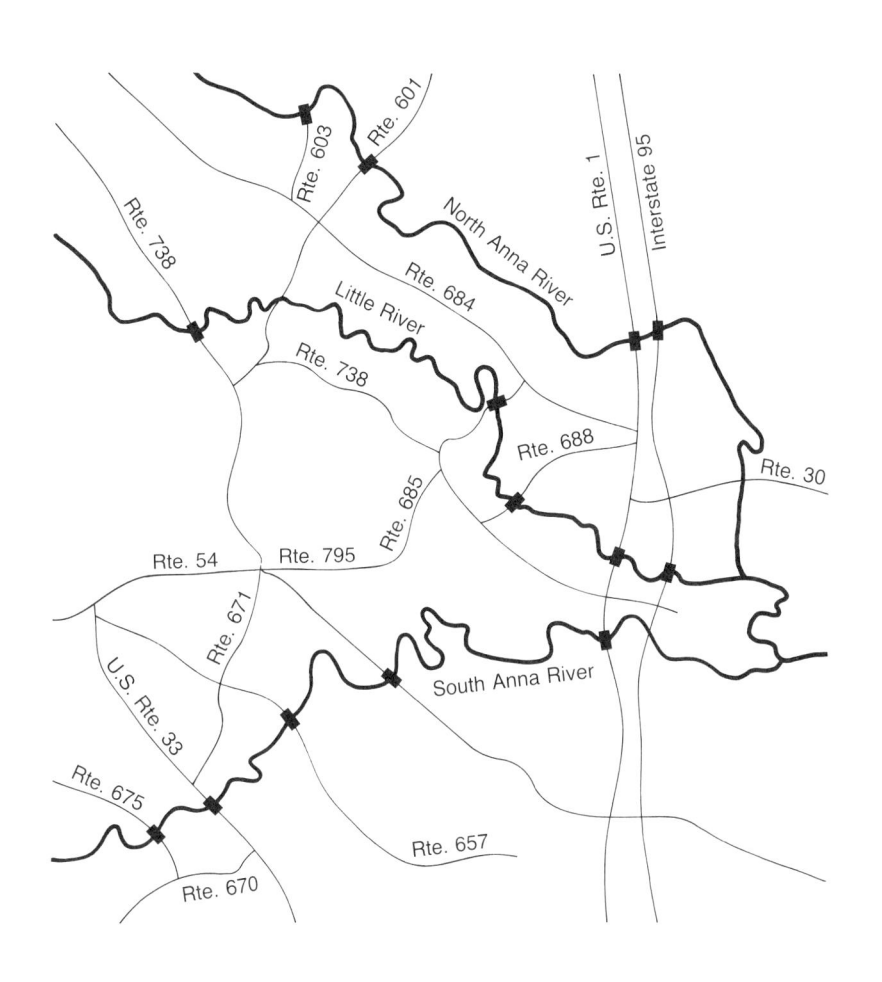

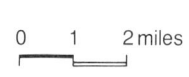

The Little River

The Little River, as its name implies, is a small stream - narrow and short -, flowing into the North Anna just above its confluence with the South Anna. From its headwaters in Louisa County the river flows through the Piedmont province as a flat, narrow, slow-moving stream. As it enters the fall zone, it completely changes its character, cutting a deep ravine through granite bedrock and flowing swiftly through a series of rapids. The scenery here is spectacular, almost alpine in character, with high, forested bluffs and cascades tumbling over granite outcroppings.

Unfortunately (at this writing) this beautiful area is not a park and not open to the public; however, Hanover County planners have identified part of the area as a potential park site for its scenic and recreational qualities. Although we have normally described only those resources that are presently in the public domain, it is mentioned here in the hope that the county's tentative plans will materialize.

South Anna River

Originating in the western piedmont province near Charlottesville, the South Anna enters the region through beautiful rural "horse country" in western Hanover County. All but two of the bridge crossings abut posted private property, with fences restricting access, leaving only one section of the river accessible from rights of way under bridges.

State Route 33 to Route 54

Access and parking is available at the Route 33 bridge along the southeast bank. According to Corbett, this section affords a nice downstream run, beginning with flat water, followed by Class I-II rapids and "rock gardens." The six mile trip takes about three hours. Fishing is said to be good in this area for bluegill, crappie, and smallmouth bass.

Pamunkey River

After the North and South Anna reach the coastal plain, they join to form the Pamunkey River. A typical coastal plain river, the Pamunkey meanders through historic farmland and lowland forest, flowing through a beautiful and wild swampy area in its lower reaches. Sections have been described as entering a virtual wilderness environment, offering unusual glimpses of wildlife along the way.

Unfortunately, although it is fairly wide and deep and well suited for fishing and boating (both by canoe and motorboat), the only public boat landing on the Pamunkey is at Lester Manor downstream below the Pamunkey Indian Reservation. It is possible to get informal access to the Pamunkey upstream by putting in canoes at any of several bridge crossings - Route 30 on the North Anna, Route 738 on the South Anna, and on the Pamunkey, at U.S. Route 301, Route 615, and U.S. 360 - about the right distance apart for downstream trips between them. Anyone

89

considering using these areas for access, however, should visit them first to make sure that parking is still allowed in the vicinity of the bridges.

The distance from U.S. Route 360 to Lester Manor Landing makes canoeing any further downstream impractical. As for motoring, the only launching area for trailered boats is at the landing.

Lester Manor Landing

>Located in King William County across the river from New Kent County. From State Route 30 travel approximately one mile east from the town of King William, then turn south onto Route 633 and drive about seven miles to the town of Lester Manor. Turn left at the Game Commission sign to the landing.

This is a good place to launch trailered boats for cruising and fishing in the vicinity. Because of the tides, canoeing is not ideal.

Pintail Drakes

Bank Fishing in Riverside Parks

Boat landings and canoe launching areas offer some opportunities for bank fishing as well; however, bank fishermen are not limited to these spots. Excellent bank fishing may also be enjoyed along the shores of several riverside parks. For descriptions and directions to the sites mentioned below, see Section III.

In Richmond miles of shoreline in the James River Parks - the Main Section, Belle Isle, the Pony Pasture, Huguenot Woods, and North Bank - are ideally suited for

Swift Creek at White Bank

bank fishing along the falls of the James, with a choice of casting into flat water or rapids. In many spots fishermen can walk out into the river on rocks where no overhanging limbs or underbrush will interfere with casting. In the future when Brown's Island is developed as a park, this may also be a good bank fishing spot just a short walk from downtown Richmond. Below the falls, Great Shiplock Park and the intermediate terminal are also favorites with many of the local fishermen.

In Petersburg the Fleet Street peninsula and small beach on the southwest bank below Campbells' Bridge, although not parks at this writing, together provide almost a half mile of accessible riverbank along the lower end of the wonderful Appomattox River rapids.

In Chesterfield County the new Henrico City Park trail leading downstream from Dutch Gap Landing will open up several small coves along the lower James River to bank fishermen. Also along the lower James, the small beach below Drewry's Bluff (Fort Darling Unit of the Richmond National Battlefield Park) is a favorite fishing area. The Appomattox River Boat Launch/park has turned out to be as popular with fishermen as canoeists; fishing is exceptionally good in this area because fish swimming upstream are blocked by the dam from going any further.

Lakes

All of the lakes in the Capital Region are either impoundments or dug ponds. Many of the smaller lakes in the region were created by dams in the 19th century to provide water power for grist mills. The mills are no longer there, but the dams and lakes have been preserved, many of these in the parks and preserves of today. Most have been stocked with fish, even, surprisingly, tiny lakes that at first appear to be merely relics or decorations in the landscape. Lakes entirely within parks and preserves are described in Section III. These include the following:

> Harrison Lake Fish Hatchery - Harrison Lake - boat landing;
> Pocahontas State Park - Swift Creek Lake - boat landing and rentals;
> Powhatan Wildlife Management Area - six lakes, two with boat landings;
> Petersburg - Lee Park - Wilcox Lake - boat rentals;
> Richmond - Bryan and Byrd Parks - small lakes;
> Hanover Wayside Park - small mill pond;
> Henrico - (in 1986-87) - Crump, Echo Lake, Deep Run, and Dorey Parks, all small ponds presently being stocked.

In addition to the Chickahominy Reservoir or Lake, as it is sometimes called (see Chickahominy River above), two major reservoirs are prime recreation areas for fishing and boating. Neither is encompassed in a park, and use of the surroundings is limited.

Lake Chesdin

> An impoundment of the Appomattox River between Chesterfield County on the north and Amelia and Dinwiddie Counties to the south. The only public boat landing, owned and operated by the Virginia Game Commission, is located in Dinwiddie County just upstream of Brasfield Dam. From State Route 601 in Dinwiddie County west of Petersburg take Route 776 north to the landing at the end of the road.

Lake Chesdin is a 3,000-acre reservoir operated by the Appomattox Water Authority as a public water supply and year round recreation area. Chesdin is a popular area for fishing, boating, water skiing, sailing, wind surfing, and swimming (in private marina enclosures). A long, narrow body of water with many inlets and coves, it is also very attractive and conducive to leisurely exploring. At quiet times explorers in canoes and rowboats can expect to see wildlife at the water's edge, and bird watching should be good.

For those who would like to stay overnight or vacation there, several private campgrounds are located near the shores. Boats may be rented, and small stores supply basic needs (gasoline, bait, tackle, and groceries). Other parcels of land surrounding the lake are privately owned residential properties.

In addition to the Game Commission Landing, four private marinas provide access to the lake. Boats with gasoline engines are allowed, but speed limits of 40-45 miles per hour apply, and all exhaust must be discharged beneath the water. The lake is patrolled continuously during the summer and periodically during the rest of the year.

The lake is well stocked with fish, including bluegill, channel catfish, smallmouth bass, pickerel, walleye, and a hybrid striped bass. Most of the fishing is done from boats, and citation size catches are not unusual.

Diascund Reservoir

An impoundment on Diascund Creek in New Kent County. To reach the only landing from State Route 60, turn north on Route 603 and travel to the end of the road.

1700-acre Diascund Reservoir is owned by the City of Newport News primarily as a water supply, but fishing and boating are allowed from April through November under somewhat restricted conditions.

A concessionaire charges a small fee for launching private boats. Only electric motors may be used on the lake. Bank fishing is prohibited. Boat rentals, bait and tackle are available from the concessionaire, who also operates a small campground along the shore.

Over the years, anglers have landed crappie, pickerel, white perch, largemouth bass, catfish, bluegill, and carp in this excellent fishing area. The open and wooded surroundings create an attractive environment. Exploring the lake is also a pleasant diversion, and likely to result in many sightings of water birds.

Resources

Information, Lessons, Outings, Rentals, and Memberships
American Red Cross - Virginia Capital Chapter
409 E. Main St., Richmond, Va. 23220
804/780-2250
Courses in swimming, canoeing, sailing, and water safety.

Bass Anglers Sportsmen's Society (BASS)
c/o L. W. Powers, Director
Central Virginia Bass Federation
14251 Pine St., Chester, Va.
Highly competitive membership organization for bass fishing only.

Chesapeake Bay Foundation
162 Prince George St., Annapolis, Md. 21401
1-800/445-5572
Estuarine and bay field trips in Virginia and Maryland.

Chesterfield County Parks and Recreation Department
Chesterfield County Courthouse, Chesterfield, Va. 23832
804/748-1623
Canoeing and other outdoor skills instruction and outings.

Coastal Canoeists
P.O. Box 566, Richmond, Va. 23204
Outings for members.

Virginia Commission on Game and Inland Fisheries (Game Commission)
4010 West Broad Street - P.O. Box 11104
Richmond, Va. 23230
804/257-1000
Fishing, boating, and hunting licenses, information and educational materials.

Float Fishermen of Virginia, Appomattox Chapter
Rte. 4, Box 35F
Appomattox, Va. 24522
Outings for members.

James River Experiences, Inc.
2971 Hathaway Road, Richmond, Va 23225
804/323-0062
Commercial rafting trips, canoeing and kayaking instruction, rentals.

James River Park Visitor Center
Main Section, James River Park, Richmond
804/231-7411
(Or write Department of Recreation and Parks, City Hall,
Richmond 23219)
Information on James River Rapids.

James River Runners
Rte. 1, Box 106, Scottsville, Va. 24590
804/286-2338
Canoe livery service - rentals and trips.

Maidens Canoe Livery
P.O. Box 336, Goochland, Va. 23063
804/556-4000
Canoe rentals and trips, shuttle service

Richmond-on-the-James
104 Shockoe Slip, Richmond, Va. 23219
804/780-0107
Lower James River Cruises and walking tours.

95

Richmond Power Squadron
Richard Zuraw, Public Relations,
Tidewater Marine
5016 Williamsburg Road, Richmond, Va. 23231
804/222-5450
Boating courses.

Science Museum of Virginia
2500 W. Broad St., Richmond, Va. 23220
804/257-0000
Sponsored outings and programs.

Sierra Club, Falls of the James Group
P.O. Box 25201, Richmond, Va. 23260
Outings for members and non-members.

Trout Unlimited, Virginia Council
Rte. 1, Box 12, Fishersville, Va. 22939
703/825-6660
Outings for members.

U.S. Coast Guard Auxiliary
c/o Larry D. Davis
8407 Kalb Road, Richmond, Va. 23229
Courses in power boat safety, sailing, and piloting.

Virginia Commonwealth University Outdoor Adventure Program
916-1/2 W. Franklin St., Richmond, Va. 23284
804/257-6043
Courses and lessons in canoeing, backpacking, rock climbing, and other outdoor skills.

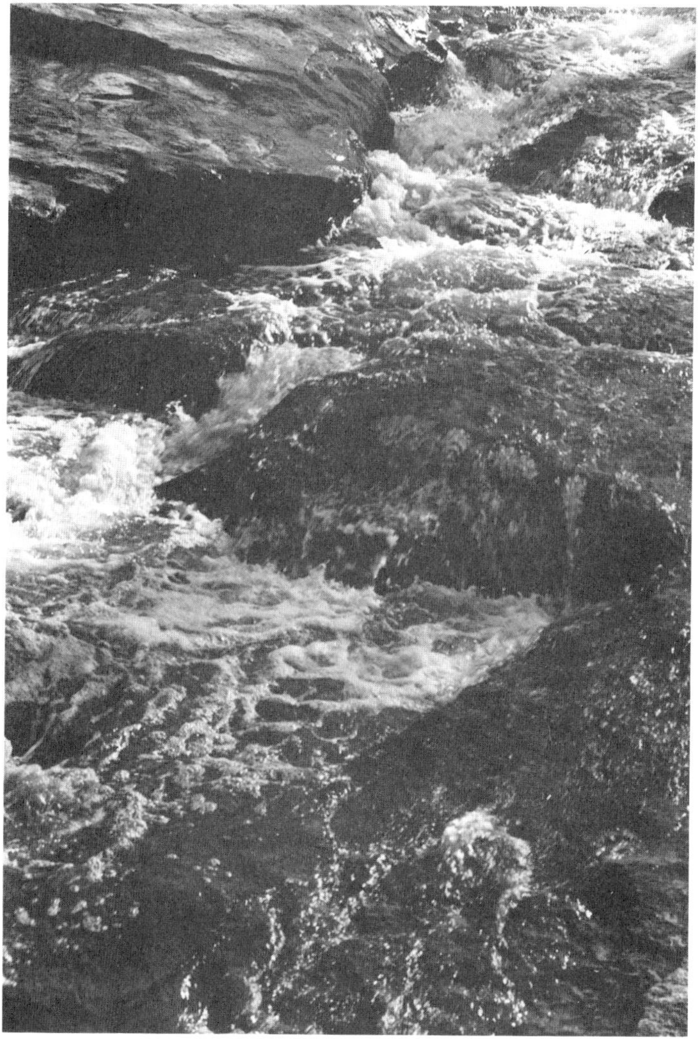

Section III

Directory of the Parks and Preserves

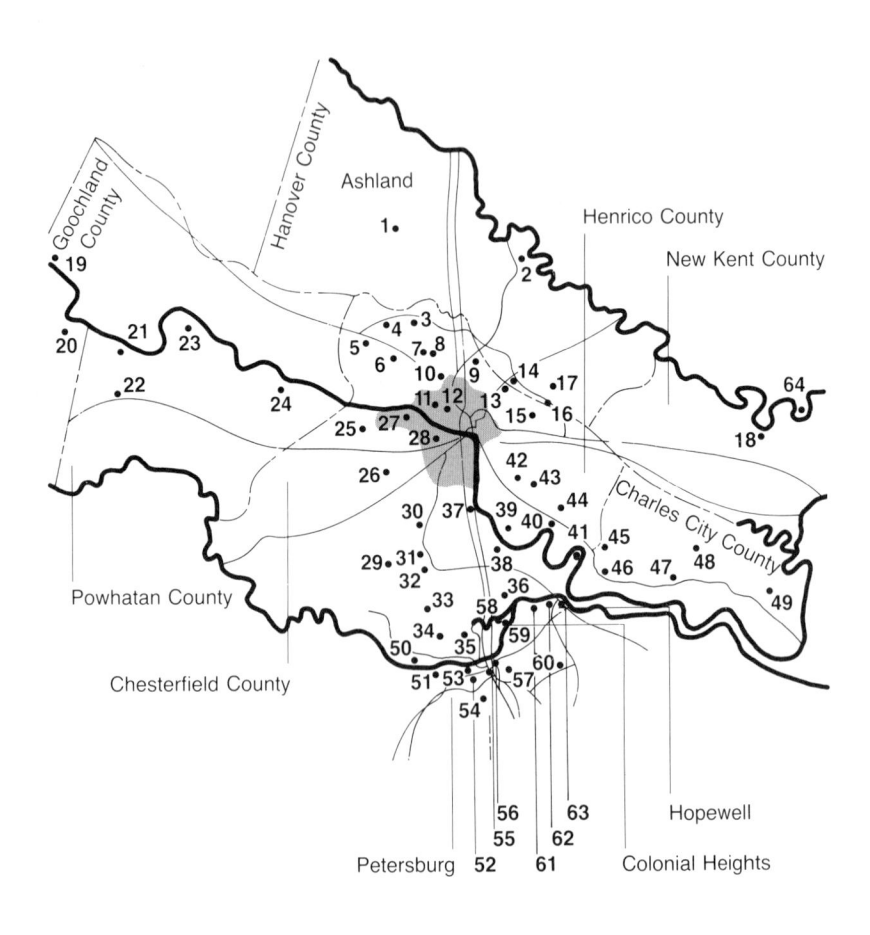

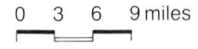

(See also Richmond Map page 125)

1. Poor Farm Park
2. Hanover Wayside
3. General Crump Memorial Park
4. Echo Lake
5. Deep Run Park
6. Cheswick Park
7. Lewis Ginter Botanical Garden
8. Belmont Recreation Complex
9. Vawter Street Park
10. Bryan Park
11. Byrd Park
12. Maymont Park
13. Chickahominy Bluff NBP
14. Beaverdam Creek NBP
15. Robinson Park
16. Watt House NBP
17. Cold Harbor NBP
18. Chesapeake Corporation Nature Trail
19. Columbia Landing
20. Cartersville Landing
21. Westview Landing
22. Powhatan Wildlife Management Area
23. Beaumont Landing
24. Watkins Landing
25. Huguenot Park
26. Rockwood Park
27. James River Park
28. Forest Hill Park
29. Pocahontas State Park and Forest
30. Iron Bridge Park
31. Court House Recreation Complex
32. Goyne Park
33. Harrowgate Park
34. Matoaca Park
35. Ettrick Park
36. Point-of-Rocks Park
37. Drewry's Bluff NBP
38. Dutch Gap Landing/Henrico City Park
39. Fort Harrison NBP
40. Deep Bottom Landing
41. Presquile Wildlife Refuge
42. Dorey Park
43. Four Mile Creek Park
44. Malvern Hill NBP
45. Harrison Park
46. Harrison Lake Fish Hatchery
47. Hillside Park
48. Charles City Recreation Center
49. Chickahominy Wildlife Management Area
50. Appomattox River Canoe Launch
51. Appomattox Riverside Park
52. West End Park
53. Fleet Street
54. Lee Park
55. Poplar Lawn
56. Blandford Playground
57. Petersburg National Battlefield Park
58. White Bank Park
59. Berberich Park
60. Prince George Park
61. Atwater Park
62. Riverside Park
63. City Point Unit Petersburg NB
64. Lestor Manor Landing

Mutual Attracton - Byrd Park

Nature Trail - Harrison Lake Fish Hatchery

National Preserves

Harrison Lake National Fish Hatchery

(354 Acres)

Located in Charles City County 23 miles east of Richmond along the north side of State Scenic Route 5, between Berkeley and Shirley Plantations. To enter, turn north from Route 5 onto State Route 658 then take an immediate right onto a short access road ending at the Hatchery.

Fishermen, hikers, and naturalists should enjoy visiting this federal preserve for the several unique features it has to offer. Harrison Lake, a 192-acre impoundment on Herring Creek, affords excellent fishing in a beautiful and secluded forest environment. The fish hatchery is of great interest, and is interpreted in a small Visitor/Environmental Education Center featuring an aquarium display and several other exhibits relating to fish and wildlife topics. In addition, an unusually appealing nature trail through a wooded area along Herring Creek provides a pleasant place to walk, with interesting discoveries along the way.

Once part of Berkeley Plantation, the hatchery property has an interesting history. Harrison Lake - like many other small lakes in the Capital Region - is an impoundment created many years ago to provide falling water-power for a grist mill. In 1934, some time after the grist mill ceased to operate, the United States Fish and Wildlife Service purchased the property, finding it ideally suited for the development of a "warm water" hatchery which could be supplied with water from the lake and mill race and drained by Herring Creek at the other end. WPA workers constructed the 24 fish production ponds, sheds with hatching tanks, staff offices, and other facilities needed to support the hatchery.

Operated by the Fish and Wildlife Service under the Department of the Interior, the hatchery propagates fish species that may be grown in ponds under near-natural conditions, where summer water temperatures reach 75-85'F. Currently 90% of the hatchery production consists of striped bass being grown to assist in restoring populations in the Chesapeake Bay. In 1980 approximately 280,000 were stocked in the James River. The hatchery also plans largemouth bass and channel catfish for stocking in military and other federally owned areas in the northeastern U.S.

To serve and inform the public better, the Service has recently converted an old residence into a Visitor/Environmental Education Center, which is open from April 1 through October 31. Also by special arrangement a staff member may be available to groups for orientation talks and the operation of an audio-visual program. This is a good starting point for a tour of the hatchery ponds, which otherwise are not interpreted. The Center and restroom are accessible to handicapped visitors.

Individuals are welcome whenever the Center is open. To make an appointment for group visits, call 804/829-2421.

The various habitats on the site support a variety of wildlife species. Bird watching is good; a platform overlooking the ponds provides a good view around the area and the edge of the woods. During a morning visit in June we also saw hundreds of tiny tree frogs climbing not only the trees, but the buildings as well!

The primitive nature trail*, which was developed by a Youth Conservation Corps group as a summer project in 1975, is a delight, not only for the interesting discoveries along the way, but also for the refreshing interpretive signs made by the YCC youngsters. They obviously enjoyed the project and threw themselves into it with enthusiasm.

Among the points of interest along the trail are examples of plant succession from field to forest, wildlife feeding grounds, point bars deposited by Herring Creek, and an old whiskey still, all charmingly interpreted by hand lettered signs. A poignant sight, which would not be understood without interpretation, is an area of shallow depressions where Civil War soldiers killed in battle were temporarily buried in 1862, while Berkeley Plantation was being used as a staging area by McClellan's troops.

Harrison Lake may be reached by a dirt road paralleling the mill race along the western edge of the hatchery property. Almost entirely surrounded by woods, the lake and a black gum swamp at its northern end can best be explored by small boats. Although beaten paths penetrate the woods for a short distance along the shore on both sides, they do not go far enough for exploring on foot. A simple boat ramp near the parking area provides access to the lake. It is important to note that Federal regulations limit gasoline motors in the lake to five horsepower, while electric motors are allowed. On a windless day, canoeing should be lovely.

Fishing from boats is said to be excellent, as the lake contains a good population of largemouth bass, bluegill, crappie, pike (chain pickerel), and catfish. Fishing from the dam is generally good unless the lake is low after a dry spell, as sometimes occurs in late summer. Shore fishing is also possible along the paths that go partway around the lake, but underbrush and low limbs may create problems with lines. State fishing regulations apply.

*The trail, being only a beaten path through uneven terrain, unfortunately is not accessible to the handicapped.

Boat Ramp

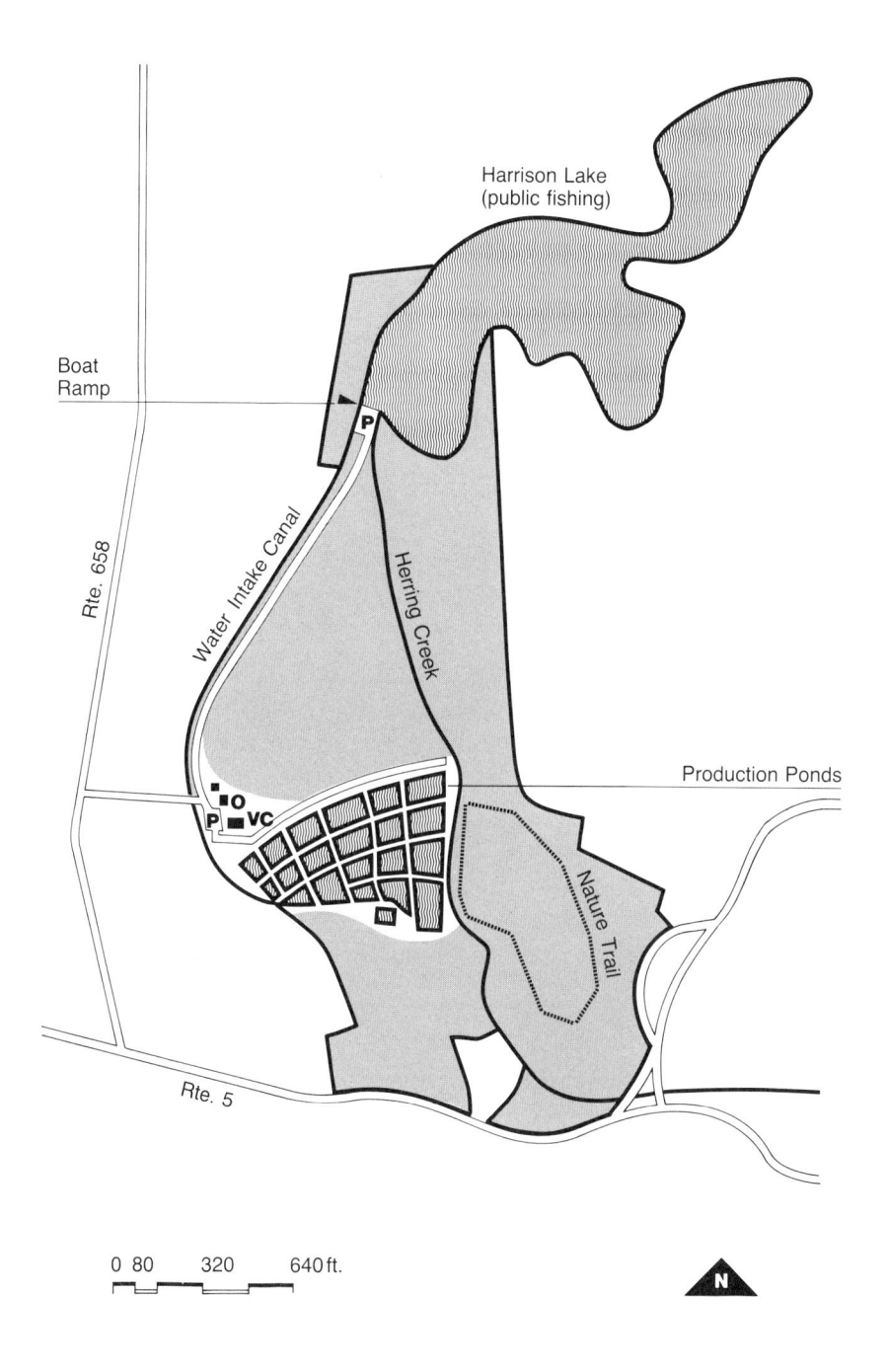

Rte. 658

Water Intake Canal

Harrison Lake (public fishing)

Herring Creek

Production Ponds

Nature Trail

Rte. 5

0 80   320   640 ft.

N

Presquile National Wildlife Refuge

(1,329 Acres)

An island in the third large oxbow formed by the James River below Richmond, five miles north of Hopewell. From Route 10 in southern Chesterfield County take State Route 827 east to the refuge ferry slip at the end of the road. Park along the edge of the road.

Transportation to and from the refuge is by a government-owned and operated ferry. For information on ferry schedules, call 804/458-7541, or write to Refuge Manager, Presquile National Wildlife Refuge, P.O. Box 620, Hopewell, Virginia 23860.

The Prequile National Wildlife Refuge (NWR), historically called Presque Isle, or Turkey Island, is a fascinating preserve established in 1952 by the Department of the Interior U.S. Fish and Wildlife Service to protect and manage the habitat of thousands of wintering-over waterfowl. Many other wildlife species are also managed, at least in the sense that their needs are recognized and their habitats left undisturbed.

Visitors are welcome throughout the year. There is a fine sense of adventure about taking the little cable ferry over to the island, anticipating what might lie on the other shore. On special occasions the ferry runs on a regular schedule all day, and an appointment is unnecessary. Another way to visit the refuge is to join a sponsored trip, such as a bird-watching expedition. (Watch the newspaper calendars for announcements of these special visitor's days and field trips.)

A brochure available at the visitor center near the ferry slip describes the habitats, plants, and wildlife, and calls special attention to the muskrat houses, wild rice, and dense stands of horsetail, a primitive plant seldom seen elsewhere in the region.

The 3/4 mile trail leads from the visitor center through a small wooded area, tidal marsh, and swamp, and across the island to the old farm and a simple picnic ground. Interested visitors will probably find themselves wishing that the trail were longer. Handicapped access is limited. Facilities are also simple; restrooms at this writing are of the portable type.

The island is a haven for the many animal species that inhabit its several protected habitats - river, marsh, swamp, woods, and farm land. Deer abound, raccoons and red fox are commonly seen during daylight hours, and muskrats and beaver are to be found along the tidal creeks on the island.

An old farm donated to the Department of the Interior now grows wheat, corn, clover and fescue, mainly for the Canada geese which graze on these crops during the late fall and winter months. With as many as 10,000 geese staying over, they can be quite a sight, both on the ground and in the air!

Curles Neck Plantation

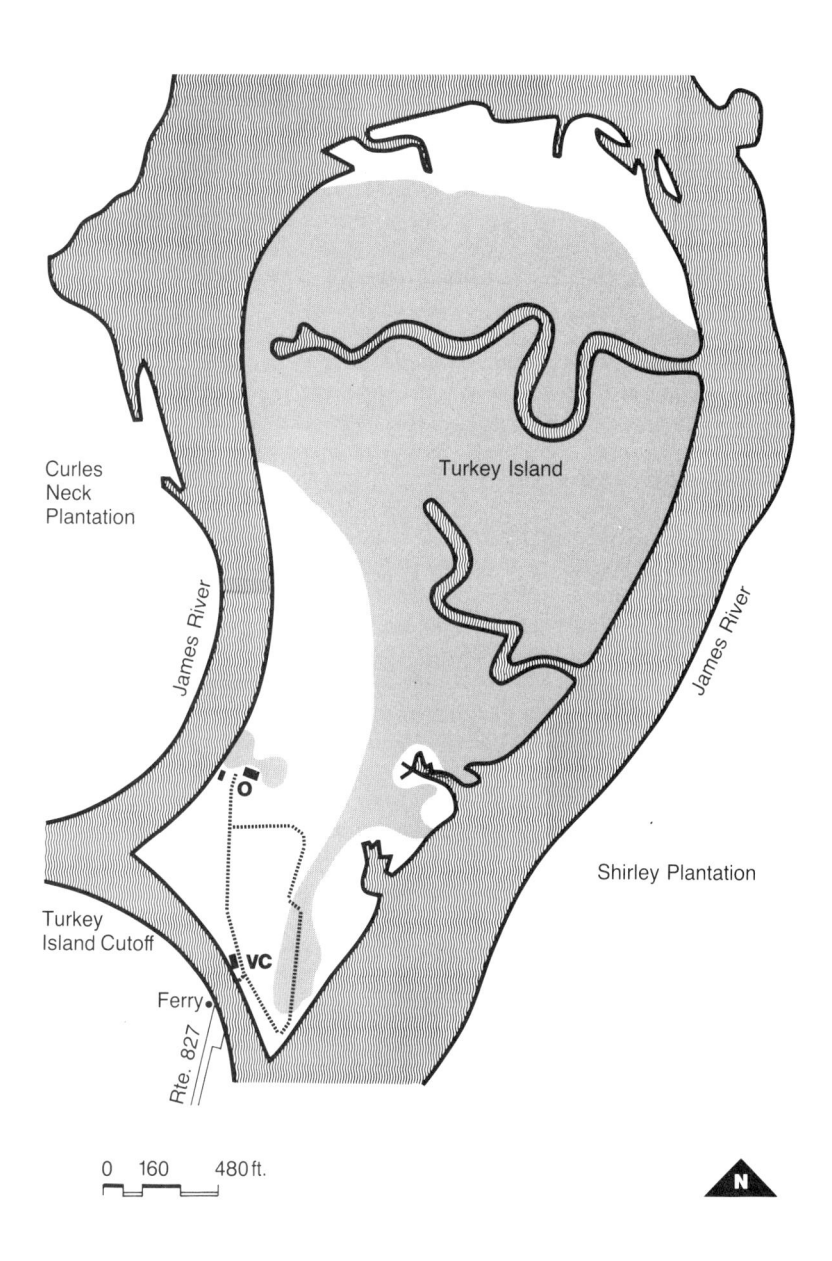

Turkey Island

James River

James River

Shirley Plantation

Turkey Island Cutoff

Ferry

Rte. 827

VC

0 160 480 ft.

N

105

A bird list for the refuge, available at the little visitor center, lists 199 species! According to Dr. Charles Blem, hundreds of ducks of several species also winter on the island. Bald eagles nest nearby and are commonly seen. Wild turkeys are often visible in early morning and late afternoon. Among the breeding birds on the island are Prothonotary Warblers, Yellow-throated Vireos, Blue Grosbeaks, Blue-gray Gnatcatchers, American Redstarts, Barred Owls, and many other species. The largest Bank Swallow colony in the region usually is active each spring along the banks of the main channel of the James River.

The swamps and marshes have substantial reptile populations. Large brown water snakes and northern water snakes may be routinely observed. Several other species of snakes occur on the island, but there are *no* records of poisonous species. (Cottonmouths do not exist there, although the species' range ends nearby.) Five-lined Skinks may be observed in the trees, and at least seven species of turtles are present in the river.

The north end of the island is still in a wild condition and inaccessible, a trackless swamp. Canoeists, however, can cross the channel (launching from the bank near the ferry slip) and enter one or the other of two little creeks draining the island, to quietly explore the area from the water. We are told that the going is easiest at high tide. (Canoeists should not venture into the main channel of the river.)

Interestingly, Turkey Island was once part of a peninsula in the great oxbow formed by the meandering James River. The island was created in 1934 when a shortcut channel was dug across the narrow neck of the peninsula to facilitate navigation. The old channel is seldom used now, and the isolation of the refuge area has probably helped to keep it a successful preserve.

The human history of the island is interesting. Archeological diggings have turned up traces of Indian habitation - arrowheads and pottery shards - as long ago as the Archaic period, and suggest that tribes occupied the area more or less continuously during the Early and Late Woodland periods as well. (See Section I - *Indians of the Capital Region.*)

As might be expected, English colonials moved in as they began to settle the area in the early 1600s. Several generations later but before the revolution, Colonel Richard Randolph farmed the peninsula and built a home there, which stood for many generations, and was taken over as General Benjamin F. Butler's headquarters in 1864. The old house was used as a staff residence until 1964, when a new dwelling replaced it.

The present use of the island is the happy consequence of its recognition as a valued wildlife habitat. The region is fortunate that Presquile was selected by the Department of the Interior to be included among the many national wildlife refuges operated by the U.S. Fish and Wildlife Service throughout the country.

State Parks and Preserves

Chickahominy Wildlife Management Area

(5,300 Acres)

Located on the eastern edge of Charles City County, bordering the Chickahominy River just above its confluence with the James River. Not shown on all state highway maps. From State Scenic Route 5 turn north on Route 623, which borders the property on the west, and proceed to Route 621, the main access road. (See map.) Turn east on Route 621 and drive four miles through the area to the main office.

From State Route 60 at Providence Forge turn south on Route 155 to Route 614, left on 614 to the first crossroads, and left again on Route 615 past Holdcroft where Route 615 turns into Route 623, then to to Route 621. Proceed as above.

As in all wildlife management areas, non-hunters are advised to visit outside of hunting season. For information about the various hunting seasons and regulations, call the Game Commission - 804/257-1000. For specific information about the area, call the WMA field office - 804/829-5336.

One of two wildlife management areas in the Capital Region (see also Powhatan WMA). Chickahominy is typical of river environs in the coastal plain. Except for the upland forests on well drained slopes, its habitats are wet - tidal marshes, swamps, beaver ponds, creeks, and lowland (flood plain) forests. Morris Creek, which flows through the area, is exceptionally beautiful and interesting, and superbly suited for fishing and canoeing. An adjoining piece of land to the south, forming a peninsula and point between river and creek, has recently been added to the WMA, increasing the access to both waters.

Most of the WMA is situated on a plateau at about 35-40 feet above sea level, although elevations vary between sea level and 90 feet, with some fine views over the river. Much of the forest has been recently cut, but is being successfully reforested, with park-like results.

Seven miles of gravel roads cross the preserve, and old logging roads (not shown on the map) used as trails and for internal access link ten parking lots. The property's design for maintenance, habitat management, and hunter penetration of the area serves admirably for hiking and horseback riding as well. Horse trailers may be left at any of the parking lots.

Wildlife species are much the same as those in the other WMAs in the region,

Morris Creek Swamp and Marsh - Chickahominy Wildlife Management Area

American Egrets

except that certain of those preferring wet habitats are more common. Copperhead snakes are also common here. (We ran over a good-sized specimen on the road, and were told to keep an eye out for more.) Hunters and hikers should wear boots and be on the watch. Game species include white-tailed deer, squirrel, rabbit, turkey, quail, snipe, woodcock, dove, and several species of ducks. The area also provides habitats for many non-game species, such as beaver, muskrat, opossum, raccoon, and mink, several reptiles, including snakes and turtles, and many birds.

109

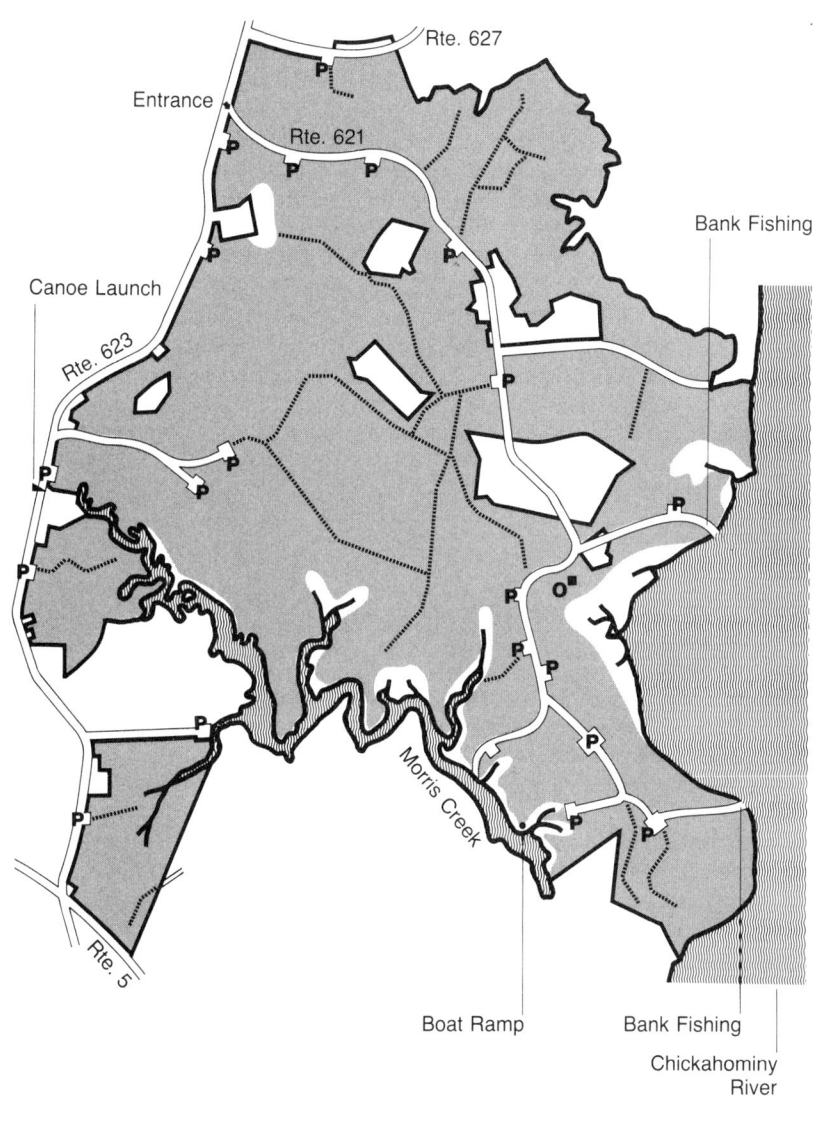

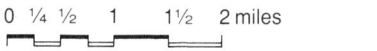

Fishing in Morris Creek, as well as the Chickahominy River, is said to be excellent year-round. Fishermen may expect to catch any of several kinds of catfish, white and yellow perch, sunfish, crappie, largemouth bass, pickerel, spot, croaker, and, during the spring runs, striped bass and herring. A new boat ramp provides access to the creek just two miles above its confluence with the Chickahominy, which makes it convenient to fish in either of these waters. It is also possible to put a boat directly into the Chickahominy in two locations, although at this writing these are not developed with ramps.

From the Morris Creek boat ramp it is possible to motor a short distance upstream before the creek becomes too shallow. This stretch is very beautiful, mysterious, and fascinating because of the tidal marshes it passes through, and the plants unique to these - among them, the tall wild rice and cattails, beggar ticks, smartweeds, pondweed, and the arrow-shaped leaves of arrow arum, arrowhead, and pickerel weed. Several of these plants are important foods for wildlife. (See Section I - *Plant Communities*.) Behind the marshes are swamps, and here, among the more familiar species found in lowland forests as well, the swamp-loving bald cypress trees also grow, their knobby "knees" projecting above the surface of the water.

Morris Creek is also the best place to see certain of the wildlife species inhabiting the management area, including many birds. The most spectacular are the great blue herons, flying low over the creek to fish. These breed in rookeries in the tallest of the swamp trees. We are told that bald eagles nesting nearby are also sighted now and then over the creek. Turtles seem to occupy every fallen log, and the swimming animals include not only ducks, but also beaver, muskrat, and mink. Other species come to the edge to drink, among them white-tailed deer.

It would be difficult to get close to these aquatic plant and wildlife communities without a boat. With a boat, however, a whole new natural world opens up! Best of all, we are told, is to put in a canoe where the Route 623 bridge crosses the creek, and paddle downstream to the landing, about a four-hour trip that should be a spellbinder. (Cars may be parked in a small parking area at the put-in spot.)

At this writing, no restroom facilities are available in the WMA, and drinking water must be carried in. These facilities will, however, become available across Route 623 from the main access road when Charles City County develops Mt. Zion, a community park planned for this location.

As might be expected from its location near Williamsburg, the WMA is in historic country, farmed as early as the mid-1600s. While few vestiges of these settlements remain today, Eagle's Lodge (circa 1690), an old dwelling and Virginia Historic Landmark, still stands not far from the field station and manager's residence. Recently restored, the house is occupied by a private owner.

Scout troops are allowed to camp with their leaders in designated areas, bringing their own equipment, provided special arrangements are made. For information, call the field office at the number above.

Pocahontas State Park and Forest

(1,791 and 5,648 Acres)

Located in the heart of Chesterfield County south of Courthouse and Matoaca Roads. Enter four miles west of the County Courthouse on Beach Road. Other entrances to the Forest are shown on the map.

Lovely, wooded Pocahontas State Park has the only public campgrounds in the region, and its surroundings and outdoor recreation features are the kind that go with camping and all day outings in the woods - an extensive trail system for hiking and nature study, a bicycle trail, horseback riding, a lake for fishing and boating, and a large modern swimming pool.

The park is situated in a rolling piedmont upland forest watered by Swift Creek and little Third Branch, one of its tributaries. The lower end of Swift Creek has been dammed to create a 2-1/2 mile long lake. Beaver Lake, a small empoundment on Third Branch, is man made, but, according to park personnel, beavers keep trying to improve it, in a continuing fight with the management, and have built their lodges on it. Nestled within the much larger State Forest and surrounded by game sanctuaries, the park is secluded and left for the most part in its natural state.

To fully appreciate the beauty and variety of its magnificent old trees and luxuriant understory - young trees, shrubs, wildflowers, ferns, and groundcovers - spend a day or two walking the nature trails of the Park. These pass through upland forest and flood plain habitats along the streams and lakes. Notice the interesting granite outcroppings exposed by millenia of weathering. Best of all, return from time to time to follow seasonal changes, progressing from the lacy foliage and delicate blossoms of spring to the robust wildflowers and flourishing growth of summer, the flaming colors of autumn, and the revealed branches of winter. Walk quietly and look for wildlife, especially birds; they are all about.

This park is an excellent place to study natural history. A good way to begin is to go on one of the nature walks, self-guided or conducted by park interpreters on summer days. Spring and fall weekend programs may also be available. A Visitor Center featuring plant and wildlife exhibits also helps to make discoveries on the trail more interesting and memorable.

Special natural history programs are conducted from time to time. Schedules can be obtained from the Park Superintendent, Pocahontas State Park, 10300 Beach Road, Chesterfield, Virginia 23832 (telephone 804/796-4255). If you happen to be in the park, you can pick one up either at the Park Office just inside the gate or at the Visitor Center. Maps of the Park are also available either place.

The 3.5 mile Grist Mill Bicycle Trail is routed through some interesting scenery, including the remains of an old grist mill in the woods, and an area in the State Forest recovering from clear cutting, (which makes you appreciate the woods, especially on a hot day). Notice the "pioneer plants" establishing themselves in this early period of plant succession. (See Section I - *Plant Communities*.) If you don't want to bring a bike, you can rent one from a concession operator in the park, in season. The granite dust trail, firm enough for bikes, also makes a pleasant surface for hiking.

If you just want to stretch your legs – walk briskly, jog, or run –, the internal park roads and connecting paths are fine to use, as vehicular traffic is restricted in many areas.

The Awareness Trail and Visitor Center have been designed for handicapped visitors, as are restrooms located in the Center and at picnic shelter #2 in the main picnic area.

Secluded sites are available for (bring your own) tent camping for a reasonable fee. The maximum stay is 14 days. Reservations are recommended for holiday weekends; the rest of the time camp sites are usually available on a first come-first serve basis. For reservation application forms call the State Ticketron Reservation Center year round at 804/490-3939, weekdays from 10-4, or the Division's Central Office at 804/786-2134.

Several group camps with cabins can be rented for a week or more. Reservation season runs from spring to fall. (Call early. These may be reserved as long as a year in advance.) They may also be rented for weekends in late spring and early fall, if available, provided reservations are made at least 90 days in advance. Scout troops, youth and church groups, and clubs are enthusiastic users.

Campers enjoy evening interpretive programs held in a natural amphitheater overlooking Beaver Lake on summer weekends. Daytime visitors (who greatly

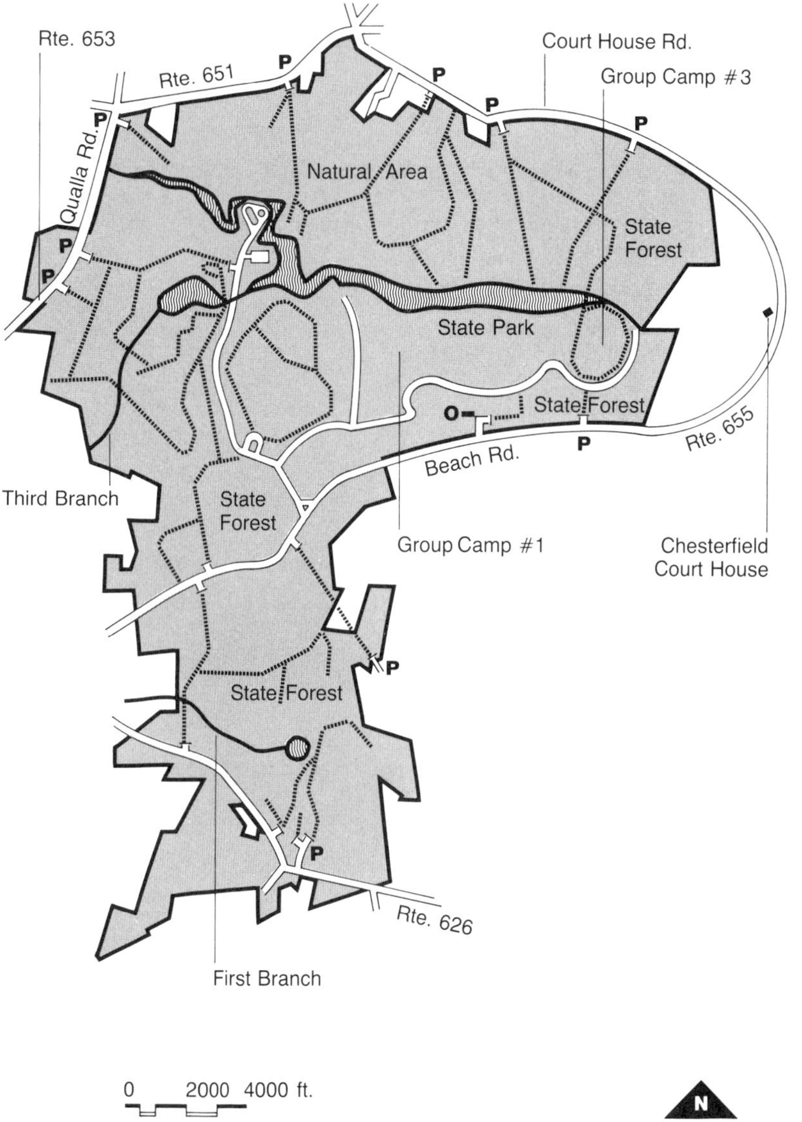
Rte. 653
Rte. 651
Court House Rd.
Group Camp #3
Qualla Rd.
Natural Area
State Forest
State Park
State Forest
Beach Rd.
Rte. 655
Third Branch
State Forest
Group Camp #1
Chesterfield Court House
State Forest
Rte. 626
First Branch
0 2000 4000 ft.
N

outnumber campers) may, of course, stay for these. Other kinds of programs may also be offered from time to time. Contact the Park Office for details.

With a state license, one can fish in any of the park's waters throughout the year. Largemouth bass, bluegill, catfish, and crappie are said to be abundant. One can also launch a boat or - in season - rent a paddle or rowboat at the public boat ramp on Swift Creek Lake. (Only electric motors are allowed.) The lake is an especially lovely and safe place for canoeing.

Also during the season, horses and ponies can be rented at the stable. (You may not bring your own horse to the Park, but you can ride your own in the State Forest.) Rental horses are gentle, and guides accompany all riders on a bridle path.

A large picnic area with three shelters and restrooms accommodates families and larger groups. A playground is located near these and the Visitor Center. Finally, there is an enormous new swimming pool, clean, and equipped with every modern convenience - diving boards at various heights, a wading pool and slide, bath houses, and a refreshment stand.

Please remember that park regulations prohibit alcoholic beverages, firearms, cutting or marring trees, or collecting plant or animal species without permission.

Originally the park and forest comprised the Swift Creek Recreation Demonstration Area, constructed in 1935 by the National Park Service, primarily for group camping. The Swift Creek Project was among the first in the country to utilize workers from the Civilian Conservation Corps (CCC), during the depression years. The area was turned over to the state in 1946, divided into park and forest, and day visiting encouraged.

Pocahontas State Forest, a multiple-use management area, is also an impressive year round recreation resource in its own right, with 25 miles of internal roads and trails for hiking/exploring and horseback riding, and 18 miles of stream, including Swift Creek Lake, for fishing.(If you wish to ride in the forest, you must bring your own horse.)

The forest is also open for hunting in designated areas, in season, except within the game sanctuary that serves as a buffer between the forest and park. Visitors other than hunters would be well advised to stay within the park or sanctuary during hunting season.

Visitors are allowed in the forest only on foot or horseback; vehicles and horse trailers must be left outside in one of the small parking areas at gated forest fire roads. (See map.) For more information and maps, stop by the Forest Headquarters located off Beach Road east of the park entrance, or call 804/796-4250.

The forest is managed under a multi-use concept, with primary emphasis on commercial timber harvesting and reforestation, and game management. The public may also cut firewood in certain areas with permission. Anyone interested

115

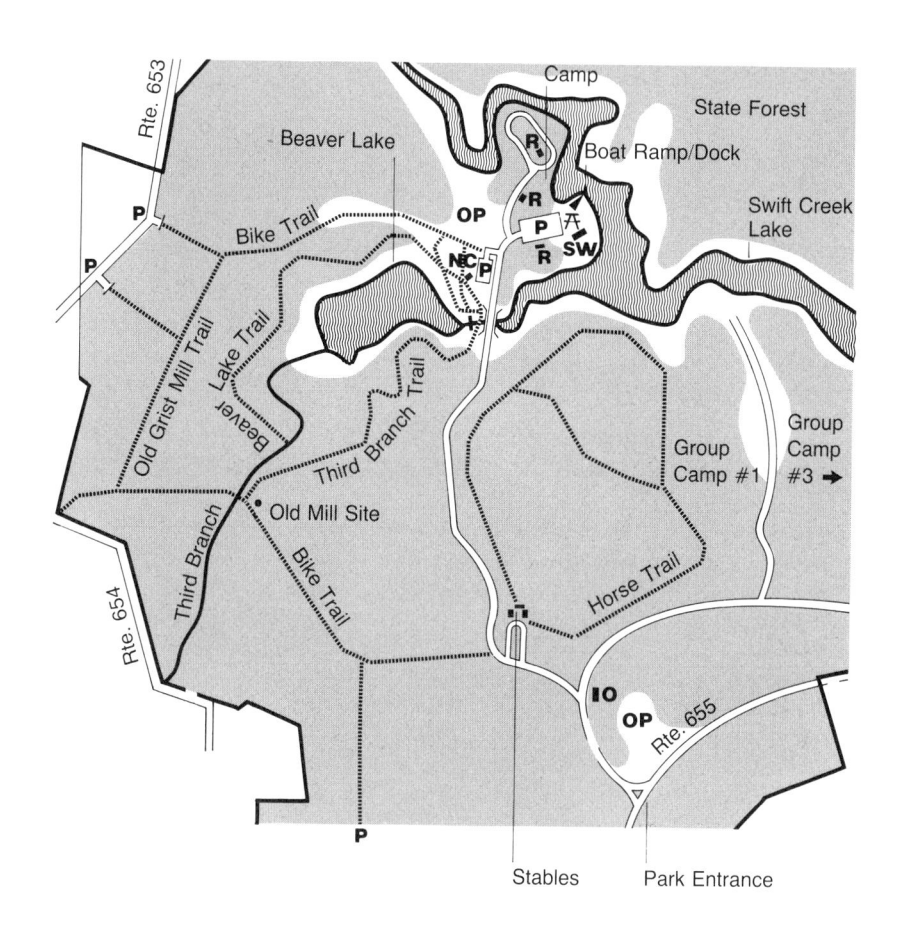

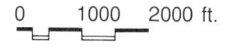

in forestry will find examples of just about every stage of management here, from newly cut, through newly seeded areas, to young, middle-aged and old tree stands.

In the 33-acre Swift Creek Natural Area, directly across the lake from the park, the forest will remain in its natural state without any controls, even of the pine bark beetle, which has destroyed many pines in recent years. By observing this tract over a period of years, it will be possible to determine how nature solves this and other problems in an unmanaged area. Trees around the perimeter are blazed with blue markings.

Changes in the forest cover - through cutting and seeding - are also made with a view to promoting diversity of plant and wildlife species, as some wildlife prefer habitats and food where grass, young trees, and sun loving shrubs can grow, especially along the edges of forests. Without management, the forest would gradually take over these clearings and discourage the game and non-game species that prefer them. Because of its diverse habitats, many species inhabit the State Forest. As you walk or ride about the forest, notice how management has affected the environment and consider all the planning that has gone into the decisions to change, maintain, or leave the forest alone.

White-Tailed Deer

Powhatan Wildlife Management Area

(4,200 Acres)

Located in Powhatan County along both sides of Route 60, about five miles west of the Powhatan County Courthouse. Not shown on State highway maps. No central road system serves the area; instead eight access roads enter it from the perimeter. (See map.) Not all of these small routes are shown on State highway maps; look for the Game Commission signs. Horse trailers may be parked at any of the eight parking lots. (Note three small enclaves of private property and be careful not to trespass.)

Non-hunters are advised to visit only between hunting seasons. For information about seasons, call the field office - 804/598-3706, or the Game Commission in Richmond - 804/257-1000.

Virginia's wildlife management areas ("WMAs") are among the finest public preserves in the state, yet they are often overlooked by hikers and naturalists in the mistaken assumption that they are reserved for hunting. These areas are owned and operated by the Virginia Commission of Game and Inland Fisheries, to provide and manage habitats for native wildlife, and for appropriate public recreation, with emphasis on hunting and fishing in season. Hunting and fishing license fees entirely support these areas.

What is not generally known is that these sizable areas contain miles of trails (including unimproved roads) that are wonderfully well suited for hiking and horseback riding, and that these activities are also encouraged by the Commission. Another advantage of the wildlife management areas is the variety of natural habitats through which the trails pass. Hiking and exploring become one and the same experience. Naturalists will find much of interest in the plant communities along the way, and an observant visitor is also bound to catch glimpses of wildlife. Of course, bird watching is good.

The Powhatan Wildlife Management Area is situated on gently rolling country - ranging in elevation from 195 to almost 500 feet - in the piedmont physiographic province of the region. Sallee Creek and several smaller tributaries flow through the area, and six small lakes, including an old mill pond, impound several of the streams along their courses.

Once part of the vast forest that covered Virginia when the early English colonists arrived, the land has undergone successive changes over the years. As was their practice, the early settlers cleared it for growing crops of tobacco, corn, and wheat. When the tobacco depleted the soil after several years, this cropland was allowed to revert to forest through natural succession. (See Section I - *The Changing Landscape* and *Plant Communities*.)

In the 1930s and '40s part of the area was converted to pasture for beef and dairy cattle, and that was its condition - part forest and part pasture and field - when the Game Commission acquired the property. This general pattern has been maintained for habitat variety.

Today much of the high ground is open, with pleasing vistas over the hills, woods, streams, and lakes. This is a splendid area to hike through, especially on a breezy day, with the grasses and wildflowers tossing in the wind. Numerous trails pass through open spaces, wooded areas, and by the lakes. Along the way, traces of old farms, a pre-Civil War dam at Finch's Mill Pond (the upper of the two Powhatan Lakes), and the ruins of the grist mill and mill race are interesting reminders of days gone by.

The lakes are routinely managed for the game fish sought by fishermen. All of the six small lakes are stocked with largemouth bass and bluegill. Some contain crappie and channel catfish from previous stocking efforts during past years. The two Powhatan Lakes also contain chain pickerel, bullhead catfish, and various sunfish which were native to the stream when the impoundments were constructed.

The smaller lakes in the southern section have cleared areas around the edges for easy bank fishing. The Powhatan Lakes in the north have boat ramps located conveniently near the parking lot. Canoes, rowboats, and small boats with electric motors are permitted. Fishing is said to be good either way.

(Note that while the northern lakes are only 1-1/2 miles from the field office on foot, they cannot be reached by car from this direction, as the service road there is closed by a gate. It is necessary to drive around the WMA on Route 684 heading north and west, then turn south on Route 625 to enter this area and the parking lot that serves the lakes.)

This wildlife management area is an excellent overall habitat for game animals, including deer, rabbits, squirrels, turkey, dove, quail, and several kinds of duck. For a copy of the Game Commission booklet on hunting seasons, species, and regulations, call the Commission (see heading), or write to the Commission on Game and Inland Fisheries, 4010 West Broad Street, Richmond, Va. 23230.

No camping by the public is permitted, but an exception is made by special use permit for Scout troops supervised by their leaders. All equipment and water must be brought in, and designated areas used. This is a beautiful environment for primitive camping, and there should be plenty to see and do over an entire weekend.

(Powhatan is one of two wildlife management areas serving the Capital Region. See also Chickahominy Wildlife Management Area.)

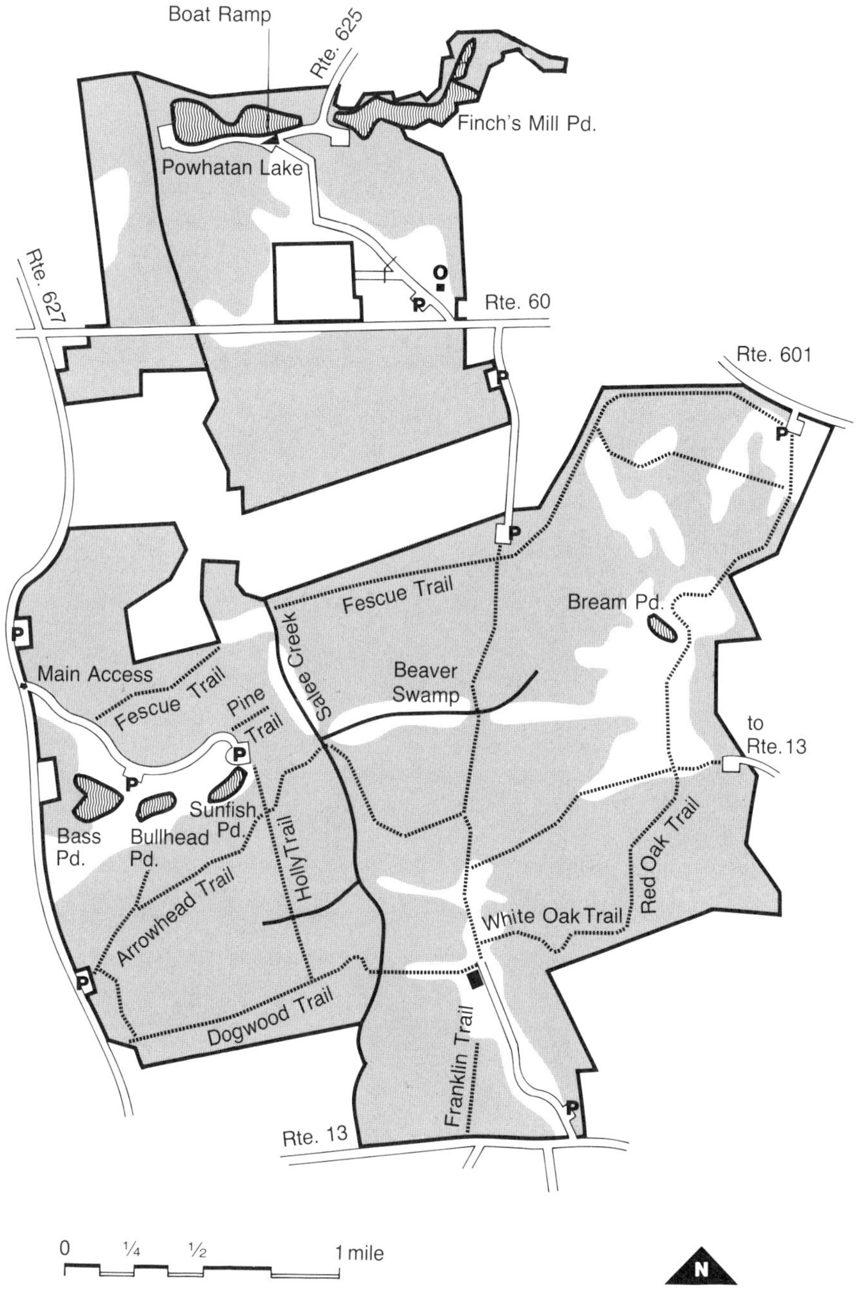
Boat Ramp
Rte. 625
Finch's Mill Pd.
Powhatan Lake
Rte. 627
Rte. 60
Rte. 601
Fescue Trail
Bream Pd.
Salee Creek
Beaver Swamp
Main Access
Fescue Trail
Pine Trail
to Rte. 13
Sunfish Pd.
Bass Pd.
Bullhead Pd.
Holly Trail
Arrowhead Trail
Red Oak Trail
White Oak Trail
Dogwood Trail
Franklin Trail
Rte. 13
0
1/4
1/2
1 mile
N

Special Places

Chesapeake Nature Trail

Along the south side of State Route 33 in New Kent County 3 miles west of the town of West Point. Look for the sign. A small parking lot is located just off the road.

Self-guided nature trails are a wonderful invention; they allow one to walk along at ones own pace, discovering and enjoying a natural environment without distractions. Several parks and preserves in the Capital Region feature self-guided trails, but for the number of fascinating discoveries interpreted in a brochure, our favorite is the Chesapeake Nature Trail in New Kent.

The nature trail passes through a portion of a 565-acre forestry complex owned and managed by the Chesapeake Corporation at West Point. As a public service, Chesapeake has set aside this area and developed the trail and brochure - the best of its kind that we have seen - for public use and enjoyment, and to give visitors some understanding of the complexity and usefulness of forests. If you enjoy hiking in a beautiful forest environment and learning something about plant communities, we highly recommend a few hours on the trail as a guest of Chesapeake.

The area through which the 3-1/2 mile loop trail passes is mainly forested sloping terrain cut by ravines, with a wide variety of upland and lowland plant species. (See Plant Communities in Section I.) A box at the entrance to the trail holds the illustrated brochures. Be sure to take one along, for interesting information about native plant species and other fascinating discoveries along the trail (including vistas, lime deposits, fossil shells, and gravestones), is keyed to numbered posts along the way, 48 in all. A centerfold map is a also a great help in deciding what fork to take when the trail branches from time to time.

Cutoff trails enable hikers to return to the parking lot without going the full distance if they choose. Some of the numbered posts or interpretive stops are along these cutoffs, a problem which creates some difficult choices on reaching the forks. The ideal solution may be to visit the trail twice, once to take the long loop, and another time - perhaps in another season - to criss cross the area along the shorter ones. (Whatever route you take, watch out for poison ivy; you are likely to encounter it long before reaching stop #44, which finally identifies it.)

One of the most pleasing sights along the way is the clear stream that flows through the forest. The trails cross the stream several times on rustic bridges and planks, and the brochure calls attention to it as an illustration of the cleansing effect of a completely forested watershed, in which very little erosion and sedimentation take place.

Part of the long loop traverses steep terrain, and walking may be a little difficult;

Racoons

use caution. No part of the Nature Trail is suitable for handicapped access, as it is merely a simple path through the woods, perhaps even part of an Indian trail used long ago.

The long loop crosses a Virginia Power Company easement, which seems a startling swath after spending an hour or two in the deep woods, but the clearing on high ground opens up a panoramic view over the Pamunkey River and the surrounding countryside. The trail across the clearing is not clearly marked, but if you simply sight across it from where you come out of the woods, you will find it picks up again on the other side directly opposite. As the trail nears the parking lot again, it skirts the edge of a 50-acre loblolly pine seed orchard, also quite a change from the natural area, but interesting as an example of pine monoculture.

As may be expected, the natural area through which the trail passes supports a variety of birds and other wildlife, including deer. An observant hiker who walks quietly may see several species of the many that inhabit the forest. The wildlife is protected; hunting is not, of course, allowed on the property.

The Chesapeake Corporation requests visitors not to remove or damage plants, fossil shells, or other items along the trail, not to build fires, to extinguish cigarettes before discarding them, and not to leave trash behind. Only day hiking is permitted. No facilities are provided. Groups of more than 10 persons planning to visit the area are asked to contact the Public Relations Department, Box 311, West Point, Va. 23181 - phone: 804/843-5000.

Lewis Ginter Botanical Garden

(72 Acres)

Located at 7000 Lakeside Avenue, in western Henrico County, north of Hilliard Road and west of Lakeside Avenue. Enter from Lakeside Avenue.

At long last, the Capital Region's first botanical garden is about to become a reality on the old Bloemendaal Farm in Henrico County. One of the few missing amenities in the region is on the way to becoming an important attraction. Horticulturists, from tenders of windowsill plants to passionate gardeners of acres, now have the opportunity to follow the planning and development of a fine botanical garden and as time goes on, to enjoy the fruits of its creation.

Once the home and garden of Miss Grace E. Arents, philanthropist and devoted gardener, Bloemendaal (flower valley, in the language of her Dutch forebears) was bequeathed to the City of Richmond, to be developed as a botanical garden in honor of her uncle, civic leader Lewis Ginter.

Miss Arents died in 1926, but under the terms of her will, her friend and companion, Mary Garland Smith, was allowed to stay in the mansion for as long as she lived, so that the property did not revert to the city until 1968. For the next several years the city used it as a nursery for street trees and other city plantings.

Finally, in response to requests from the horticultural community, the Lewis Ginter Botanical Garden was established in December, 1982. Under a special arrangement with the city, the development and operation of the Garden has been entrusted to a private foundation created to do justice to it, and to administer the trust fund left for this purpose by Miss Arents. The Garden is entirely supported by this fund and grants and contributions.

Over a period of two years, the foundation - the Lewis Ginter Botanical Garden, Inc. - has planned and raised additional funds for a start up, and in the fall of 1984, Mr. Robert S. Hebb, a distinguished horticulturist and authority on botanical gardens, became the director.

The old-fashioned garden setting creates a perfect environment for a botanical garden reflecting a historic past. The Bloemendaal property goes a long way back to a land grant in 1742. Over the years, the land was owned by a succession of farmers and millers (one of whom built the old mill pond on the property). Patrick Henry also owned the farm for two years while he was governor. In the late 19th century Major Lewis Ginter bought several acres for his Lakeside Wheel Club, a quaint turn-of-the century institution. Cyclist members rode out from Richmond to socialize in the club house that is now the Garden headquarters. Major Ginter left his estate to his niece, and she purchased the Wheel Club House and added to the property, which eventually became her home, and her garden.

The objectives of the Garden are: to develop an extensive collection of native Virginia plants, so as to assist in their preservation and promote their appreciation and use; to assemble and display a broad range of the world plants that can be grown in this area; and to carry out related programs of research, education, service, and publication.

At this writing, plans for the Garden and related programs are under way. Over the years, much of Miss Arents's original garden has been lost, although many of the old trees and the plantings close to the mansion still remain. A new landscape plan will preserve the best, and carry out her ideals and the objectives of the Garden in the finest manner possible. The goal is a garden that will take its place among the best in the world.

Mr. Hebb, who is the author of a book on perennials, among other horticultural works, is planning a comprehensive collection of the perennials that will thrive in this area. Other elements of the master plan include extensive displays of bedding plants, changing with the seasons, a marvelous woodland garden laid out in the romantic English style, and in another section of woodland and surrounding fields, a comprehensive collection of native plants of the southeastern United States. As time goes on, greenhouses and a conservatory will be added.

The Mid-Atlantic Chapter of the American Rhododendron Society is already at work helping to plan the English gardens. Also under way is a seed exchange program with 350 botanical gardens around the world. The Garden will serve as a testing ground for the introduction and dissemination of new plants for landscaping in this area. It will also serve as a living laboratory for use by educational institutions throughout the state with undergraduate and graduate programs in botany and horticulture, and stimulate interest in younger students through programs relevant to secondary public schools. A botanical and horticultural library, with lending privileges for members, and an herbarium will be started in the near future.

Although the design and landscaping will neccessarily take several years to accomplish, a beginning is being made, and the Garden will be open to the public even in the initial stages of its development. Various programs will begin in the fall of 1985. Among the possibilities are landscape seminars, horticulture classes for gardeners, and courses for teachers and school groups. Many of these will be the first of their kind in the area. The grandest of all events will be conducted tours of botanical gardens in the U.S. and abroad. Watch the newspapers for announcements.

Memberships are presently available for $15 a year and up. Benefits will include the newsletter, program announcements, and opportunities for participation in various activities. Interested volunteers will be trained to assist in the garden, programs, and other functions that especially appeal to them. The beautiful Mansion House serves as the Garden headquarters, and is also available to the public for seminars, conferences, receptions, weddings, and other events in keeping with the Garden. For information, call 804/262-9887.

Richmond Parks

The Richmond City park system is the oldest, largest, and most varied in the region. The first city parks Libbie Hill, Gamble's Hill, and Monroe) were created in 1851 to beautify favored residential areas. As the city grew, other neighborhood parks were added, each of which still reflects the designs and traditions of a period in Richmond's history. Some of these are also historic sites with a fascinating past. Most now have recreational facilities and children's play areas.

Each of the four major landscaped parks has a different origin and a character all its own. Byrd was the first, and owes its existence to the persistence of one Colonel Cutshaw, a city engineer in the late nineteenth century, who was determined the city should acquire and develop the site as a park, and succeeded in persuading the City Council to agree to this. Forest Hill began as a commercial amusement park at the end of the "Old 230" trolley line. When the family automobile and the lure of the road replaced the trolley and the amusements, attendance dropped, and the city purchased the property, converting it to the beautiful passive park it is today. Bryan and Maymont Parks were magnificent family estates bequeathed to the city for the enjoyment of the public.

Fortunately all four of these major parks are close to bus lines and therefore accessible to visitors without the use of automobiles.

The James River Park was the first of the natural parks to be developed within the city. Federal and state matching funds for urban parks were a valued contribution toward the project. Its purpose was twofold - to acquire an outstanding natural area for the public to enjoy, and to open up the river for recreation. When the Main Section opened in October, 1970, the Richmond James became accessible to the public for the first time in modern history. The other three riverbank units were acquired and developed during the years that followed.

The trend to natural parks along the river continues with plans for improving access to Belle Isle, and its development as a park, perhaps to be used as an outdoor recreation center focusing on use of the river and related skills. Brown's Island and other properties on the north shore are to be landscaped as riverfront parks and grounds to create an appropriate downtown approach to the river and the island. Unfortunately, public funding is not as readily available as it has been, and considerable private contributions may be needed to implement these plans.

Other additions proposed in the City Master Plan include the development of a historical park focusing on the old Pump House and the James River and Kanawha Canal below Byrd Park (see canal information under *Great Shiplock Park*), and also a riverside trail extending along the north bank of the James from Oregon Hill to the Powhite Bridge. The timetable will depend on availability of funds for these projects.

Other natural areas acquired by the city include three parcels of upland forest in

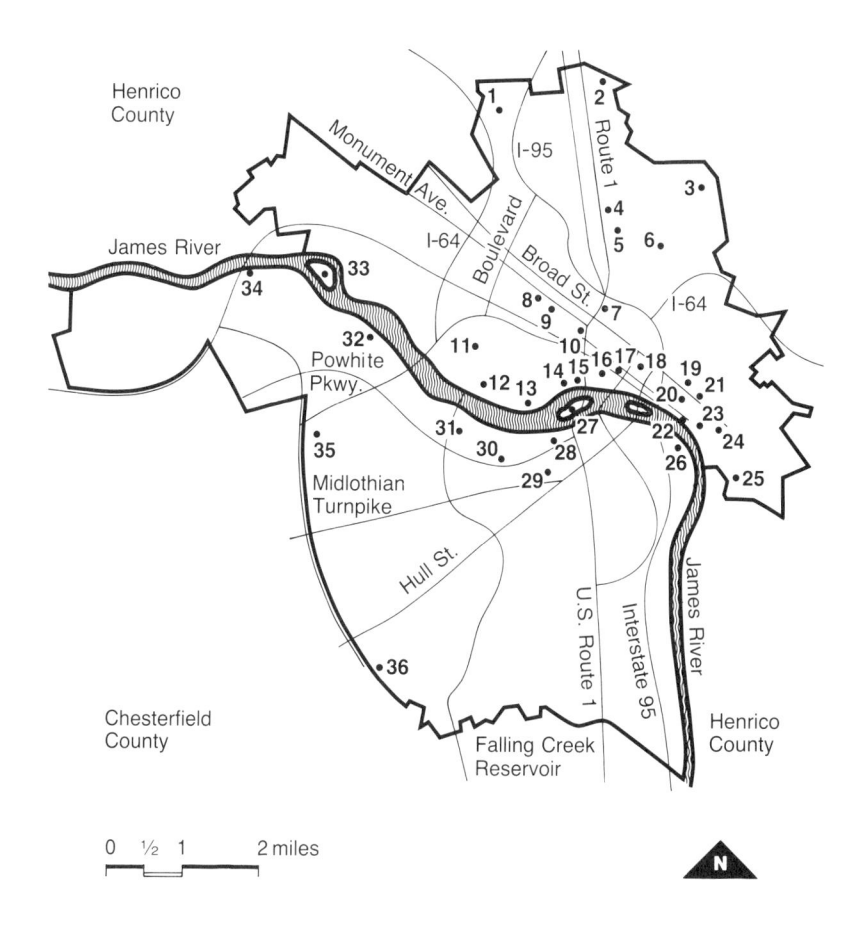

1. Bryan Park
2. Pine Camp
3. Highland Park Plaza
4. Pollard Park
5. Battery Park
6. Cannon Creek
7. Abner Clay Park
8. Meadow Street Triangle
9. Lombardy Triangle
10. Monroe Park
11. Byrd Park
12. Maymont Park
13. James River Park: North Bank
14. Riverside Park
15. War Memorial
16. Gamble's Hill
17. Kanawha Plaza Park
18. Capitol Square
19. Jefferson Park
20. Taylor's Hill Park
21. Patrick Henry Park
22. Great Ship Lock Park
23. Libbie Hill Park
24. Chimborazo Park
25. Powhatan Hill Park
26. Ancarrow Landing
27. Belle Isle
28. James River Park: Main Section
29. Carter Jones Park
30. Forest Hill Park
31. Wayside Spring
32. James River Park: Pony Pasture and Wetlands
33. James River Park: Williams Island
34. James River Park: Huguenot Woods
35. Powhite Park
36. Pocosham Park

125

the area annexed in 1970 - Powhite and Pocosham Parks, and the Stony Point natural area. Powhite is in the process of being developed as a passive park with nature trails and overlooks. Pocosham will be treated similarly. The development of the Stony Point property will be delayed until the use of the surrounding properties has been determined and plans for the extension of Chippenham Parkway have been completed.

In addition to extensive recreation programs carried out at community centers, gyms, playfields and playgrounds, the city sponsors annual festivals in several parks, the famed Dogwood Dell free summer concert series, and nature programs, the best of which are carried out in the James River Park. The development of the Belle Isle Center will add new programs and a new dimension in recreational use of the James.

Ordinary use of the parks is free. Large group activities require a permit. Group picnic shelters and indoor facilities may be reserved for a fee. A few restrictions - no alcohol or firearms may be taken into any city park. Loud car or transistor radios are considered a nuisance.

For up-to-date information about programs and special events in the parks, watch for schedules in the public libraries, check the calendars of events in the newspapers, or call the Bureau of Recreation in the Department of Recreation and Parks - (804) 780-8607. For picnic shelter reservations and use permits, call 780-8785. For information about the James River Park and related programs, call 231-7411, for Maymont Park information, 358-7166.

Grand Old-fashioned Landscaped Parks
Bryan Park

(230 Acres)

Located at the intersection of interstates 95 and 64. Enter from Bellevue Avenue. The major park roads are one way. Exits are via the Hermitage Gate and on Bryan Park Avenue. Take the Lakeside #24 bus East or West, which goes right by the park. During heavy use periods non-city residents may be charged an entrance fee of 50 cents per automobile on weekends during azalea blooming season and $2.00 per visit for the remainder of the summer.

Every year during the azalea season (April through mid-May) thousands of visitors come to Bryan Park to enjoy a display of over 50,000 blooming plants, including more than 50 species covering 12 acres of the park. Adding to the garden's beauty are a small lake and fountain surrounded by hundreds of white dogwoods also in bloom during the early spring, a setting chosen for many weddings.

Beyond the azalea garden the park extends in a rolling topography of lawns and wooded areas, through which trails wind for walking, jogging, and bicycling in all seasons. Many are level enough for handicapped access. After a snowfall the slopes are popular for sledding.

Bryan Park Fisherman

Young's Pond, a major attraction of the park, is surrounded by pleasant lawns where one can sit in the sun and watch or feed the waterfowl. Fishing is permitted and may yield perch and catfish, but because of runoff into the pond swimming is not allowed. At one time, before the days of refrigeration, ice was cut from it and stored in what used to be called an ice house. Old stones from a grist mill can still be seen adjacent to picnic shelter #1.

Acres of lawns may be used for active recreation; there are no "keep off the grass" signs. Four tennis courts are available. Picnicking facilities include group shelters and tables with barbecue pits at scattered sites.

Many fine old trees shade the open areas and grow in wooded stands as well, providing habitats for woodland animals that coexist with park visitors. Several of these have been identified and labelled as pre-civil war specimens. A nature walk leads to Jordan's Branch and a marshy natural area. According to Dr. Charles Blem, ornithologist, the various park habitats attract many species of birds, and the park is one of the few sites in the area with albino grey squirrels.

The park was a gift to the City from Mrs. Joseph Bryan in memory of her husband, a prominent civic leader and newspaper publisher. Visitors knowing this will appreciate the living memorial that has brought pleasure to so many over the years.

Sunbathing Rocks

Bryan Park Ave.

Hermitage Rd.

Young's Pond

Falls

R
P
☶2
☶ 1 ☶ P
P
Young's Pond ☶
P
Keeper's House

Jordan's Branch

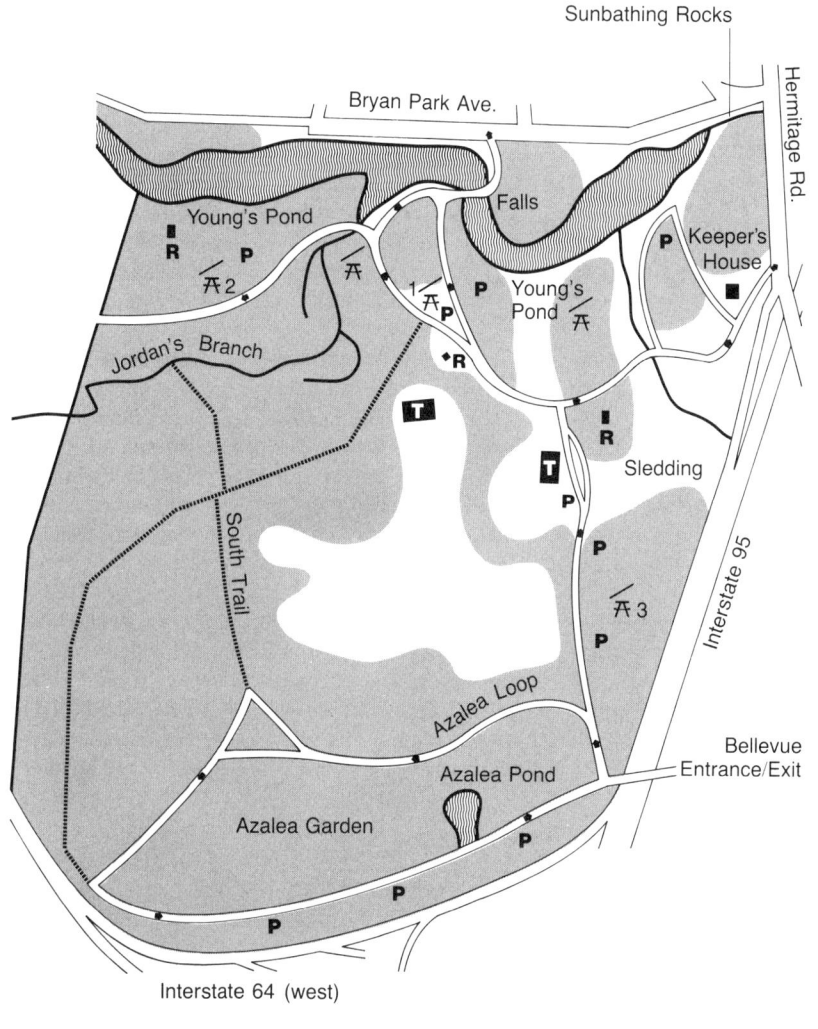

♦R

T

R

T
P
Sledding

South Trail

P

P
☶ 3
P

Interstate 95

Azalea Loop

Azalea Pond

Bellevue Entrance/Exit

Azalea Garden

P

P

Interstate 64 (west)

0 150 300 ft.

N

129

Byrd Park

(300 Acres)

Located in the near west end on both sides of Boulevard just north of the bridge. The park is adjacent to Maymont Park east of the Boulevard. There is no main entrance; roads lead into the park from adjacent city streets. Parking is allowed along the park roads unless otherwise indicated by signs. The Robinson #3 bus stops at the eastern end near the lakes; the Robinson #4 stops near the Carillon and tennis courts.

Byrd is a beautifully landscaped park on gently rolling terrain featuring tree-shaded lawns, three man-made lakes, tennis courts, ball fields, a Carillon tower (a World War I Memorial) presently used as a recreation center, and an amphitheater aptly named Dogwood Dell, where free concerts and plays are performed on summer evenings. In addition to the Dell series, a number of other events are held in the park throughout the year, including annual tennis and baseball tournaments, art exhibits, dance festivals, patriotic celebrations, and a Christmas pageant. (Watch the Calender of Events in the papers for announcements.)

The atmosphere is often festive and always relaxed. A number of asphalted paths wind through the park, making it ideal for walking, jogging, or biking. A one-mile fitness trail has several exercise stations. The extensive lawns may be used for free play (ball, frisbee, kites, etc.). After a snowfall, sledding is allowed on Reservoir Hill. Picnic tables with grills are scattered throughout designated areas. Group shelters with fireplaces and four to six tables must be reserved by calling ahead.

Byrd Park Geese and Friend

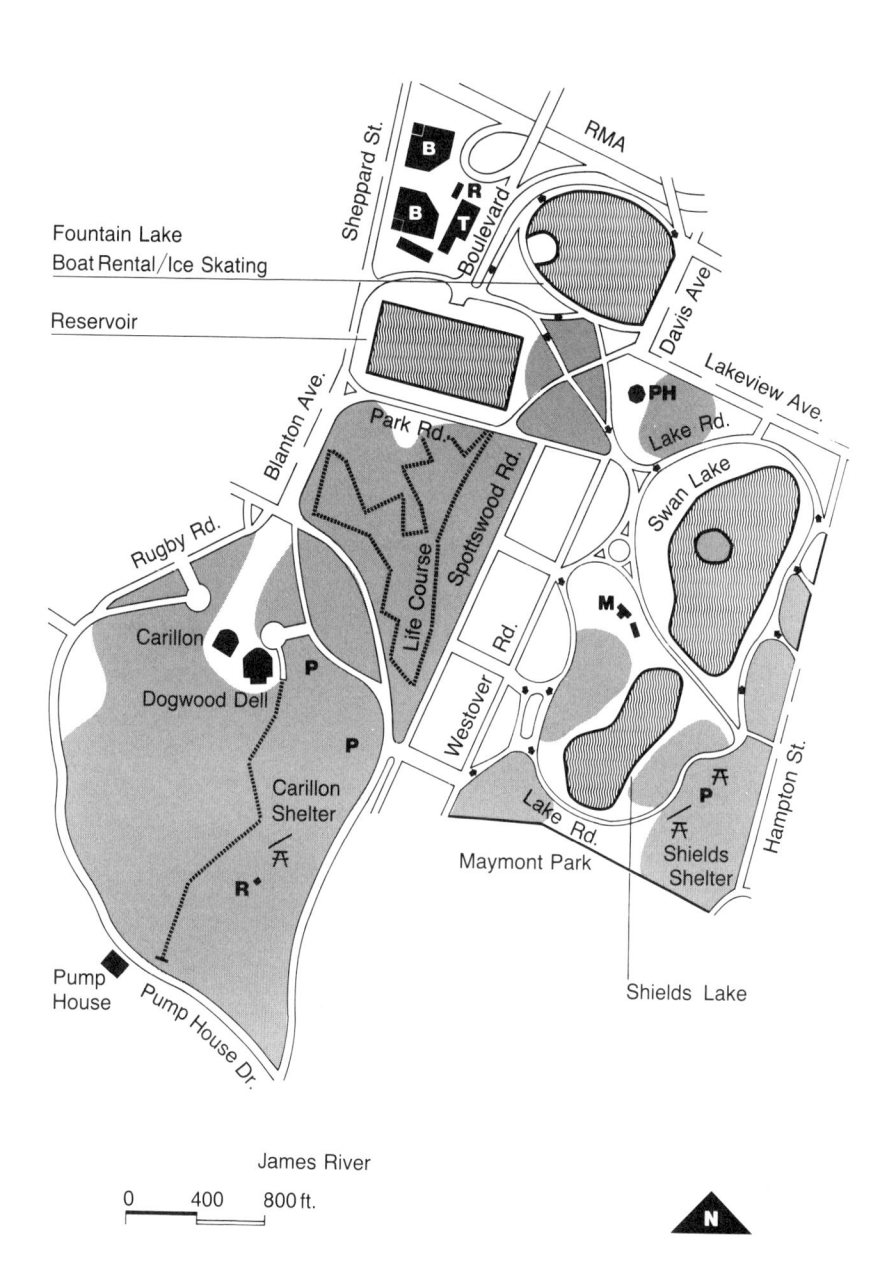

Fountain Lake
Boat Rental/Ice Skating

Reservoir

Sheppard St.

Boulevard

RMA

Davis Ave.

Lakeview Ave.

Blanton Ave.

Park Rd.

Rugby Rd.

Life Course

Spottswood Rd.

Lake Rd.

PH

Swan Lake

Carillon

Dogwood Dell

P

P

Westover Rd.

Carillon Shelter

R

Lake Rd.

Maymont Park

P

Shields Shelter

Hampton St.

Shields Lake

Pump House

Pump House Dr.

James River

0 400 800 ft.

N

131

Skating on Fountain Lake - Richmond Times Dispatch/George Lamm

Each of the lakes offers a different diversion. Swan Lake is literally for the birds; geese in great numbers live on Sanctuary Island in the middle of the lake, swimming over to the shore for handouts of bread. They are quite tame and will walk up to anyone who feeds them. Bring children and stale bread, lots of it. Fishing is allowed in Swan and Shields Lakes, which, surprisingly, contain hungry smallmouth bass, carp, catfish, and other species. Fountain Lake is the only place in town for paddle boat enthusiasts. On hot days they love to paddle around the fountain and get drenched from the spray. (Five dollars will buy an hour.) After a hard freeze the lake is also a popular place to skate.

An interesting old park house is available for meetings. This building has been made accessible to disabled visitors. Restrooms in the Field House near the tennis courts and in the Carillon are also accessible to the handicapped. as are the paths where slopes do not present a problem.

The park was named in honor of William Byrd II, founder of Richmond. In the early days the New Reservoir Park Trolley Line ended in a small amusement park within the larger park, and carriage rides around Fountain Lake were a popular concession. The Carillon and Dogwood Dell were public works projects dedicated in 1932.

Forest Hill Park

(119 Acres)

Located along Forest Hill Avenue between 34th and 42nd Street, extending irregularly north to Riverside Drive across from the Main Section of the James River Park. The main parking lot is just off 42nd Street a block from Forest Hill Avenue. The Forest Hill buses #70 and 71 and the Huguenot bus stop near the park entrance.

Named for its forested slopes, old Forest Hill Park combines natural and landscaped environments in a magnificent relief that invites exploring. Reedy Creek, pretty as a mountain stream, tumbles through a deep ravine ending in a 3-acre man-made lake at the northern end of the park. A steep, stepped path follows the course of the creek through the woods down to the lower level and continues as an asphalted trail around the lake. Another steep path, also with steps, descends from the parking lot on the other side of the ravine, creating a loop trail for walkers (and joggers) who don't mind the climb.

A trail leads north from the end of the lake, where Reedy Creek runs out again, ending in Riverside Drive across from the service entrance to the James River Park (Main Section.) To pick up the Buttermilk Trail, cross Riverside Drive. In dry weather it is possible to walk under the drive through one of the large culverts draining Reedy Creek into the James.

Reedy Creek - Forest Hill Park

James River Park

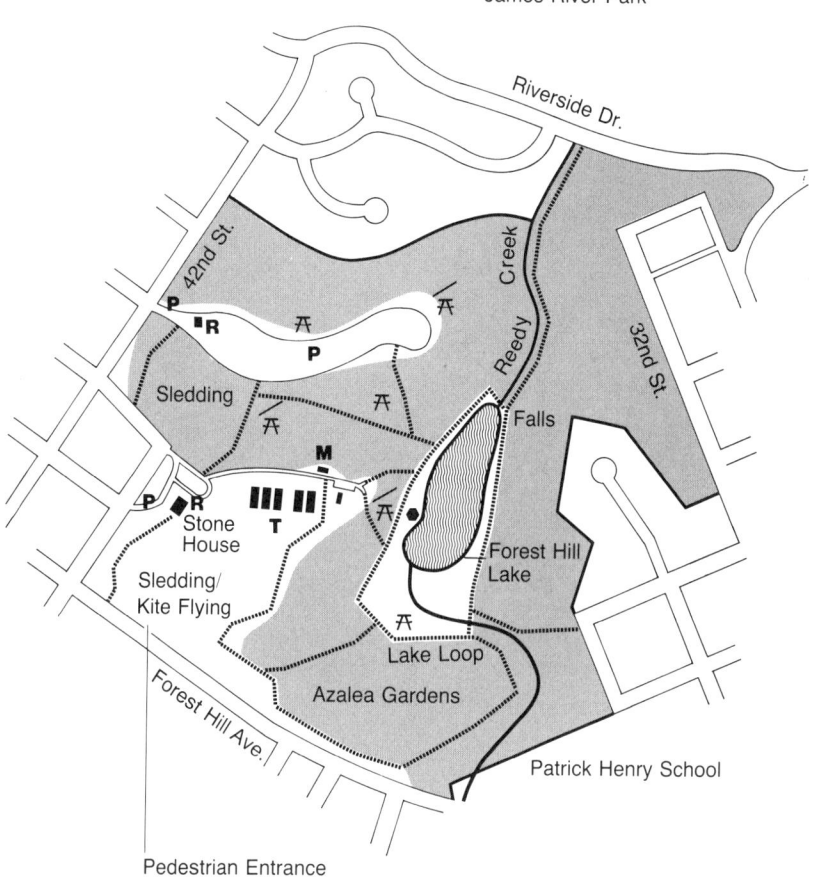

Photo by Lyn Woodlief

Visitors who appreciate fine stonework will admire the low walls and stone walkways and risers constructed in the 1930s of granite quarried nearby. These are features one seldom sees in parks developed today; you will also see these used extensively in Battery Park.

The Old Stone House (circa 1836) near the park entrance at Forest Hill and 41st Street was the first Southside Branch of the City Library and was built of granite quarried on the site. Today it is available for meetings of civic associations.

At the upper level along Forest Hill Avenue a clear expanse of lawn may be used for free play and is especially fine for flying kites and sledding. Along one side, adjacent to 34th Street, a lovely small azalea garden has been planted with cuttings donated by the Norfolk Botanical Garden. Every year in April when the azaleas begin to bloom, the Westover Hills Civic Association celebrates spring with a colorful Azalea Festival attended by thousands thronging the park, some in turn-of-the-century costumes, all in holiday mood.

Also at the upper level, convenient to the parking lot, are most of the picnic tables and group picnic shelters, as well as several tennis courts. Paths are fine for biking - until one begins to descend.

Handicapped visitors should use the park with caution, staying at the upper level. Even here uneven brick and cobblestone walkways may present problems. Still it would be a shame to miss the park altogether because the environment and the views are worth experiencing. Picnic Shelter #1, designed to accomodate wheelchairs at the table, may be reserved for groups or families with handicapped members. The adjacent restroom is also accessible for handicapped visitors.

The park's quaint history adds to its charm. It began at the turn of the century as an amusement park at the end of the "Old 230" trolley line. Its purpose was to promote ridership on the trolley during weekends, a common practice around the country in those days. The Forest Hill Amusement Park prospered into the 1920s, but was closed in 1925, as were many amusement parks in that period of change. The property was acquired by the city in 1934 and redeveloped mainly as a passive park in its present form. For a taste of the days gone by, attend the Azalea Festival.

James River Park

Maymont Park

(105 Acres)

Above the north bank of the James River between the Carillon in Byrd Park and Hampton Street. Two entrances with parking lots serve the park, one at the northwest corner, and one on the east side. From the Boulevard just north of the Bridge turn east at the Maymont sign to the Spottswood Entrance and the Children's Demonstration Farm. The main entrance is on Hampton Street opposite Pennsylvania Street. (To reach Hampton, take Meadow south and turn right on Colorado.) Or take the Robinson #3 bus to Meadow and Pennsylvania and walk one block west to the entrance.

(Park hours from April to October are 10-7, the rest of the year, 10-5. Exhibit hours are 10-5, Tuesday-Sunday June 1-September 2, the rest of the year, 12-5. The Emporium (Gift Shop) is open 10-5 Tuesday-Saturday, 12:30-5, Sundays. The exhibits and the Emporium are closed Mondays, except on major holidays.)

Maymont is a magnificent Victorian estate bequeathed to the city in 1925 by its owners, Major and Mrs. James Henry Dooley. In recent years the old family mansion, estate buildings, and landscaping have been preserved and lovingly cared for, so that today Maymont is a park of exceptional beauty and charm. The Virginia

Gazebo - Maymont Park

0 60   240   480 ft.

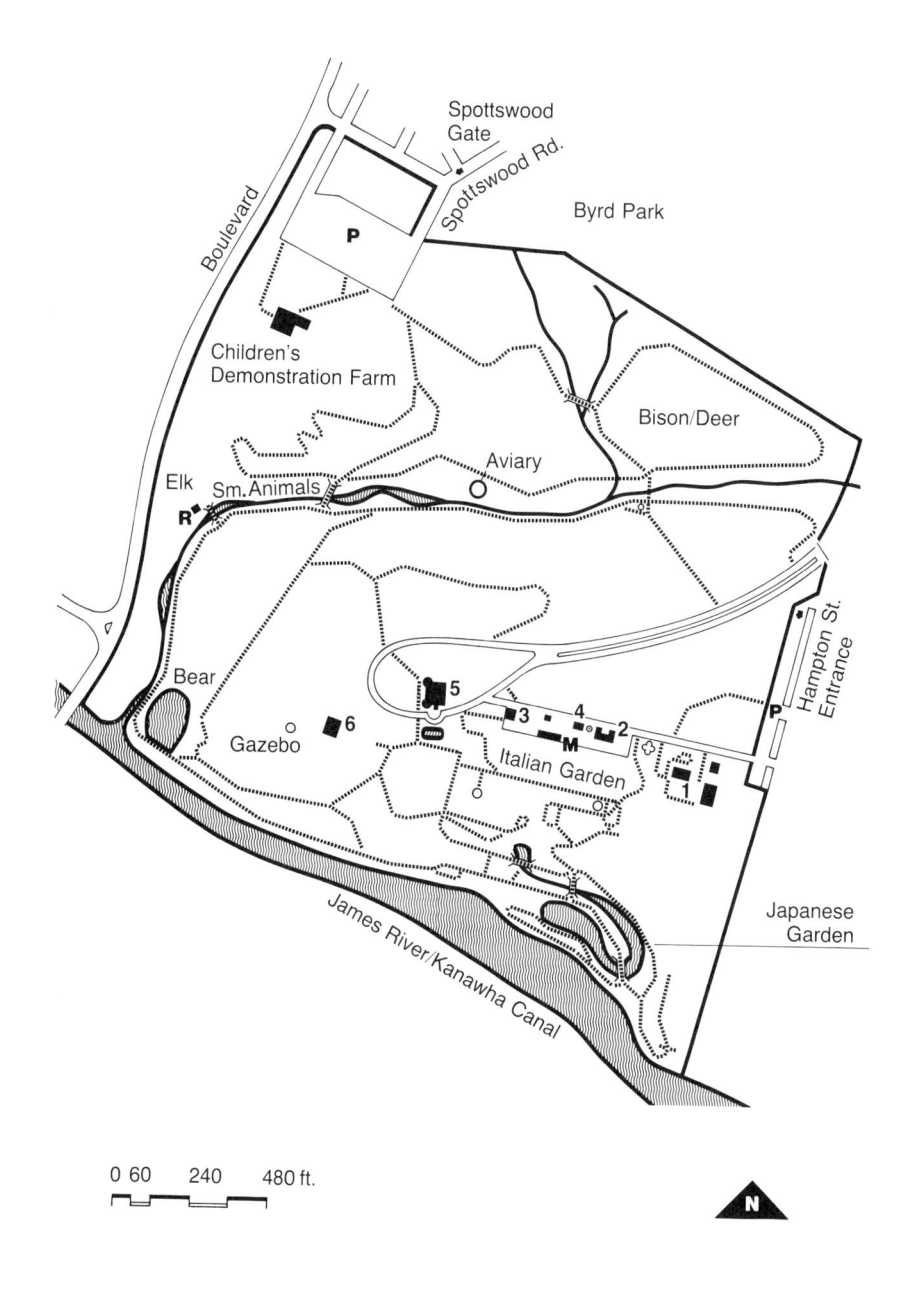

N

1. Parsons' Nature Center/Visitors' Center
2. Carriage House
3. Emporium
4. Assembly Hall
5. Maymont House
6. Mausoleum

139

wildlife habitats and Children's Demonstration Farm added since 1925 have greatly enriched the pleasure of young visitors.

The park's setting on lawnswept hills, with stately trees and pleasing vistas, is a perfect environment for walking and relaxing in the out of doors in all but the most inclement weather. The park is managed by the Maymont Foundation under an agreement with the City, and its staff and volunteers are dedicated to the comfort, enjoyment, and safety of visitors.

The Mary Parsons Nature Center located in the old stone barn just inside the Hampton Entrance is a good place to start a tour of Maymont. Be sure to stop at the desk for self-guided tour booklets and information about guided tours and programs. The Center contains interesting exhibits on natural history; other exhibits intended to orient the visitor to the park are planned for the near future when this facility becomes the official Visitor's Center. (The Emporium also houses an information center at the present time.)

Tours are a good way to get acquainted with Maymont; after you become familiar with the grounds, you will want to return to your favorite places. Adults will especially enjoy the House, the gardens, and the estate in general. Children like to go everywhere in the park, but particular favorites are the wildlife habitats, Children's Demonstration Farm, and the Emporium.

The arboretum includes many American species and also a number of exotic imports, some rarely seen in this country. Some have been designated State Champions distinguished by their height and circumference. They have been sited to create lovely vistas which have a natural look, but which are actually designed by human artistry. Many are labelled and keyed to the self-guided booklet on trees.

Each of Maymont's gardens has a different character and appeal. Don't miss the small formal herb garden outside the Visitor/Nature Center. Like most herb gardens, it is rather unobtrusive but interesting for its design and variety of plants. The Italian Garden on a hillside terrace, with its classic pergola, is a favorite spot for weddings held in the park, and a mecca for rose fanciers all summer long.

Below the Italian Garden stone steps descend alongside a classical cascade and waterfall flowing over granite outcroppings to the restored Japanese Garden below. Maymont describes its Japanese Garden as incorporating an "encyclopedia of traditional styles." The result is an enchanting miniature mounded landscape with reflecting pools, stepping stones, and bridges, all surrounded by old trees and Japanese plantings. When weddings are held here, the guests, instead of throwing rice, are traditionally given pellets of fish food to feed to the golden carp in the pools, in a gala celebration of life.

Visitors interested in history will enjoy a tour of Maymont House and a charming collection of old carriages contributed by Elizabeth Scott Bocock, daughter of one of Major Dooley's business partners. Administrative offices are now housed in the upper story of the Carriage House. Carriage rides, for a small fee, are available on

Maymont Children's Demonstration Farm

weekends during the warmer months from 1-4 PM; other rides are available by arrangement.

Wildlife habitats were a gift of William B. Thalhimer. Bison, deer and elk range on the northern and western slopes of the park. Bears live in an old quarry with their own pool a short distance from the Japanese Garden. Now and then bear cubs arrive, frolicking to the delight of visitors until they (the bears) become too old and dignified. Small animals (beaver, racoons, and waterfowl) have their own habitats in a stream valley between the hills.

The highly popular Children's Demonstration Farm is located on a hill at the western end of the park at the Spottswood entrance. A model barn and fenced paddocks house domestic farm animals -- horses, cows, goats, sheep, rabbits, pigs, and chickens. Nutritious food pellets for feeding the animals are available for a small fee. Each spring a crop of baby animals arrives, to the delight of visitors.

A favorite stop for everyone is the Emporium located in an original estate structure near Maymont House. Items for sale reflect Maymont's orientation to nature, gardens, and life at the turn of the century. Many are inexpensive enough for children to purchase. The present Information Center and Boehm Porcelain collection housed within the store and the store itself are manned by volunteers; proceeds go to the Maymont Foundation. Refreshment stands are located next to the Emporium and the Children's Farm.

Handicapped visitors should avoid trying to cross the park, as a deep valley separates the hills on the east and west sides. Fortunately the two entrances make it possible to get to both the Children's Farm and the area near Hampton Street. Both the Farm and the Nature Center have handicapped-equipped restrooms. Access to the Maymont House or low-lying areas may be a problem. For suggestions ask at the Visitor Center.

A few activities are restricted. Because the paths are for pedestrians and handicapped visitors, bicycling, roller skating, and skate boarding are not allowed, neither are organized ball games or kiting. (These activities are allowed next door in Byrd Park.) Joggers and picnickers are welcome (however, outdoor cooking grills are not permitted.).

The Maymont Foundation offers highly successful programs for school groups, as well as weekend programs and activities for both children and adults. The latter may be announced in the newspapers, but a more reliable source of information is the newsletter, which you can receive by becoming a member of Maymont Foundation. For information on membership or volunteer opportunities at Maymont drop by the Visitor Center or call 358-7166.

Everyone is invited to two wonderful annual events sponsored by the Foundation - a candlelit Christmas Open House on the second weekend in December and an Old Fashioned Fourth of July celebration. If you like festivities, be sure to attend, if possible escorted by children.

The Richmond James and the James River Park System

The James River Park was an answer to many prayers when its four river bank sections opened early in the 1970s, providing public access to the Richmond James for the first time in modern history. While these river banks in themselves are beautiful and fascinating natural areas often visited for their own sake, taken together with the river, they create a magnificent recreation area along the famed Falls of the James which has to be seen to be appreciated.

The James River crosses the seven mile fall zone as it courses through Richmond, dropping over a hundred feet in rapids alternating with stretches of quiet water. Studded with wooded islands and flowing most of its distance between natural river banks overhung with trees, the James in Richmond is a scenic, ecological, and recreational treasure in the midst of the metropolitan area.

The Richmond James is also rich in human history going back thousands of years. Archeological diggings reveal that Indians inhabited its shores as early as 12,000 BC, fishing its waters where fishermen cast their lines today. It was at the foot of the rapids that the first English explorers, Captains John Smith and Christopher Newport, came ashore on May 23, 1607 to plant a wooden cross on the north bank, to the amazement of the watching Indians.

It was on a hilltop overlooking the James - thought to be on the site now occupied by Powhatan Hill Park - that the Indian Chief Powhatan entertained his strange guests in an encounter that marked the beginning of colonial history in the Richmond region. It was along the north bank below the falls that the first English outpost was established, followed by settlements on both sides of the river, in those days the only transportation corridor to the east. The riverbanks have seen many changes since those times, including wars and the progress of peaceful times.

The rapids and shallows along the fall line were an obstacle to navigation until the first section of the James River and Kanawha Canal was completed in 1795. From this time on until the railroads were built canal boats carried people and goods around the falls, and as the system was extended, all the way to Buchanan at the western base of the Blue Ridge Mountains.

Today sections of the old canal and several locks remain as fascinating remnants of the past, the walls of hand-hewn stone testifying to the enduring quality of the materials and workmanship of that time. Part of the canal is still in use, carrying water from the river to the Richmond water treatment plant. Parts of it can be seen from the bridges and several vantage points on the north shore - some sections with water still flowing through them, and others dry and resembling ancient ruins. The first lock has been restored and can been seen in Great Shiplock Park. Two locks have been preserved by Reynolds Metals Company, and other restorations are planned in what will some day be the Old Pumphouse Park.

The exceptional scenic, historic, ecological, and recreational values of the Richmond James have led to its designation by the Virginia General Assembly as a State Scenic River, called *The Scenic and Historic Falls of The James*. The designation gives official recognition to the resource and also serves to protect this magnificent sector of the James from changes that could lessen any of these values.

The James in Richmond lends itself to many kinds of recreation, including exploring, boating, fishing, and simply cooling off on a hot summer day. During normal to low flow periods in warm weather the river is ideally suited for canoeing, kayaking, rafting, and "tubing" (floating downstream in oversized inner tubes), provided of course that sensible safety precautions are taken. The river in Richmond provides the finest white water canoeing and kayaking of any city in the country. By embarking and returning at appropriate spots, it is possible to choose quiet flatwater or rapids ranging from the easiest to the most difficult to negotiate - class I-VI rapids in canoeing language. Commercial rafting trips run by the James River Experiences provide thrilling, but safe (though wet) rides down the falls.

The City regulates boating for reasons of safety. Life jackets are required when the river level rises above five feet. Entering the river without a special permit is prohibited above nine feet; no entry is allowed at twelve feet - flood stage. (For information about river levels, call 231-7411.) Maps and information are available and posted at several access locations in the James River Parks.

Fishing is excellent from boats, the banks, and rock outcroppings that form giant stepping stones into the river. On hot summer days "rock hopping" combined with wading, sunning, and body surfing in certain of the tamer rapids are popular forms of recreation.

The City of Richmond officially discourages swimming for safety reasons because supervision is impossible. The city is not liable for accidents, although it does attempt rescue and recovery operations (sometimes at considerable cost, which may be charged to the rescued.) Nevertheless, the beauty of the river environment and the joy of a cooling dip prove so irresistible to so many on hot summer days that it would be difficult to enforce an ordinance against swimming. Instead, common sense and caution are urged. During low flow periods in shallow water near shore, a mere dip can be safe, but river currents, holes, and obstacles that create traps make swimming potentially dangerous at all times.

A few precautions for those who attempt swimming anyway

-Know how to swim well. Never swim alone, or when the river is high.

-Stay close to shore and out of the main channel.

-Be wary of deep holes. Swim only where you can easily regain your footing, preferably in water no more than waist high.

-Never jump or dive into the river.

-(For dumped canoeists) When in rapids, float feet up and pointed downstream. (Do not attempt to stand up until safety is reached.)

-Avoid "strainers" - tree limbs in the rapids.

-Do not start the big rapids from Belle Isle east.

Is the river clean enough for contact recreation? This question is often asked, but seldom answered because conditions vary from time to time and from place to place. Heavy rains pollute the river everywhere for several days until the material in the runoff has moved downstream or settled out. Mud in the James is a pretty good indication that the river is still carrying runoff. When it clears, the water above the water supply treatment plant - roughly above the Powhite Bridge - is relatively clean and safe for contact recreation. Downstream - from about 42nd Street east - some of the heavy storm runoff flows into sewer pipes, causing them to discharge directly into the river at several points, and it takes awhile before the water reaches relative cleanliness. Still further downstream, below the 14th Street Bridge, the sewage treatment plant discharges effluent into the river, and though this is chlorinated, unnecessary contact is not recommended at any time in this area.

(For information about the natural history of the James, see Section I. For more on fishing and boating, see Section II.)

Postscript

Now and then news of a drowning in the Richmond James reminds us of the hazards of careless use of the river and underscores the need for following safety practices and using caution at all times. The City government may from time to time strengthen its safety ordinance by restricting use of the river in certain areas. Anyone planning to use the river should be aware of the rules and regulations and observe these as minimal guidelines.

The James River Park System

The parks occupy over 450 acres of lovely open and forested floodplain and upland slopes along the shores and islands in the river. Entirely natural in character, they preserve flourishing plant communities and animal habitats as they have existed for hundreds of years. The floods that sweep over them from time to time have saved them from development that would surely have occurred otherwise.

The four riverbank sections and two major islands that make up the system each have their own special character that is different from all the rest, and each is adjacent to a segment of the river with its own individual characteristics. The features they share are natural beauty and fascinating natural history.

Over 400 species of flowering plants have been catalogued in the parks, and over 150 species of birds have been sighted and listed by the Richmond Audubon Society. This is a good place to see ospreys, now making their comeback from endangered species status. Many other small animals inhabit these natural areas, and deer frequent the more isolated islands, sometimes swimming to shore to browse. Some of the parks also contain historic sites. Some have a few facilities appropriate to natural or historic areas; others are without any facilities.

Access to fishing is one of the greatest appeals of these parks, especially where rocks in the river or channels make it possible to cast without interference from tree limbs and bushes. Fishing for smallmouth bass, channel catfish, and bream is excellent. The highly prized striped bass and also shad and herring migrate through in April and May.

In addition to the park rules that apply throughout the city, special James River Park regulations prohibit taking glass containers into the parks because of hazards from broken glass in the river. (The only other common hazard is poison ivy.) Canvas shoes should be worn when wading; glass, alas, is likely to be present on the river bottom.

The City Naturalist watches over the parks, provides interpretive programs, and organizes work parties for volunteers willing to spend a few hours improving the park. Guided walks and pamphlets (available in the Visitor Center in the Main Section) focus on topics such as the ecology of the flood plain, the history of man in the area of the James River Parks, geology of the park, wildflowers, and trees. The Audubon Society conducts bird walks regularly, and various hiking clubs schedule walks through the parks. Watch the papers (calendars of events) for announcements. For park information call 804/231-7411.

Main Section

(213 Acres)

Located along the south shore between the Lee and Boulevard Bridges. Enter from Riverside Drive opposite 42nd Street or 22nd Street (a short walk from the bus stop - Forest Hill #70 or 71 - on Riverside Drive at the south end of the Lee Bridge.) Canoeists may park along the drive opposite Hillcrest Road and take canoes into the park through the service entrance and under the railroad tracks through a large culvert.

The first and largest of the James River Parks encompasses the floodplain of the south bank between the Lee and Boulevard Bridges, the wooded slopes above it, and numerous small islands closely paralleling the shore. The river also comes into the park, branching into small streams as it flows among the islands. Even the rocks in the river seem to be an extension of the park. This is a fine place to get close to the river.

The Visitor Center is also located in this section close to the river, near the service entrance, midway between the two pedestrian bridge towers. A visit to the Center is highly recommended.

The two main entrances from Riverside Drive lead to attractive parking lots under the trees. (These fill up early on summer weekends.) From each of these a pedestrian bridge crosses to an open tower of unique design, with steps descending to the floodplain below. At 22nd Street this little walk among the treetops is an adventure in itself. The views are spectacular, overlooking the river, rapids, rock outcroppings, wooded islands, bridges, historic Hollywood Cemetery on the opposite bank, and to the east, the City skyline. If you have binoculars or a camera with a telephoto lens, you will enjoy using them here.

The sloping, stepped paths to the pedestrian bridges may create difficulties for handicapped visitors, and the parapets may obscure the view for people in wheelchairs. Fortunately, a similar view and an even better look at Belle Isle may be had from a pullout/overlook off Riverside Drive just west of the Lee Bridge. This is also the place to observe a panorama of raging rapids during floods.

A service road enters the park at grade level midway between the park entrances. (See map.) With special permission, this entrance may be used to transport handicapped visitors to the Visitor Center and the service road within the park. Park personnel must escort vehicles across the railroad tracks. The Center and restrooms within are accessible to handicapped visitors, as are picnic shelters and several of the trails, including one that goes to the river's edge (a good fishing spot). For information regarding permission and arrangements, call 231-7411. Advance notice is helpful, as personnel are not always available.

The service road is also the only practical route for taking canoes into the park for launching into the major (for experts only) rapids downstream, and for taking

Map

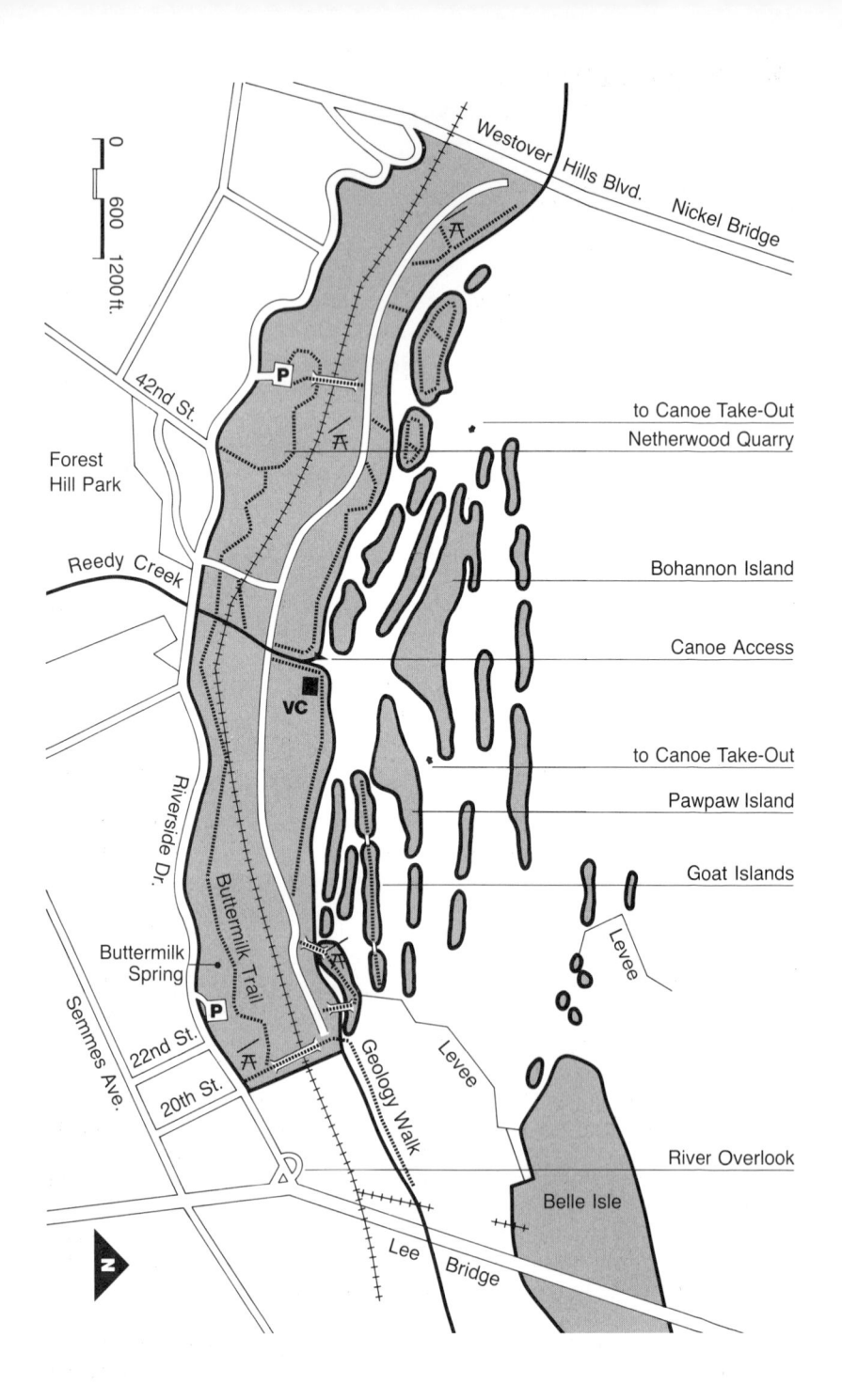

- 0 / 600 / 1200 ft
- Westover Hills Blvd.
- Nickel Bridge
- 42nd St.
- Forest Hill Park
- Reedy Creek
- to Canoe Take-Out
- Netherwood Quarry
- Bohannon Island
- Canoe Access
- VC
- to Canoe Take-Out
- Pawpaw Island
- Goat Islands
- Levee
- Riverside Dr.
- Buttermilk Trail
- Buttermilk Spring
- Semmes Ave.
- 22nd St.
- 20th St.
- Geology Walk
- Levee
- River Overlook
- Belle Isle
- Lee Bridge
- N

148

Pedestrian Bridge - James River Park

them out from the novice (beginner's whitewater) run, which starts at the Pony Pasture Section three miles upstream. Put-in and take-out vehicles can come as close as the railroad tracks while loading or unloading, and may be parked along Riverside Drive just outside the service entrance. The launch area is behind the Visitor Center.

The Southern Railroad tracks and fenced right-of-way separate the upper and lower levels of the park, creating an awkwardness which has been solved for the most part by the pedestrian bridges and stair towers. Near the service entrance a very large culvert provides passage under the tracks.

Goat Island Bridge - James River Park

On entering either of the parking lots you can choose to remain at the upper level and take the Buttermilk Trail, which goes through a deep forest in an east-west direction, or follow a path to the pedestrian bridge-tower and the steps to the lower level. Most visitors are irresistibly drawn in this direction - to the view, the floodplain below, and the river. This is a good choice for the first-time visitor, because it also leads in the direction of the Visitor Center.

The two-mile Riverside Trail extends east-west beween the little islands near 42nd Street and the masses of rock outcroppings in the river across from Belle Isle. When the river is low, you can walk across them all the way to the island. (See *Belle Isle* below.)

These rocks are part of a massive granite "pluton" with a fascinating geological history. It is thought to have been formed from molten rock squeezed up through cracks in the earth's crust some 500 million years ago when the African "tectonic plate" collided with the North American plate. It remained, solidified, and has been worn smooth by the river over millenia. (See also Section I - *The Changing Landscape*.) The great boulders resting on the outcroppings were carried downstream by the force of the river during floods.

From the trail leading westward at the 22nd Street entrance the views are mostly of islands and the narrow channels of the river flowing between them and the shore. Rustic bridges make it possible to cross over to one of the islands. The three Goat Islands, connected to one another by bridges, could at one time be reached by a small hand operated ferry, but this was damaged in a flood and unfortunately has not been replaced. At this writing the only way to reach them is by walking on the levee to a point closest to the easternmost island and hopping across the water on stepping stones *when the river is low.*

Notice on the map how the islands are clustered in rows paralleling the shore. They are moving downstream, continually being eroded on their upstream ends and "growing" on the downstream ends, where sand and silt are being deposited, creating more island material.

Notice the beds of water willows (named for their resemblance to the leaves of willow trees) growing in the river, blooming in June and July. These plants are sure indicators of shallow water. Fishing is excellent from this shore. These channels are also beautiful canoeing waters.

Other than the river itself, the greatest charm of this section, as in other units of the park, lies in its magnificent trees, shrubs, wildflowers, ferns, grasses, and mosses, and its many birds.

The Riverside Trail between the pedestrian bridge towers leads through woods and meadows to the Visitor Center, an attractive rustic building at the edge of the river, midway between the towers. The Center is open on weekends and by appointment, and when the park naturalist is in his office, which is located in the building. Among its features are exhibits on the natural and cultural history of the park; the excellent interpretive pamphlets are free. A drinking fountain and clean restrooms add to its attractions for hikers.

At this point you can turn the trail into a loop by walking under the tracks and taking the Buttermilk Trail back to the parking lot, for a total of one mile, or continue on to the next pedestrian bridge tower and ascend to the Buttermilk Trail for a two mile hike (or jog) in all.

The Buttermilk Trail is a wooded roller coaster following the contours of the slope. It is at its loveliest and most interesting in the spring when the delicate "ephemerals" - short-lived spring flowers - appear. This is the time to take a wildflower walk with a naturalist who knows where and what they are. (Watch the newspapers for announcements of wildflower walks.) A little side trail will take you by the dry Netherwood Quarry, where you can get a good look at the Petersburg granite that underlies the park. These rock faces are favorites with rock climbers for practicing and teaching.

Small picnic shelters are located throughout the park, and there are endless pleasant spots for picnicking without tables. Fires, however, are not permitted.

151

Belle Isle

(65 Acres)

> Located in the James River underneath and west of the Lee Bridge. At this writing the only way to reach it by foot is across the rocks from the Main Section when the river is low. A high dike along the island shore must be surmounted by improvised ramps or steps. Greatly improved access is being planned. Call the James River Park regarding guided tours and the latest information about access.

Belle Isle is indeed a "beautiful island" suspended in time between a fascinating past and a future yet to be realized. The City Master Plan calls for the island, which is owned by the City, to be developed as a park at some time in the future. If all goes well, Richmond Renaissance will participate in developing a river oriented outdoor center, with access via a footbridge from the north shore and improved access from the south shore. In the meantime the forest is creeping back, and only the adventuresome visit this scenic, historic, and mysterious island, except to reach the rocks alongside the rapids in summer.

Like the great flat rocks in the river, Belle Isle is formed of granite. The wearing of the rock and silt carried downstream have deposited its soil, to which has been added humus from the forest that now occupies the island and provides a habitat for wildlife.

All traces of its Indian inhabitants have long since vanished, at least on the surface. It is recorded that Captain John Smith bought the island from Chief Powhatan in 1608, and that it subsequently passed through many hands. In 1815 a wooden dam was built from the south shore to get power for a nail factory on the island. Old Dominion Iron and Steel took over the factory in 1832, operating it for 144 years until the City bought the property. Workers lived in houses (long since gone) on the island. A Virginia Power plant was constructed in 1905. These facilities have fallen into disrepair and, despite their historic significance, may ultimately be torn down. Avoid them, as they are unsafe.

The island is full of interesting discoveries, among them a little old stone building, perhaps a snuff factory dating back to 1815, and an abandoned granite quarry filled with water, which has become a scenic attraction, a challenging rock climbing site, and a favorite fishing spot. (This will be a featured attraction in the Renaissance plan.)

Perhaps the most notorious period of the island occurred during the Civil War when it became a squalid tent city for more than 30,000 Union prisoners of war. One wonders how many walked across the rocks to freedom when the guards were not looking!

The map shows the landmarks on the island, its relationship to the Main Section, and the location of the rapids on the west and north. (A levee has diverted the river to the north side of the island for water power, leaving very little between the island and the south shore.) The rapids in this area are *for expert canoeists only!* The inflatable rafts of the James River Experiences run these safely, however, with a guide in each raft. Their trips break for lunch here on the big flat rocks, which are also favorite spots for fishermen, spectators, and sunbathers.

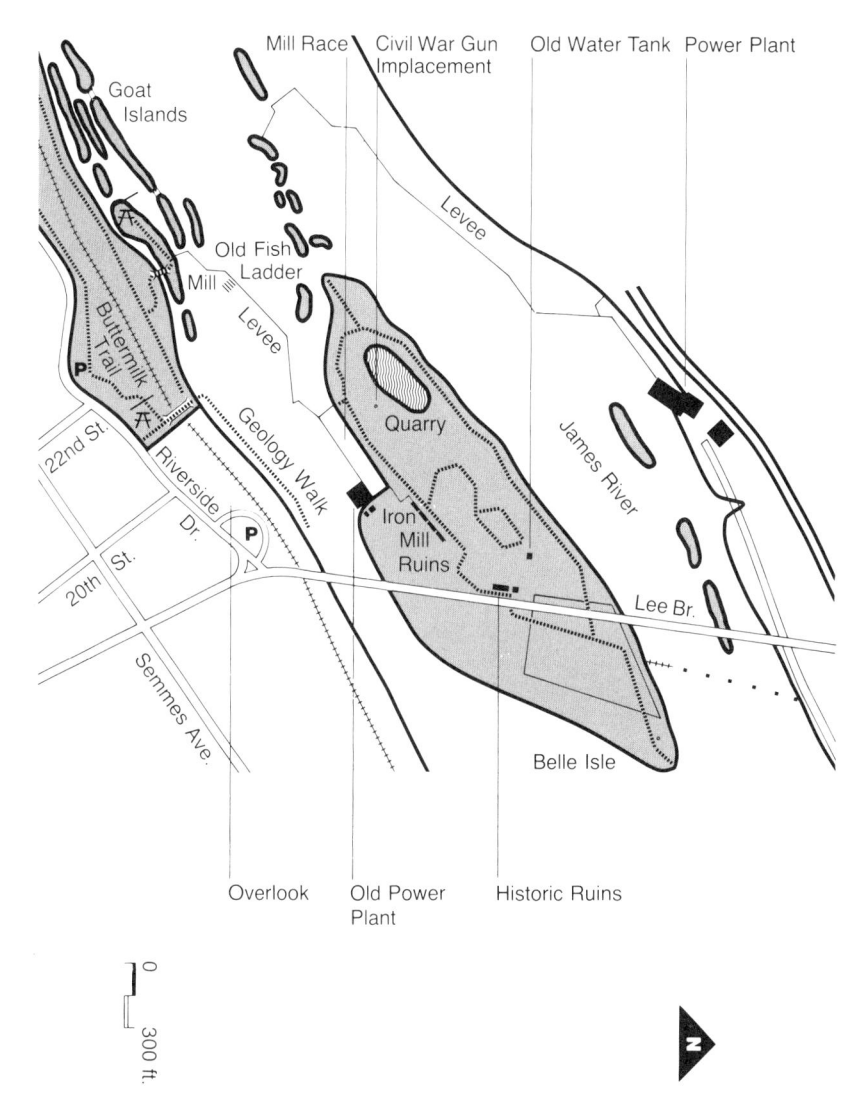

A loop trail goes around the island and out to both ends, with an inner loop to its highest point, where a fine view may be enjoyed. It is a good idea to take a map along, as there are currently no signs or markers on the island. Copies of the map included here are available at the Visitor Center in the Main Section, along with interpretive pamphlets.

North Bank Park/Texas Avenue Annex

(6 Acres)

Located along the north bank between the Mt. Calvary Cemetery on the east and Maymont Park on the west. The entrance is at the end of Texas Avenue five blocks east of Maymont. By bus, take the Robinson #3 to the intersection of Texas and New York Avenues and walk south.

Across the river from the Main Section, the heavily wooded North Bank Park is like a small mirror image in many respects. From the attractive parking lot a path leads down the steep bank to a pedestrian bridge and open tower with steps down to the floodplain. Thick vegetation obscures the view of the river in the growing season, but the crossing over the Kanawha Canal is interesting at any time of the year.

Here, as in the Main Section, islands parallel the shore, and the river runs through channels overhung with trees. A series of small rapids adds to the beauty of the scene from the trail, and rocky ledges create attractive places to rest and picnic.

This park is, however, less developed, and its only trail may be almost overgrown in places. (Poison ivy is rampant; wear long pants.) The linear trail leads west for about 3/4 mile, petering out at a large culvert; to return, one simply doubles back. Here and there the channel is shallow enough to wade across to one of the islands for a little exploring. The scenery is beautiful and the water tempting at normal levels, but unfortunately it is polluted after heavy rains. Fishing is good in many locations away from underbrush and overhanging trees.

There are no facilities in the park. The descent is steep, and the trails primitive and unsuitable for handicapped access. This area is relatively unknown and seldom crowded. Its wildness creates a sense of adventure not experienced in more developed parks.

The Pony Pasture and the Wetlands

(100 Acres)

Located off Riverside Drive 1.7 miles east of the Huguenot Bridge. From Forest Hill Avenue turn north on Hathaway Road alongside the Stratford Hills Shopping Center. Hathaway becomes Longview; continue to the end of Longview. Take a short right and left onto Riverside Drive to the park entrance. No bus lines serve this area.

The Pony Pasture, named for ponies that once grazed here, is a lovely section of floodplain along the south bank where the rapids begin. In normal to low flow conditions, especially in the leafy seasons, this is one of the most beautiful river environments in the City. The river here is open, sunny, and shallow, with gentle, sparkling rapids flowing among the many large flat rocks and patches of water willow. The water is relatively clean. Canoes may be launched for the three-mile trip ("beginner's whitewater") down to the Visitor Center in the Main Section. A large, well designed parking lot is located close to the riverbank. Inevitably the park and river have many visitors on summer days.

The river scene in summer is often a curious one, resembling a montage of recreational activities. All at the same time in the same place, people enjoy hopping from one rock to another, or sunning themselves - perhaps in beach chairs with their coolers - socializing, wading, and body surfing down the gentle rapids. In the very same area canoeists, "tubers", and rafters thread their way among the rocks or

"The Rocks" - James River Near the Pony Pasture

pull their craft up onto them to rest and reconnoiter, visit, or take on passengers. Kayakers paddle upstream to take the rapids in the midst of all this, and fishermen cast from rocks as far removed from the crowd as possible.

Anyone wanting to join the scene should plan to arrive early; the parking lot is often filled before noon on weekends. To have it all (or almost) to yourself, go on a weekday or walk downstream a short distance where fewer people find their way.

The park itself is worth discovering. Several trails lead from the parking lot through an old field maintained to demonstrate plant succession, (see Section I - *Plant Communities*) and over a small wooden bridge to a marsh known as the Wetlands. The old field is covered with riotous plant growth, including great patches of wildflowers in season - violets in March and April, clusters of blue and purple spiderworts in May, multiflora roses and daylilies in June, and a variety of other species throughout the summer. Unfortunately poison ivy also thrives throughout the park; beware. Stay on the trails.

In the deep woods the yellow flowering spicebush graces an otherwise bare forest during the last two weeks of March. Another interesting little tree is the pawpaw, with flowers like brown tulips and edible fruits that look like mottled pears, ripening in September.

Although nature puts on its greatest show from April to October, the park is an interesting place to walk at any time of the year. Bird watchers schedule outings throughout the year, (early spring is best) always with many sightings, as the variety of habitats in turn attracts a large diversity of species. (See Section I - *Wildlife*.)

156

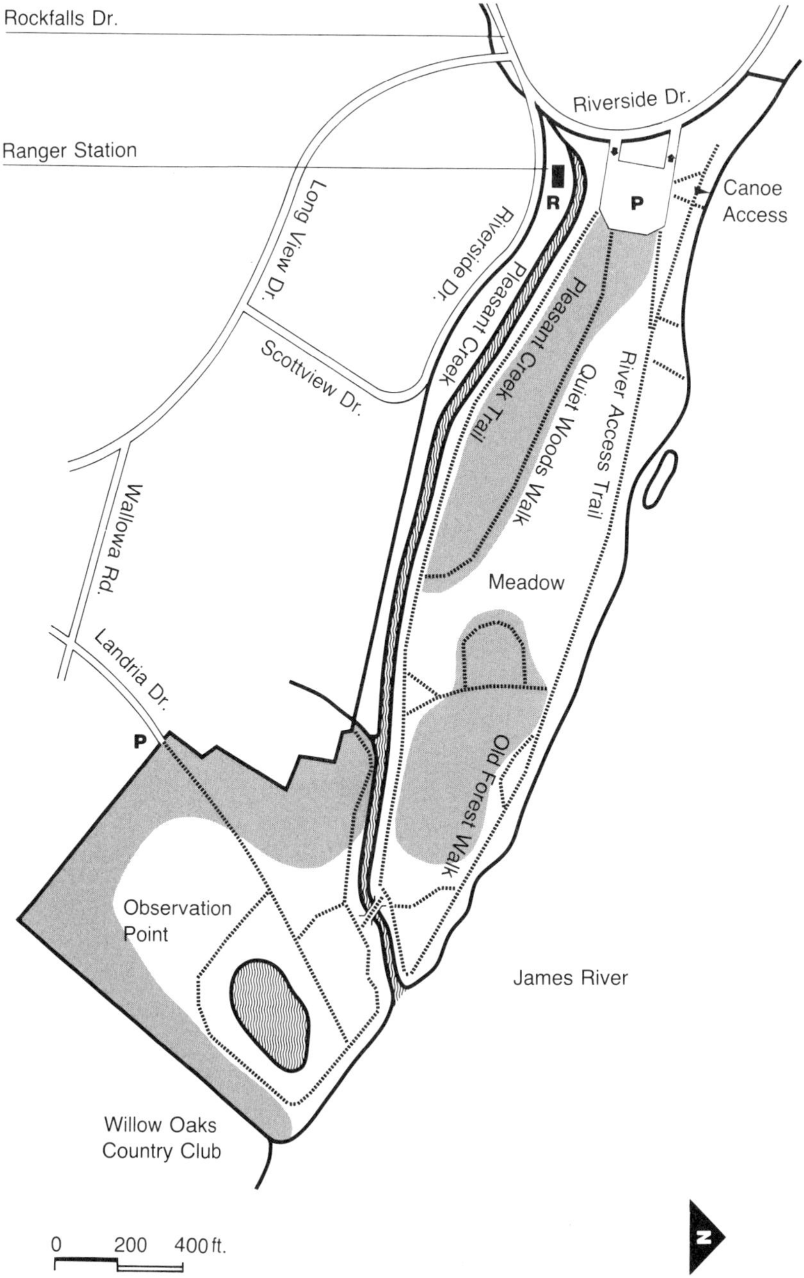

Rockfalls Dr.
Riverside Dr.
Ranger Station
R
P
Canoe Access
Long View Dr.
Riverside Dr.
Pleasant Creek
Pleasant Creek Trail
Quiet Woods Walk
River Access Trail
Scottview Dr.
Wallowa Rd.
Meadow
Landria Dr.
P
Old Forest Walk
Observation Point
James River
Willow Oaks Country Club
0
200
400 ft.
N

The ranger station adjacent to the parking lot has restrooms, equipped for handicapped visitors. Unfortunately, even at best the trails are too uneven for good handicapped access, but one of the prettiest and most interesting spots in the park is readily accessible by a good path from the parking lot. On summer mornings at the end of the path, from a bench overlooking the river, one can often watch wild ducks teaching their young to dive, swim upstream and coast (one could almost say merrily) back down the rapids, while great blue herons fish in the shallows a cautious distance away. This scene alone is worth a visit time and again.

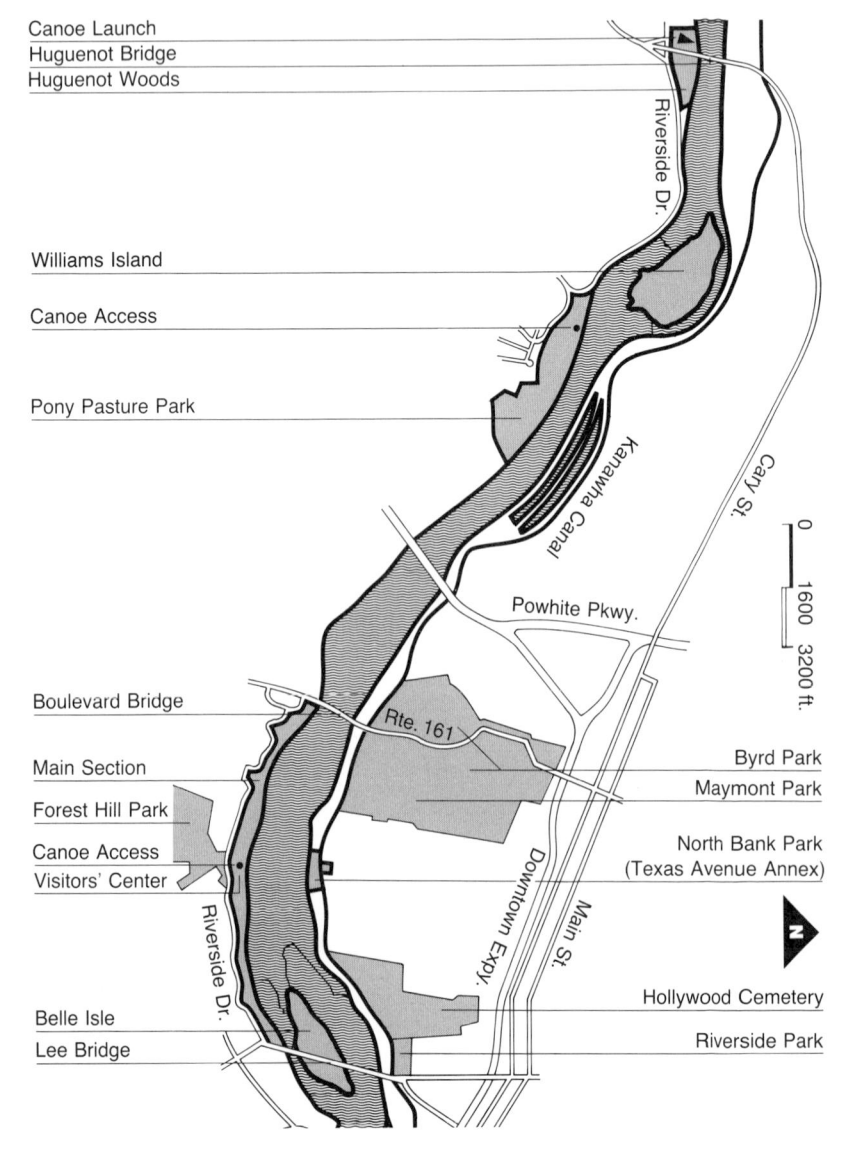

- Canoe Launch
- Huguenot Bridge
- Huguenot Woods
- Riverside Dr.
- Williams Island
- Canoe Access
- Pony Pasture Park
- Kanawha Canal
- Cary St.
- Powhite Pkwy.
- Boulevard Bridge
- Rte. 161
- Main Section
- Byrd Park
- Maymont Park
- Forest Hill Park
- Canoe Access
- North Bank Park (Texas Avenue Annex)
- Visitors' Center
- Riverside Dr.
- Downtown Expy.
- Main St.
- Hollywood Cemetery
- Belle Isle
- Lee Bridge
- Riverside Park

0 — 1600 — 3200 ft.

The Huguenot Woods

(30 Acres)

Between the south shore and Riverside Drive on both sides of the Huguenot Bridge from Southampton Road to Rattlesnake Creek. (Do not be alarmed. The name is a misnomer; rattlesnakes are *not* found in this region.) At this writing a parking area is being developed off Southampton Road along the western edge. Cars may also park in a small pullout along Riverside Drive. No bus route serves the area.

Huguenot Woods - Lowland Forest

Westernmost of the James River Parks, the Huguenot Woods Park is like a secret garden unknown to thousands of motorists who cross over it on the Huguenot Bridge every day. Its attractions are for those who enjoy a quiet place to walk, fish, birdwatch, or otherwise commune with nature. In addition, a new canoe launching area being developed on the site will provide an ideal access to the river between Bosher's and Williams Dams for exploring the waters and islands and flatwater fishing in the area.

The park is at its best when the trees are in foliage and the ground is dry. In summer the deep shade is cooling and the peaceful environment is a happy contrast with crowded conditions in other parks. Not many wildflowers grow in these woods, but in August you may find enormous hibiscus flowers blooming along the edge. (Picking them is prohibited. The flowers only last one day anyway.)

A fascinating feature of the woods, most conspicuous in winter, is a number of ancient grapevines growing up to a foot in diameter and grotesquely contorted from having climbed and fallen with generations of larger, shorter-lived trees. Do not swing on them, as they may break.

At the eastern edge, where Rattlesnake Creek flows into the river, a sand bar has created a tiny beach with a shallow incline, good for fishing and wading with care, when the river is low. Three trails enter the woods to join a long path paralleling the riverbank, one at either end and one from the parking pullout on Riverside Drive. These are uneven and interrupted by small ravines here and there. Unless they are improved in the future, they should not be attempted by anyone with serious handicaps; however, a splendid railed outlook at the end of Southampton Road is designed for access by everyone. The view over the river is fine, especially at sunset.

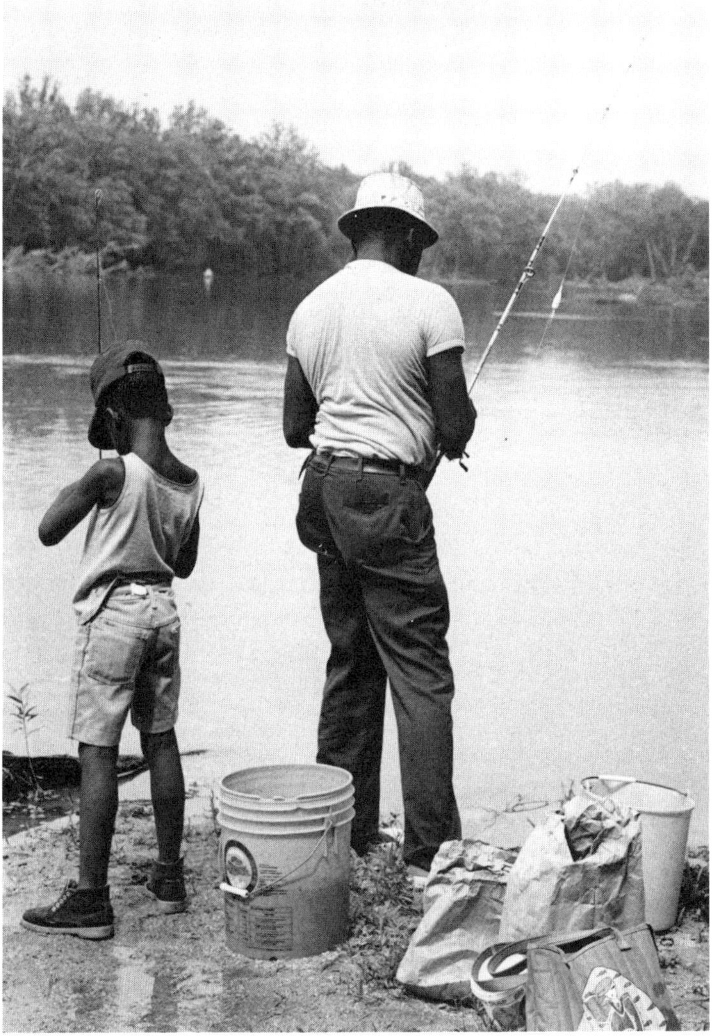

Williams Island

(95 Acres)

Located midstream from about a mile below the Huguenot Bridge to the first of the rapids opposite the Pony Pasture. The only access is by canoe or by foot with great care over Williams Dam *when the water flowing over it is very low - that is, below ankle height* .

A pocket wilderness covered with floodplain forest, Williams Island has been left undeveloped all these years because it is prone to flooding, and is for the most part protected from visitors because it is surrounded by water, with no bridges. Not yet formally part of the James River Park system, the island is owned by the City and is intended for inclusion in the future. In the meantime, the trails that used to surround and cross the island are overgrown, except for a short path along the shore, where a sandy beach is visible from the dam. This is a favorite swimming place in summer when the river is low. Youngsters used to swing into the water from grapevines hanging from the trees. Now that the vines have broken, they continue the tradition using ropes.

Plant and animal communities flourish undisturbed on the island, including not only those common to the area, but also many that have grown from seeds washed down from higher elevations. We have seen the rare Virginia bluebells and American basswood there, among other plants not often seen in Richmond. Deer live on the island (a wildlife sanctuary, of course), occasionally swimming ashore to browse.

Williams Dam extends from the south shore to the island, with an extension to the north shore on the other side. It is a low dam intended only to divert water into the Kanawha Canal and thence to the water treatment plant when the river is low. During low flow periods this is one of the best fishing spots in the state, where you can fish both above and below the dam from the same position; however, it is only safe to walk on the dam when the water flowing over it is lower than ankle height. At higher levels the current may push one over to the foot of the dam, where the hydraulic action has caused many drownings. The warning bears repeating; stay off the dam if the water is above ankle height.

Riverside Drive between the Huguenot Woods and the Pony Pasture

Although not a park road, we include this section of Riverside Drive because it connects two parks and serves as a lovely scenic drive. This is the only place in the region where a road follows the riverbank closely, affording glimpses of the James only a few feet away. Disabled passengers should especially enjoy this opportunity to see the river close up. A natural canopy of trees shades the road, and an understory of native shrubs and wildflowers lines it on both sides. The drive is also a fine place to walk, jog, or ride a bike when traffic is light. (Unfortunately there is no footpath or bikeway, and traffic is heavy on summer weekends.) The distance between the two parking lots is 1-1/2 miles. Williams Dam is about midway between them.

Historic Neighborhood Parks of the East End

Chimborazo Park And National Battlefield Park Visitor Center

(6 Acres)

Located along East Broad between 32nd and Elam Streets, sloping down to Williamsburg Road to the East. Take the Church Hill buses #41 or 51 directly to the park.

Among the first sites selected by the City for public parks were hilltops in historic Church Hill. Chimborazo was one of these. Situated on a promontory above the James River, the park commands a fine view over the river, the old City Wharf and tobacco warehouses, the city skyline to the north and west, and Fulton Bottom and Powhatan Hill to the south. Ambitiously named for a mountain in the Andes, the park's elevation is 162 feet above sea level. From this vantage point it is also possible to see the several terraces created by the ancient James River during the periods when the ocean advanced as far west as the present site of Richmond. (See Section I - *The Changing Landscape*.)

A stone mounted at the edge of the upper level bears a bronze plaque inscribed "An old Indian stone removed from and now overlooking Powhatan Seat, a royal residence of King Powhatan when Captain John Smith and his fellow adventurers made the first permanent English Settlement..." Legend has it that this was the stone on which John Smith laid his head before being rescued by Pocahontas.

If you have never seen the Statue of Liberty, here is your chance. A small replica donated by Boy Scouts stands on a pedestal on the lawn, facing east just like the original in New York Harbor.

During the Civil War a large Confederate hospital occupied the hill, but this was demolished afterward, and the site was acquired as a city park in 1874. Today the National Battlefield Park Headquarters and Visitor Center is located on the park grounds in an unusual arrangement between the City and the Department of the Interior.

The grounds mainly consist of lawn shaded by fine old specimen trees. This is a pleasant spot for a picnic on the grass. Free play is permitted - frisbee, ball tossing, kiting, etc. A recently installed Parcourse Fitness Cluster is scientifically designed to be used by both the able-bodied and handicapped, including paraplegics.

The Visitor Center of the National Battlefield Park, a major tourist attraction, is housed in a stately building on the grounds. Exhibits and an orientation film introduce visitors to the history of the 1861-65 defense of Richmond and map out the Battlefield Tour taking in over 100 miles and nine other locations in the area. A courteous and knowledgeable staff is there to answer questions. There is also a small gift shop with books and slides pertaining to the Civil War in the Richmond area. A visit to the Center is highly recommended. (See also *Richmond National Battlefield Park.*)

165

Great Ship Lock Park

(4 Acres)

Along Dock Street at the end of Pear Street. Follow Dock Street east under the railroad trestle to Pear. Turn right (toward the canal) to enter. By bus, take the #52 Montrose or # 53 Darbytown on Main to Pear Street and walk down the hill to Dock and the entrance.

Great Ship Lock Park was created by the City of Richmond in 1976 to celebrate the Bicentennial, and to insure the preservation of the Great Ship Lock at the entrance to the old Kanawha Canal. Despite its out-of-the-way location, the park is well worth a visit to see the fascinating lock and the mechanisms that used to lift barges and boats, including sea-going vessels, above the river. Here canal boats started their passage west to the Great Turning Basin, and up the canal around the seven mile stretch of rapids and shallows which had made upstream navigation impossible for the early settlers.

A kiosk in the park provides an interesting history of the James River and Kanawha Canal, and in particular the Great Ship Lock, with maps and old photographs showing some of the ships that have passed through it. The canal was an engineering marvel, needed in those days when overland transportation was hampered by the difficulties of building and maintaining roads and bridges over difficult terrain and rivers. Boats could only maneuver below the fall line, and above it only where the water was deep enough and not obstructed by rapids.

The challenge in overcoming obstructions on land and water was to create a system combining the easiest solutions along a continuous route. The Virginia General Assembly began discussing a James River and Kanawha Canal as early as 1765, but the impetus that generated the survey, design, financing, and construction of the canal came from none other than George Washington! The legend on the kiosk describes the project in summary.

"Washington dreamed of a transportation system that connected the Tidewater of the James River at Richmond with the eastern foot of the Rocky Mountains. The only portion that was completed was the canal, river, and (wagon) road complex from Richmond on the James to Point Pleasant on the Ohio River - no mean feat itself...The dock is the tidewater terminus of the entire 485 mile system of canal, turnpike, and steamboat navigation linking the James River and Kanawha rivers, serving as an essential transportation system between the east and west."

The story of the canal is a long and fascinating one. The first survey for the section around the Falls in Richmond was made in 1786, and construction from Westham to Belle Isle completed three years later, with extensions and many additions and improvements as time went on. In 1800 an eastern terminus within the heart of the city, known as the Great Basin, was completed, creating docks in the commercial district, and allowing boats and barges to be turned. All that was needed was a connection with the tidewater to the east, so that boats coming up the James could enter the canal, and boats going down, the tidal river.

The first connection consisted of a series of wooden locks, a lower dock, and a wooden ship lock, but these soon deteriorated and had to be replaced with new ones made of granite blocks and sturdier timbers. (At the same time, much of the rest of the canal was undergoing repair and replacement.) By 1840 the canal had reached Lynchburg, by 1851, Buchanan through a total of ninety lift locks for a total lift of 728 feet.

In 1854, nearly seventy years after the canal was begun, the Great Ship Lock was completed, along with the canal and lock system that connected it with the Great Basin. The Tidewater Connection, as it was called, consisted of five locks in a line running east of Byrd Street. Each of these locks had a lift of 13 feet 8 inches, for a total lift of 68 feet 4 inches between 13th and 9th Streets, an amazing engineering feat, and not an easy one to finance in those days.

As the principal means of shipping, the canal was very important to Richmond in those days and for another quarter of a century. It was responsible for much of the city's prosperity and contributed a cultural element as well, with passengers travelling on packets as far as Lynchburg, under pleasant - though crowded - social conditions, and in the late 1870s taking evening excursions to the pumphouse to dance in its upstairs pavilion. (The stone pumphouse still stands, though its pavilion has fallen into disrepair.)

The first canal boats used for shipping were wooden "bateaux," fifty to sixty feet long and five feet wide, propelled by poling. Later, specially designed freight boats and passenger packets built to the maximum size were hauled by mules along the towpath.

In 1880 the canal was purchased by the Richmond and Allegheny Railroad, and essentially replaced as a transportation system. Part of it was filled in, and most of the rest left dry and falling into ruin. Today only remnants of the canal and towpath survive. There is a great deal of sentiment in Richmond for preserving and possibly restoring certain segments, and a beginning has been made by Reynolds Metals Company.

After the demise of the canal, the Great Ship Lock was never again an important gateway to the west. The recent restoration was mainly a salute to its historicity, but happily it still contains water, and is operable.

To see the Tidewater Connection double locks 4 and 5 and the old stone 13th Street Bridge spanning the canal, visit the Reynolds Metals Company at 12th and Byrd Streets, where these handsome relics have been preserved for the enjoyment of the public. Picnic tables in an attractive setting around the edges can be rented for parties. The atmosphere is delightful, and on hot summer days the flowing water in the shade creates an environment at least ten degrees cooler than that of the rest of the city.

The City Master Plan calls for the eventual restoration of the three-mile locks just west of the old pumphouse and the pumphouse itself in a historical park, for which the property has already been acquired, and there is talk of recreating the concession canal boat excursions.

This is a fascinating area, where you can actually see three canals running parallel to one another - the newest, the old, and the oldest - and examine the construction of the two that are dry. Unfortunately, until the new park is developed, the area has to be fenced off at this time for reasons of safety. Fortunately, regular tours are offered by the Virginia Canals and Navigation Society. (For information, call 804/288-1334.)

James River and Kanawha Canal

Jefferson Park

(8 Acres)

Situated on a terrace between Marshall and Clay Streets west of Jefferson. To approach it from above, park along Jefferson or Clay. Steps lead up from the lower level at Marshall and 19th Streets. The nearest City buses are the Church Hill #41, Jefferson 45, and the Fairmont 43 (Pike or Peter Paul.)

A pleasant neighborhood park developed in 1911 for its location on high ground, Jefferson is also worth a visit for its view of the city skyline and historic Shockoe Valley. The grounds are mainly landscaped in tree shaded lawns, with a small bandshell and tot lot as added features. In the days before air conditioning neighbors sought out the park for the cool breezes it catches on hot summer days and evenings, which are still enjoyable for people who prefer to be outside at times like these.

As in many other city parks, there is more here than meets the eye. Sitting in the sun, it is hard to believe that underneath the park an old train lies buried in a tunnel constructed in the 1870s, which collapsed in 1925. Today old tracks leading into the hill are an erie reminder of the sealed off tunnel and its imprisoned contents. Better to enjoy the sunshine and the breeze, and forget about what lies beneath.

Libbie Hill Park

(12 Acres)

Located along East Franklin Street between 28th and 32nd Streets, sloping steeply down to Main. The closest bus is the Main #53.

Situated on a high bluff overlooking the bend of the James, Libbie Hill Park commands a splendid view of the city to the north, south, and west. This is a charming little park created in 1851 to enhance a neighborhood of fine homes, now undergoing restoration. Over the years it has retained its peaceful character of lawns shaded by great old trees. An old enclosed gazebo is now a park house (warmed by a potbellied stove) used for meetings of civic groups. Steps lead down to a lower level terrace and Main Street.

The most conspicuous feature of the park is a 70 foot high Confederate Soldiers and Sailors Monument, a bronze figure of a soldier standing on a column reproduction of Pompei's Pillar. History records that its dedication in 1894 attracted 100,000 people, which must have been just about everyone around at that time. An annual Memorial Day observance still commemorates the sacrifices of those who gave their lives in the war.

From the eastern end of the park you can look down on the valley called Sugar Bottom, once named Bloody Run after a fierce battle between settlers and marauding Indians in 1656. The settlers fought on the side of the Powhatan Indians of the lower James against the Monacans of the upper James. The Monacans were victorious.

The park was named after Luther Libbie, a prominent local business man whose mansion once stood on the hill—and whose warehouse was converted into the infamous Libbie prison for captured Union soldiers during the Civil War.

Although mainly used as a neighborhood park today, Libbie Hill is well worth a pilgrimage by anyone interested in a historic place, a quaint atmosphere, and a place to relax while taking it all in.

Patrick Henry Park

(One Square Block)

Located on Broad Street directly opposite Old St John's Church between 24th and 25th Streets. The Broad Street #41 and 51 buses go right by it.

This tiny landscaped square was developed in 1964 as a tribute to Patrick Henry, who made his famous "Give me liberty or give me death" speech in the church across the way. Separated from the sidewalk by a low brick wall, it mainly serves as a neighorhood retreat and a place for tourists to rest after visiting the historic St. John's Church and cemetery.

Powhatan Hill

Powhatan Hill

(14 Acres)

Located in the curve of Williamsburg Road, where it turns east opposite Hatcher Street. To park, turn up Northampton Street to Goddin on the upper level. A recreation center across the street has parking facilities. To get there by bus, take the Main #53.

This little hilltop park is one of the most historic sites in North America. It was here the Indian Chief Powhatan (father of Pocahontas) entertained Captains John Smith and Christopher Newport on May 23, 1607 when they came ashore after having sailed up the James from their landing at Jamestown. Smith later purchased the hill, naming it "Nonsuch" for its unexcelled beauty.

Here you can sit on a bench at the edge of the hill overlooking the James and reconstruct the pageantry of this encounter between the hospitable (at least at first) Indians and their unexpected guests from across the sea, more than three and a half centuries ago. Today the city skyline and urban scenes have replaced Powhatan's view, but the basic landscape is the same. Walk down the steps and turn up the sidewalk on Northampton Street. There, set into the stone retaining wall, you will find the plaque commemorating this strange and historic event.

The park and its associated neighborhood recreation center also feature a playground, ballfields, and a swimming pool. The slope of the hillside is a favorite place to sled after a winter storm.

Powhatan Hill

172

Taylor's Hill Park

(2.6 Acres)

Situated on a hillside between East Franklin and Grace above 21st Street. Park at the end of Grace west of 22nd Street. Or take the Church Hill #41 or 51 bus on Broad and walk over to Grace.

Would-be visitors may have a hard time finding this park because some of it is on a 45 degree slope. When you arrive at the end of Grace Street you will still wonder where it is because all you notice at first is a drop off and a plaque interpreting the magnificent view of the city skyline. As you face the downtown area to the northwest, you will see the park extending down the hill to the right below the WRVA radio station, with no access in that direction. On the left, however, a steep road for pedestrians only leads down the hill and around the old Monte Maria Convent. From here steps descend to a grassy terrace at 21st and Franklin Streets. This is an interesting environment of old streets and buildings and new construction where revitalization is taking place.

The entire hill, originally called Council Chamber Hill, was named after William H. Taylor, a prominent nineteenth century merchant and local civic leader. Taylor's love for the hill prompted him to build three homes there over the years. The hill has also been home to many well known Richmonders, including Elizabeth Van Lew, who was scorned as a Union sympathizer during the Civil War. The city acquired this small portion of the hill in 1882 to preserve the superb view from its heights.

Downtown to Belvidere

Capitol Square
(Virginia State Capitol Grounds)

(12 Acres)

South of Broad Street between 9th and Governor Streets.

A beautifully landscaped oasis in the heart of downtown Richmond, Capitol Square serves as a year-round landscaped passive park as well as the grounds for the State Capitol. First time visitors to Richmond should by all means tour Thomas Jefferson's Capitol, where the Virginia General Assembly has met since 1788. Interpretive tours run continuously during business hours seven days a week.

The grounds are also interesting as well as lovely. The graceful white brick Governor's Mansion, built in 1813 and occupied continuously ever since, occupies the north east corner. An imposing statuary group depicts George Washington astride his horse, with famous contemporary leaders surrounding him in characteristic postures. Other statues of famous Virginians are placed here and there throughout the grounds.

During the legislative sessions from January to March the Capitol is an especially interesting place, bustling with legislators, their aides, State agency personnel, and lobbyists, in addition to the usual groups of visiting school children and tourists. Yet even then, in spite of all the bustle, the grounds manage to be peaceful and inviting, with people strolling about, taking pictures, feeding the pigeons and squirrels, and relaxing on the lawns or benches.

At noon time on pleasant days at any time of the year, the square is a favorite place for Richmonders working downtown to bring a sandwich and meet friends for a social hour in a pleasant environment. Probably more than any other place in the region, it typifies a successful urban central park in every way.

If you happen to be there around noon and haven't brought a lunch, you can buy a sandwich in the snack bar on the ground floor of the Capitol to take outside while surveying the scene from one of the benches. Who knows —you just might rub shoulders with the Governor.

Kanawha Plaza

(4 Acres)

>Canal Street between 6th and 7th Streets, across from the Federal Reserve Building. By bus take the Forest Hill #70 or 71 or the Huguenot bus.

Richmond's newest park is a showcase of landscape architecture created to enhance the environment from Main Street to the James, which it does splendidly. Colorful flower beds are changed with the seasons. Paths and inviting benches are strategically situated for strolling and sitting. This is another favorite spot for people who work in the business section to bring a lunch on a pleasant day.

If you are interested in modern urban architecture, cross the street to the Federal Reserve Building and walk about its marble plaza. Its spacious open design and grounds are worth seeing. An intriguing fountain, designed with moving metal wands, incorporates wind and water chimes as well, creating a fascinating attraction, especially when lighted at night. A lawn sweeping down the hill behind the building ends in a small park-like area, which although not public property, serves to visually grace an area returning from the desolation of neglect.

Capital Square

Gamble's Hill

(9 Acres)

Along Arch Street (one block south of Byrd) between 2nd and Fifth Streets. Park along the street. The hill is now private property. By bus, take the Forest Hill #70, or 71, or the Huguenot bus and get off at 2nd and Arch.

Gamble's Hill was one of Richmond's first parks, established in 1851 for its sweeping view of the James River and the old James River and Kanawha Canal. It was also considered to be an important historic site, as historians of that time believed it was here that Captain John Smith planted a cross in 1607, laying claim to the New World for England.

In 1907 the Association for the Preservation of Virginia Antiquities placed a granite cross on the hill to commemorate the event. After the park was acquired by Ethyl Corporation for its corporate headquarters, the cross was moved to Shockoe Slip (at the southern end of 12th Street), which may be closer to the actual site. In exchange for the hill, the city has acquired Brown's Island below it as a future riverside park.

Ethyl Corporation allows visitors to stroll along its hillside drive overlooking the river. The view is interesting and beautiful, and the grounds are appropriately landscaped and well kept.

From the western end of Gamble's Hill you can walk to the Virginia War Memorial by heading south on 2nd Street and over a small bridge, then up the steps to the War Memorial grounds.

Virginia War Memorial

(3 Acres)

A short distance west of Gamble's Hill, along Belvidere just north of the Lee Bridge. Using public transportation, take the Forest Hill #70 or 71 or the Huguenot bus. Ask to be let off at the War Memorial.

Virginia War Memorial

Virginia's memorial to its World War II and Korean war dead stands on a beautifully landscaped hillside overlooking the James River. The memorial itself is an open pavilion made of marble and glass, with a sculpted figure of a weeping woman representing Virginia mourning her dead. Thousands of names are inscribed on the walls as a poignant reminder that those who died are not forgotten.

An attached building houses a small auditorium which may be reserved by agencies and civic groups for special programs (generally dealing with public affairs.) The surroundings and ample parking make this an ideal facility for a small conference.

From the grounds of the War Memorial you can walk either to Gamble's Hill by descending the steps at the eastern end and crossing a little bridge to the foot of the Hill, or to Riverside Park by following the road that sweeps around the lower part of the grounds and under the Lee Bridge to the park.

West of Belvidere

Fan Parks

The Fan District of Richmond was originally part of the old Town of Sydney laid off in 1817. The town's street pattern resembled a fan and created many triangularly shaped roadway intersections, with leftover parcels landscaped by the City. Two of these became charming little parks, which have retained their old fashioned atmosphere over the years, and are still enjoyed by the neighboring townhouse residents.

Meadow Triangle, located in the Meadow Street-Stuart and Park Avenue Triangle, features an intimate enclosure with benches and a sandbox, surrounded by a graceful old wrought iron fence and rose garden. A bronze soldier - monument to the First Virginia Infantry Regiment - presides over a flower bed, and there is just about lawn enough for small children to run, while supervising adults rest and visit.

Lombardy Triangle, where Park and Hanover come together, is a tiny brick-walled enclave and garden with shade trees and play equipment for the little ones.

Monument Avenue Median from the Stuart Circle Monument to the Boulevard constitutes a mile-long greenbelt enjoyed as a public open space by many of the residents along the Avenue. Stately monuments of famous Virginians lend interest to the intersections, and attract visitors from all over. Joggers have beaten a controversial path, which continues to be used as a sort of right-of-way, and walking the dog is now an accepted use as well. The neighborhood turns the median into an old fashioned promenade at Easter, and a wonderful festival ground for children on May Day. Everyone is invited.

Historic Hollywood Cemetery

Along the north bank west of Riverside Park, between Cherry and Harrison Streets. Drive south on Laurel, turn right on Albemarle to the entrance at Cherry one block west. By bus, take the Laurel #11, get off at Albemarle, and walk west.

Hollywood Cemetery is included here, although it is not a park, because the historic section is interesting and beautiful, overhung with ancient trees and full of the atmosphere of days gone by. Presidents Monroe and Tyler are buried here along with six governors of Virginia. Especially poignant is the grave of Jefferson Davis, President of the Confederate States during the Civil war, surrounded by members of his family, including the tiny headstones of children who died in infancy. Thousands of Confederate soldiers also lie here in a special section devoted to them.

Visit Hollywood on a pleasant day when the warm sunshine brightens the otherwise somber atmosphere. Stop at the headquarters just inside the entrance for a map showing the way to the historic section. Stroll about and discover headstones bearing familiar names in history. This was the chosen resting place of many of Virginia's most illustrious citizens.

Monroe Park

(7.5 Acres)

>One Square block bounded by Belvidere, Laurel, Franklin, and Main Streets. By bus take the Grove #15, Westhampton 16, or Laurel 11.

Surrounded on all sides by busy streets and major buildings, Monroe Park epitomizes the value of a landscaped square in an urban environment. Planted long ago with fine old trees, its lawns and flower gardens tended, the park creates a peaceful island west of downtown Richmond in an area bustling with activity.

In 1851 when the city first acquired the property for a park, it was intended to generate new residential development of high quality by providing an attractive public garden as its focus. As the years went by the park was successively used as a fairground for agricultural exhibits, a Civil War training ground and hospital site, and a field for a new sport called baseball. Finally in the 1870s it was returned to its original purpose, designed pretty much as it is today, and enjoyed as a promenade through the 1920s, when society moved at a slower pace.

The old residential neighborhood has given way to many changes. Today the park faces a public auditorium, (the Mosque), the Sacred Heart Cathedral, Grace and Holy Trinity Episcopal Church, a hotel, apartment house, and high rise student dormitories. It sits between major thoroughfares leading to and from the downtown area and the Lee Bridge and forms the only significant open space in the Virginia Commonwealth University complex, serving in a way as an adjunct to its campus. Students and faculty members join the residents of the neighborhood in enjoying the park grounds, and it absorbs them all with ease.

The old fashioned park design is interesting and lovely, with its graceful center fountain and radiating paths. Many of the trees are old and stately. Most of the young trees are flowering species, gracing the park in spring. The old music stand is now a park house. A small playground has been added. Walking through the park is a very pleasant way to get across the block in every season of the year. The paths are also well suited for jogging, with detours along the sidewalks. Curb cuts, the flat topography, and paved walkways ease the way for handicapped users.

Riverside Park

(7 Acres)

Across Belvidere from the War Memorial. Along the hilltop above the Kanawha Canal to the edge of Hollywood Cemetery. Take Laurel Street south to the end, or 2nd Street south and west (Veer right under the bridge.) By bus take the Laurel #11 and walk south from Albemarle or the Forest Hill #70, 71, or Huguenot bus along Belvidere; get off at China, and walk over to Laurel.

Another of Richmond's old parks chosen for their location above the river and the sweeping views from their heights, Riverside Park dates back to 1889. Tucked behind the old Oregon Hill neighborhood, Riverside seems rather forgotten today, and in need of rediscovery. Take a little time to walk about and view the Kanawha Canal from above, and beyond it the river, Belle Isle, and the south shore. From the western edge of the park one can also get a good view of part of old Hollywood Cemetery.

Also near the western edge steps lead down to the old canal towpath. One can still walk west along it for some distance, where the canal boats used to be pulled upstream by mules before the railroad made the canal, towpath, (and mules) obsolete.

A quaint old enclosed gazebo on the hillside harks back to the Victorian era of the park's beginnings, and the peaceful atmosphere contributes to a contemplative visit or an undisturbed picnic.

To reach the cemetery entrance, follow Cherry at the western end of the park to Albemarle. It is also possible to walk to the War Memorial by following the road at the eastern end under the Lee Bridge to the Memorial grounds. (A one-way street prevents driving under the bridge in this direction. In a car you have to cross Belvidere to the War Memorial.)

Community Parks of the Northside

Abner Clay Park

(2 Acres)

Located in Historic Jackson Ward where Old Brook Road runs into Leigh Street.

A new neighborhood park created during the recent Jackson Ward Revitalization program, and named after a respected leader in that effort, Abner Clay is a pleasant green block in an area of old homes and new development. The park features lighted ballfields, tennis courts, a tot lot, large grassy open space for free play, and a small plaza with an open shelter for seating.

Riverside Park

Battery Park

(12 Acres)

Along Hawthorne Avenue between Wickam and Dupont, two blocks east of Chamberlayne Avenue. Enter from Overbrook, which crosses the park. One way streets may cause some confusion. By bus take the Chamberlayne #37, get off at Overbrook and walk east.

Battery is a beautiful and busy park nestled in a narrow valley, which was once the site of a Confederate battery. The park's topography, which varies 27 feet from the surrounding area, is a particularly interesting aspect of the park and is responsible for its unusual configuration. The slopes are planted with flowering shrubs, dogwoods and larger hardwoods, creating a lovely setting enhanced by granite steps and walkways.

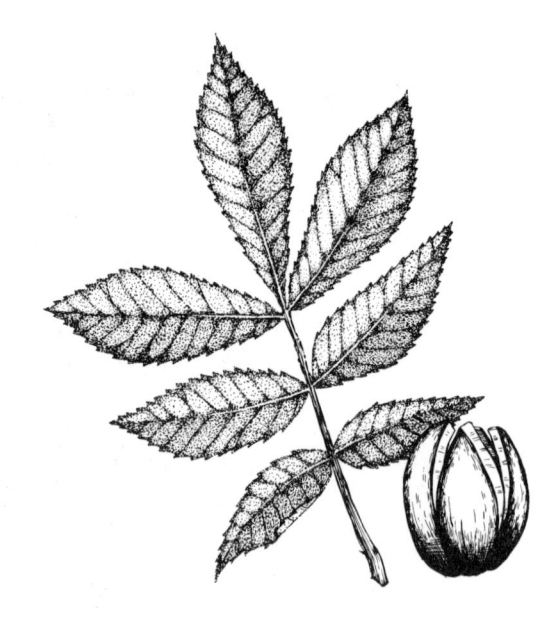

Mockernut Hickory

185

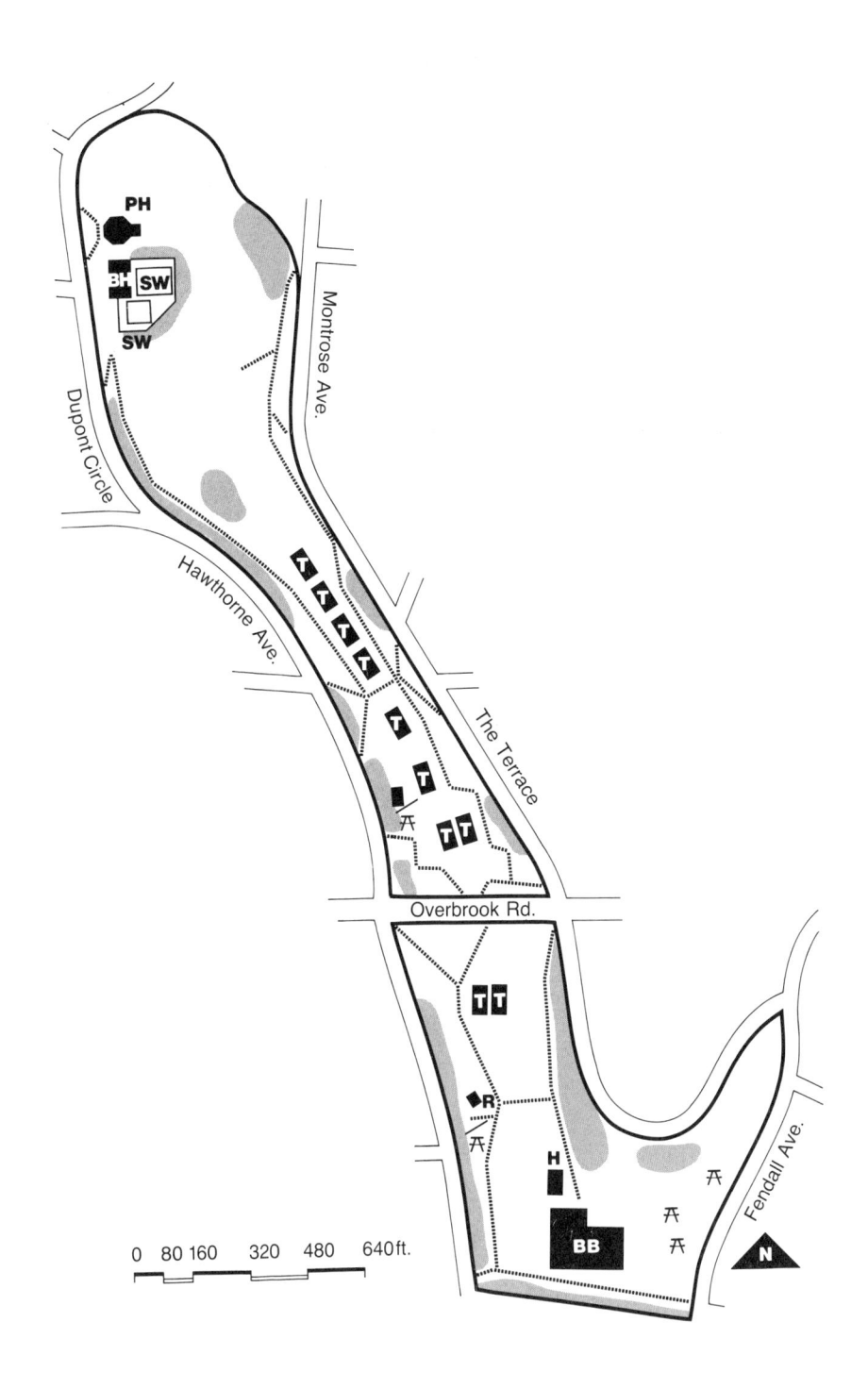

Cannon Creek Natural Area

(5 Acres)

> Located along the historic two-lane Richmond-Henrico Turnpike between Brookland Park Boulevard and Vale Streets.

Reminiscent of the old wayside parks, the natural area runs along a mile-long section of the narrow Cannon Creek valley. Surplus land belonging to the City, it was designated as a natural park at the request of neighbors who wanted to protect the native plants and wildlife habitat and make the area accessible for public enjoyment. A simple trail, maintained only by use, follows alongside the creek (which now runs only in wet weather) under large old trees, allowing the visitor to enjoy a natural experience in an area that is otherwise totally developed.

Between Dove and Vale Streets the valley widens into a shaded 3-acre picnic area with old but usable tables and fireplaces. At one time a natural spring located here was a source of pure water, but today a sign warns that it should not be used. While the picnic area is mainly used by neighborhood residents, it is available to anyone.

Highland Park Plaza

(Two City Blocks)

> Pollack Street between first and Carolina Avenues.

A homey old neighborhood park, with grass and benches under big old trees. Facilities include two tennis courts, horseshoe pits, and for the children, a playground and sandboxes.

The park is nicely lighted and, because of its level topography and curb cuts, accessible to persons with disabilities, although at this writing, an old community house on the grounds was not.

Pine Camp

(40 Acres)

Located along Old Brook Road between Bellevue and Azalea Avenues, just inside the City limits. Enter from Watkins Road. By bus take the Chamberlayne #37 on Chamberlayne, get off at Watkins and walk one block east to Old Brook.

Pine Camp is primarily a community recreation center on attractive landscaped grounds, with paths for walking or jogging, a 1-1/2 mile fitness trail, and a small nature trail along Horse Swamp Creek. A grove of loblolly pines creates a pretty setting for picnicking.

Recreation facilities include a combination baseball/soccer field, basketball courts, a playground, and a Community Center with a small theater, activity rooms, and an art gallery. A wide range of recreation programs includes classes in arts and crafts, dance, activities for senior citizens, and nature walks. The Center is mainly used by Northside residents, but its programs are open to all, including Henrico citizens. Schedules are available from the City Department of Recreation and Parks.

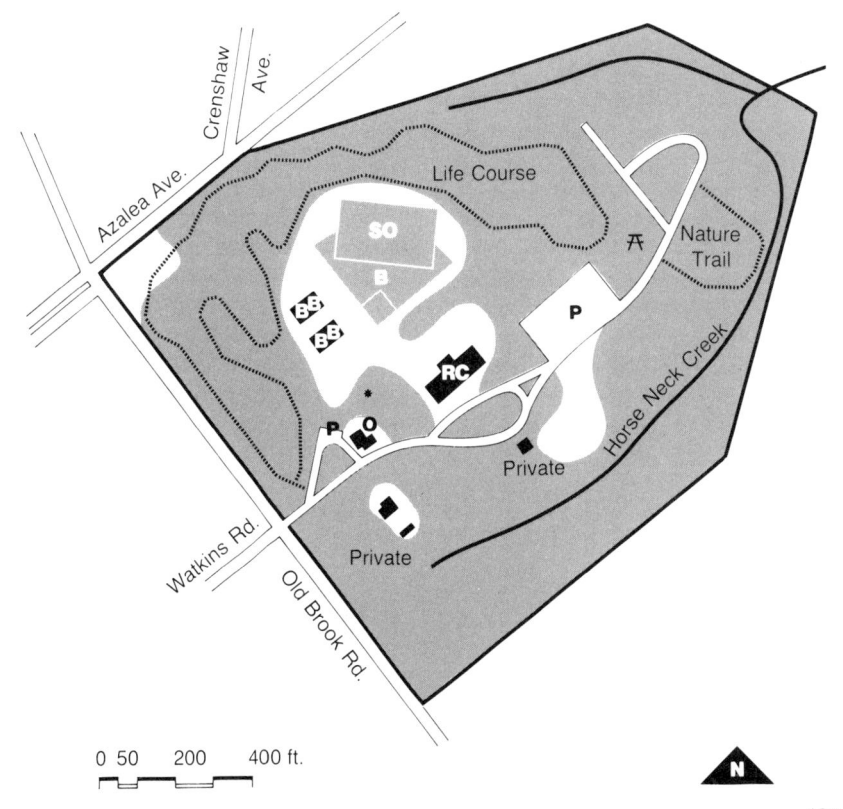

Pollard Park

(3.6 Acres)

Located at Chamberlayne Avenue and Brookland Park Boulevard, reaching to Hawthorne Avenue and Ladies Mile Road. The Chamberlayne #37 bus stops by the park.

A lovely old fashioned neighborhood passive park, Pollard is simply a peaceful oasis in which to relax on benches under big old trees. Lawns, flower beds, and an old gazebo add beauty and atmosphere.

The park manages to fit an astonishing variety of recreational facilities into the little valley, and still leave paths for walking or jogging, picnic areas, and spots for relaxing on the grass. Visitors in search of athletic facilities will find tennis, basketball, and horseshoe courts, and a swimming pool. Programs are carried out in a Community Center, which is also available to civic groups for meetings.

Community Parks South of the James

Carter Jones Park

(12 Acres)

Located in south Richmond, bounded by Bainbridge and Perry, 27th and 29th Streets. By bus, take the Midlothian #63, to 27th and walk two blocks north, or the Forest Hill #70 or 71 to Semmes and 27th and walk three blocks south.

A neighborhood park, Carter Jones also features Fonticello Spring, one of the few natural springs of potable water left in Richmond. People who appreciate spring water come from miles around to fill bottles to take home. (Do not, however, expect to see the water coming out of a bucolic environment; the spring is protected by a large concrete structure, and the water comes out of four spigots.)

Park facilities include lighted ball fields, tennis courts, a basketball court, horseshoe pit, and children's play area. Several picnic tables are scattered about, and there are plenty of grassy areas for free or open play (ball tossing, frisbee, etc.), and relaxing. Level topography, paved paths, and curb cuts make the park accessible to handicapped visitors.

The city conducts recreation programs in the park, including nature interpretation. Schedules are available from the Department of Recreation and Parks.

Pocosham Park

(86 Acres)

Along the east side of Chippenham Parkway to Hey Road, on both sides of Walmsley Boulevard. A small parking lot is located at the end of Templeton Road off Pocosham Road, which is reached via Hey Road. No city buses serve the area.

Like Powhite Park, Pocosham is a lovely natural upland forest with many old trees that have survived logging in the past. Several informal paths crisscross the woods, and the sparseness of the underbrush makes walking easy, even without trails. The park as a whole is still undeveloped, but a small parking lot, created to serve a totlot and basketball court along the edge, can be used by those wishing to walk around in the woods as well. No sign directs one to the rest of the park at this writing. You are pretty much on your own finding your way around. Just head into the woods and try to remember where you came from.

An old logging road leads north from the basketball court and connects with a beaten path down to the creek. Other paths and old roads present themselves as one goes along. The best access to the area is where Walmsley crosses Pocoshock creek; however, there is no sign identifying the park here either, and no parking is allowed. To enter or exit from this spot, you have to be dropped off or picked up. There is plenty of level space to pull off the road.

Boundaries are not marked, so it is especially important to lean over backward to avoid trespassing. As the park is developed, these problems will be overcome.

Pocosham Creek

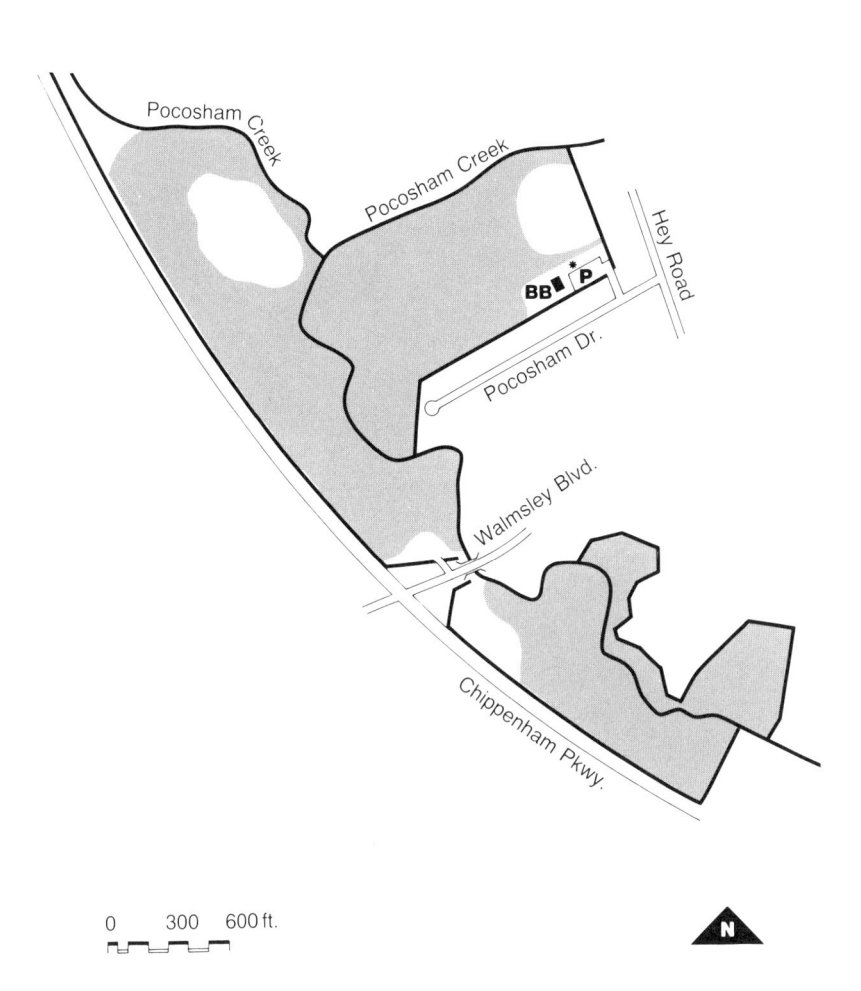

Pocosham Creek

Pocosham Creek

Hey Road

BB * P

Pocosham Dr.

Walmsley Blvd.

Chippenham Pkwy.

0   300   600 ft.

N

191

Powhite Park

(100 Acres)

Along the east side of Chippenham Parkway between the Powhite Parkway and Jahnke Road. Enter from the westbound lane of Jahnke Road between Hiokes Road and Chippenham Parkway. The Forest Hill #71 bus (marked Chippenham Hospital) stops at Hiokes Road.

Powhite Park, the latest of Richmond's parks to be developed, is situated in a natural upland forest sloping steeply into ravines and a beaver pond surrounded by a marsh and swamp. Walking along its foot trails through so much beauty and such fascinating habitats, it is hard to believe that one is less than a mile from a busy intersection and several shopping centers. The city in its wisdom has preserved a nearly pristine environment for hiking and nature study in an area where it will be a priceless resource in the years to come.

Beaver Pond - Powhite Park

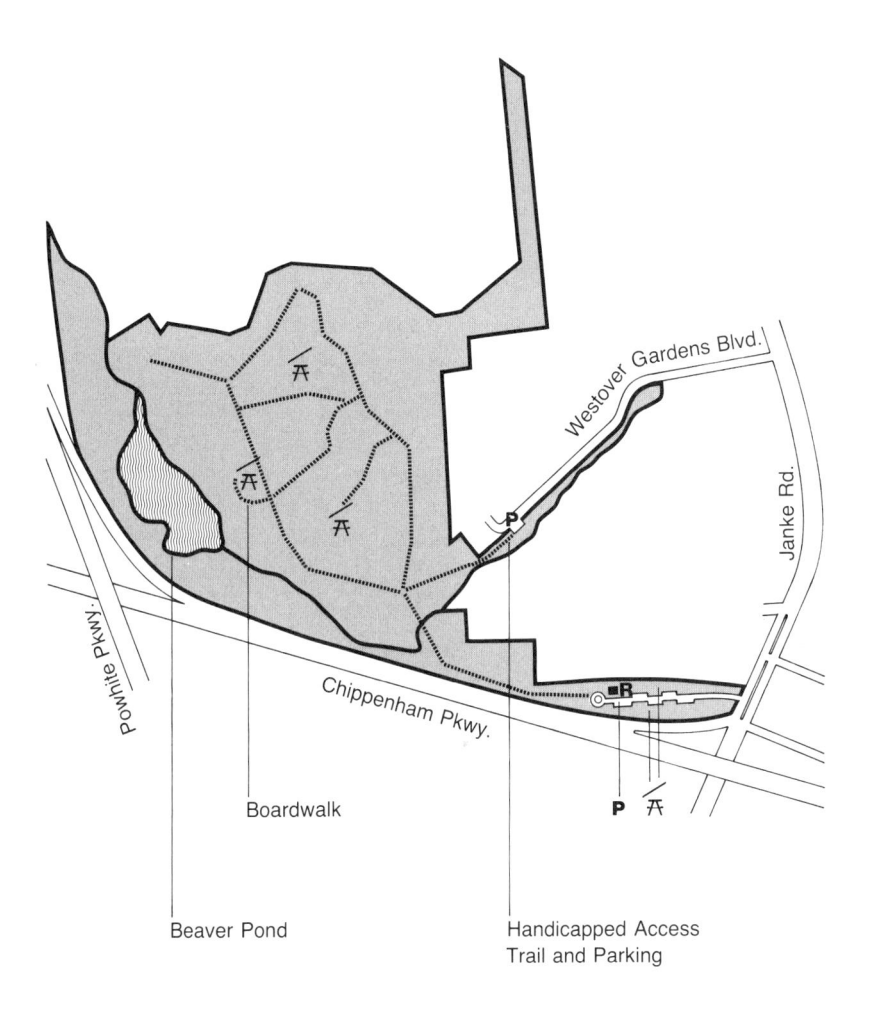

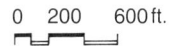

Boardwalk

Beaver Pond

Handicapped Access
Trail and Parking

0   200   600 ft.

N

Among the fascinating sights in the park are trees being cut and felled by beavers. If you have never seen the work of these industrious creatures, take a look at the pond they have created by damming Powhite Creek with the trees they have gnawed in two. Several trees are still standing with deep notches in them, perhaps to be finished off or fall from being weakened; meanwhile they illustrate the process.

Another treat the park has in store for the discerning visitor is a feast of blueberries in August. Look for the bushes on high ground.

Phase I of the park development (beginning in the spring of 1985) calls for a small parking lot (for 20 cars) just inside the entrance, with picnic shelters and restrooms (equipped for handicapped visitors) conveniently nearby. Altogether nearly two miles of trails and paths will loop around the park, including a half mile designed and surfaced (asphalt) for handicapped access.

An especially appealing feature of the park will be the pond overlook from a boardwalk, with a picnic shelter from which to enjoy the view. It should be possible from this aspect to get a glimpse of wildlife, including birds of the habitat. Another picnic shelter is planned for high ground in the middle of the park. While neither of these will be close to parking, their seclusion and the views they afford should more than make up for the inconvenience of carrying in food.

Future plans include extensions of the boardwalk, two more pond overlooks, and additional picnic shelters.

Wayside Spring

(One Acre)

In a ravine below New Kent Road opposite Prince George, seven blocks west of Forest Hill Drive. Look for a low stone wall and a rustic sign.

A natural ravine with a small spring of pure water, visited by many with their bottles from home. The field stone wall and steps, contributed by the Westover Hills Garden Club, lead down the wooded slope to the spring and a little trail paralleling the ravine. This is a lovely place to come for water, or a pleasant little walk, especially in spring when wildflowers decorate the way.

Persimmon

Chesterfield County Parks and Recreation

Chesterfield is fortunate in having within its boundaries a national wildlife refuge, an exceptional Civil War fort, a major state park and forest, and a growing county park system, including impressive natural areas and historic sites. All are described in the following pages.

The Parks and Recreation Department is young, but a great deal has been accomplished in a decade. Beside several complexes that are strictly athletic, seven parks (most of which also have some athletic facilities) and a canoe launching area have been completed. Two more parks are in the development stage, and future plans call for additional sites, including natural areas, that will add considerably to the total recreational resources in the county.

Chesterfield is obviously guided by a philosophy that is highly responsive to public needs and desires. The variety, location, and careful design of its parks and facilities, clear and attractive signs, high maintenance standards, and attention to special populations - the handicapped, for instance - all add up to enjoyable park experiences for people of many interests.

The parks are open to all without charge; however, certain group facilities, such as the large picnic shelters, ball parks, and the county stadium and stable complexes are rented under special arrangements. Garden plots in Rockwood Park may also be rented during the growing season. For information, call 804/748-1623.

Understandably, park rules and regulations prohibit the use of alcohol and firearms in the parks, and of fires other than in designated grills.

Beside maintaining existing parks and developing new ones, the Department carries out extensive recreation programs that go far beyond the traditional sports and community center activities. New kinds of outdoor programs focus on natural and cultural history, adventures, and instruction for those who want to learn or improve their skills in various out-of-doors activities.

Seasonal brochures describing all programs and events are available at county schools, libraries, and other community locations. Mail-in registration is held prior to the beginning of each program session in January, May and September. Non-residents and those who can not get to these locations may obtain brochures by calling the Department's administration office - 748-1623.

Responding to a growing interest in outdoor skills and adventures, the Department conducts outings and classes in archeology (if possible, including digs), backpacking, biking, bird watching, canoeing, caving, fishing, sailing, skiing, windsurfing, and many others. Enjoyment and learning are the objectives. Many of these are held in the parks and preserves of the county, but others involve day or weekend trips to places as far away as the coast or the mountains. All programs are open to the general public, whether or not residents of Chesterfield County. A fee is charged for most of these.

The popular week-long summer camps for youth also focus on adventure challenges and outdoor skill building, such as canoeing, sailing, rock climbing, hiking, and camping. The youngsters have a wonderful time and come away with new skills they can enjoy for the rest of their lives.

In keeping with the Department's sense of responsibility toward special populations, several therapeutic recreation programs are geared to handicapped youth and adults, and to senior citizens with special interests.

Nature awareness is built into all of the outdoor programs. In addition various special natural history programs are held almost every week in the parks. These include guided nature walks of general or specific interest, including, of course, birding trips. A small nature center at Rockwood Park presents exhibits on wildlife, ecology, and the history of the Rockwood Park area. The "great outdoors" comes indoors during a Winter Lecture Series held monthly on a variety of interesting topics. Special school programs are provided on request.

Programs and tours focussing on Chesterfield's long and fascinating history are also part of the Department's repertoire. Several of the parks (Rockwood, Point of Rocks, and the planned Henrico City Park) are historic sites, and as such, interpreted for interested visitors. One of the most exciting events is a realistic Civil War "muster" put on by uniformed volunteers at Point Of Rocks Park in the fall.

Other annual events in the parks celebrate seasons and holidays - an Outdoor Odyssey, May Fest, July 4th Extravaganza, Rainbow of Arts, Halloween Happening, and Legendary Christmas. Entertainment may include performances by the Department's co-sponsored groups, such as the Virginia Bluegrass and Country Music Foundation, the John Rolfe Players, Brandermill Community Theater, and various square dance groups. Watch the papers and local calendars of events for announcements.

Appomattox River Boat Launch

Located in the Ettrick district of southeastern Chesterfield County on the north bank of the Appomattox River, just below Brasfield Dam. From State Route 602 take Route 669 (Chesdin Road) south to its ending.

Actually a small park with a canoe launching facility, this area is also a good spot for bank fishing and picnicking. One of its attractions is a good view of the water pouring over Brasfield Dam.

The launching facility consists of wide concrete steps down to the river, suitable for carrying down canoes, kayaks, inflatable rafts, and other small craft, but not for boats requiring ramps.

This is the put-in spot for a canoe or kayak trip down the rapids of the Appomattox River as it crosses the fall zone (designated throughout this stretch as a State Scenic River). An Appomattox River Map with descriptions of the rapids along the route, safe river levels, and other information important to canoeists, is posted here. A color-coded river gauge indicates water levels at any given time.

Point of Rocks Park—Richmond Newspapers

Established Major Parks

Point of Rocks Park

(174 Acres)

Located along the southern boundary of Chesterfield County in the Bermuda District, at the junction of Enon Church and Ruffin Mill Roads. The park is approximately two miles southwest of Virginia Route 10 and three miles east of Interstate 95. From Route 10 turn west on Enon Church Road (look for signs to the park). From Interstate 95 exit at Ruffin Mill Road and drive east.

One of Chesterfield County's finest services to the community has been to acquire natural and historic areas of exceptional interest and beauty, and to make them accessible to the public. Point of Rocks is an outstanding example of a park that takes advantage of existing features and turns physical obstacles into opportunities.

Also in accord with County practices, the park includes an athletic complex close to the entrance, and well removed from the natural area beyond. Facilities include a football field, two lighted ballfields, and six lighted tennis courts. A playground and restrooms (equipped for handicapped visitors) are located in the same area. Three attractive small group picnic shelters are placed at the edge of the natural area, close to parking, and two overlook the river along the Ashton Creek Trail.

Situated where Ashton Creek flows into the Appomattox River, Point of Rocks features a wide variety of upland and lowland forest, meadow, marsh, and aquatic habitats and wildlife. Its topography on a high terrace sloping steeply down to the creek, river and marsh, and its natural features have caused it to be used at various times in the past as prehistoric Indian villages, a colonial plantation and customs wharf, major Civil War encampments, and for turn-of-the century red ochre mining.

Its location on high bluffs (used for lookout, signalling other tribes, and defence from the lowlands) was of great advantage to the Indians who inhabited the Point as early as 10,000 years ago, and up to the time when the English settlers displaced them around 1620. Fish and game were plentiful, and dugout canoes could travel from the site up Ashton Creek and down the Appomattox. Another resource that contributed to their long period of residence was the presence of quartzite, which they used for making arrowheads. It is easy to see how they came by them; quartzite cobblestones are still lying on the surface in Cobblestone Creek, which the trail crosses. The name Point of Rocks, however, derived from a large rock outcropping 80 feet above the river, just downstream from the park. (Much of this was quarried after the Civil War.)

The ubiquitous Captain John Smith explored the area in 1607-1608. The land was

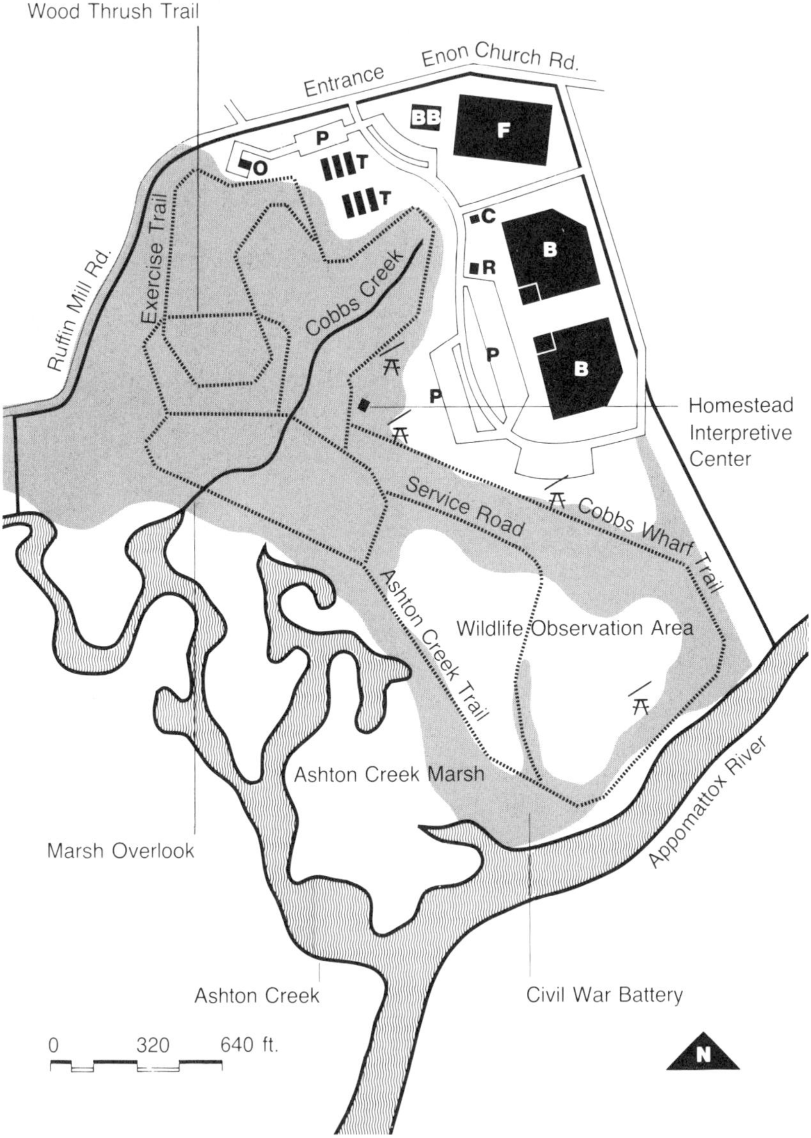
Wood Thrush Trail
Entrance
Enon Church Rd.
BB
F
P
O
T
T
C
B
R
B
P
P
Ruffin Mill Rd.
Exercise Trail
Cobbs Creek
Homestead
Interpretive
Center
Service Road
Cobbs Wharf Trail
Ashton Creek Trail
Wildlife Observation Area
Ashton Creek Marsh
Appomattox River
Marsh Overlook
Ashton Creek
Civil War Battery
0
320
640 ft.
N

Marsh Overlook - Point of Rocks Park

first patented in 1642 and was part of the Bermuda Hundred Stockade established by Sir Thomas Dale in 1611. Ambrose Cobbs operated a plantation on the property during colonial times, complete with a customs wharf on the Appomattox, now marked as a historic site. The land was used for centuries for tobacco, small grain, and cattle farming.

In 1864 Union troops under General Butler captured Cobbs Plantation/ Cobb's Hill and established a signal tower, field hospital, and Fort, which was used as a staging area for attacks on the Petersburg Railroad to the southwest across Ashton Creek. (See Petersburg Battlefield Park.) The mounded earthworks built as a defense against the Confederate Army forces guarding the railroad lines can still be discerned.

The well constructed trails are unavoidably steep in places, and often stepped, owing to the topography; unfortunately these conditions make it difficult for handicapped visitors to use them. Under special circumstances arrangements can be made to provide transportation to the main marsh overlook via a service road. For information call the Department of Parks and Recreation.

All trails begin at a demonstration homestead developed by relocating an authentic old log cabin and corn crib from other sites on the park property. The Homestead features indoor exhibits including arrowheads and artifacts from colonial times and the Civil War occupation, as well as displays on the natural history of the park. Be sure to pick up one of the self-guided Ashton Creek Trail pamphlets to take with you along the way. These are keyed to numbered posts along the trail, and although they only scratch the surface, they highlight the most important features to be seen.

The trail, marker posts, and the pamphlet were projects of the Youth Conservation Corps (YCC) in 1980-81. Its most outstanding features are the marsh overlook platforms and a boardwalk extending some distance into the marsh, giving visitors a close look at the rushes, reeds, flowers, grasses, and wild rice growing in it.

Ashton Creek Marsh, which makes up almost half of the park, is representative of the rapidly disappearing freshwater/tidal marshes so important to the ecology and economy of Virginia. A wide variety of very productive marsh plants growing here provide food and shelter to fur-bearing mammals, young game, commercial fish, waterfowl, and many other species. This is a fascinating environment worth visiting in every season to see it in all its changing aspects. The marsh was contributed to the County by Continental Forest Industries.

Many species of wildlife inhabit the park, among them beaver, deer, fox, wild turkey, and many birds. Recently the Department of Parks and Recreation has added a wildlife observation area with over fifty plant species intended to attract song birds and also small rodents, which in turn attract foxes. A large bird blind at the edge of the area and above it allows as many as fifteen people to observe wildlife at the same time, without being noticed. (Taxpayers who check off refunds to the Non-Game Program of the Virginia Division of Game and Inland Fisheries should note that a contribution from this fund made the bird blind possible.)

Interpretive programs are planned by a professional naturalist. Up to date schedules are published from time to time and widely distributed throughout the county. For a copy, ask at one of the county libraries or call the Department of Parks and Recreation, (804) 748-1623.

Rockwood Park

(161 Acres)

Northeast of the intersection of Courthouse Road (Route 653) and Hull Street Road (US Route 360). Entrances from both roads.

Two thirds natural and historic area, and one third developed for intensive recreational use, Rockwood Park has something for just about everyone. The park is situated on an upland forest which was once part of Rockwood Plantation along Falling Creek, where the Gregory family lived for five generations. Gregory's Pond, which forms its eastern boundary, was created by an impoundment for a grist mill which operated at the plantation from the 18th into the 19th century. Ice was cut on the pond, and ice pits and an old road used to haul the ice can still be seen in the natural area.

Today Rockwood is one of the region's most popular and diversified parks, offering a wide range of recreational facilities. Consistent with Chesterfield's park design policies, the athletic complex is located nearest the entrance and parking lot, and buffered from the natural area by less intense uses. Even the commotion generated by an enthusiastic crowd watching a baseball game never seems to penetrate the quiet of the nature trail on the slope below.

The athletic area includes nine tennis courts, two basketball courts, and seven ballfields, all of which are lighted for night use. This area also includes picnic areas

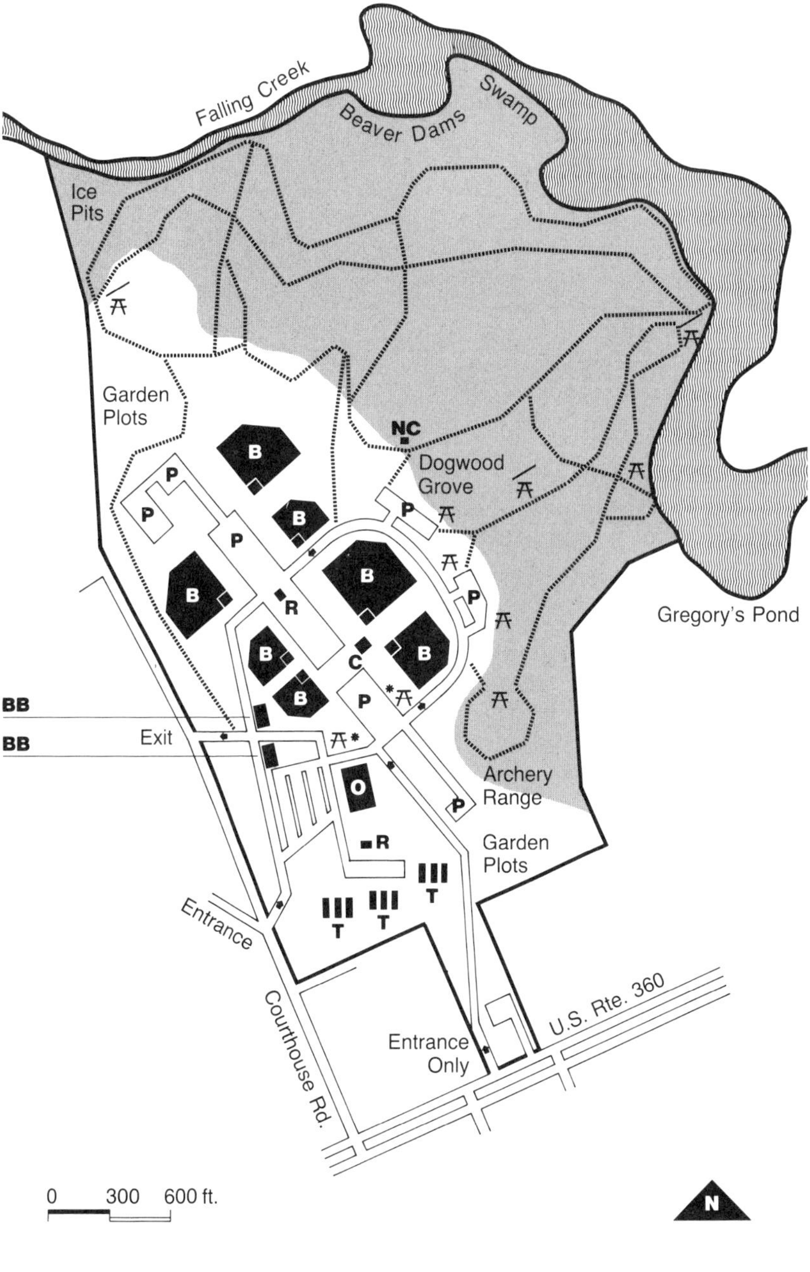
Falling Creek
Beaver Dams
Swamp
Ice Pits
Garden Plots
NC
Dogwood Grove
Gregory's Pond
B
P
R
C
O
T
BB
Exit
Archery Range
Garden Plots
Entrance
Courthouse Rd.
Entrance Only
U.S. Rte. 360
0 300 600 ft.
N

with tables and grills, several play areas with innovative equipment, a concession building, and restrooms equipped for handicapped visitors. Community garden plots may be rented. Friendly park personnel are on hand much of the time.

Four attractive group picnic shelters are located in pretty spots along the edge of the natural area, conveniently close to the circular park road. The region's only large tournament archery range, with a variety of target distances, is tucked into a secluded area, safely away from the beaten path. A fitness trail with exercise stations shares the path into the woods and also provides a firm surface for handicapped access..

Be sure to stop by the rustic little Nature Center at the head of the nature trail. The exhibits on plants and wildlife are all taken from the park. Permanent exhibits will spotlight the Rockwood Swamp, animal tracks, a Nature IQ game, and history. The self-guided Gregory Pond Trail pamphlet available at the Center calls attention to natural and historic features along the way, some of which one might not otherwise notice.

3.4 miles of nature trails (with smaller loops) wind through an old beech forest and along the edge of the creek, a small swamp, and a beaver pond. Gregory's Pond, although it is privately owned, also borders and contributes to the lovely setting. The trails are wide and well marked, bridging ravines, traversing some slopes on switchbacks, and stepped on steeper slopes. Joggers use these too.

In spite of the nearness of intense suburban development and the activities on the upper level, wildlife, including reclusive species, still flourish in these habitats. If you walk quietly early in the morning, you might catch a glimpse of a beaver, or white tailed deer. Bird watching is good, and guided nature walks are highly recommended.

The Community Parks of Chesterfield

Four neighborhood parks dedicated in 1976 complement the major parks in the growing Chesterfield system. All of these provide some athletic facilities (ball fields, tennis courts, etc.), picnic areas, modern play areas with those appealing wooden structures, ample parking lots, and restrooms equipped for handicapped visitors. Paths have been designed and compacted for handicapped access as well. To the extent that the size and original setting permits, all also have at least a small natural area, even if only a fringe of trees, and shade has been a consideration in locating the picnic and play areas.

In addition to the parks, five strictly athletic complexes have been developed in the north and central parts of the county. The Courthouse Complex is unusual, in that it includes an old half-mile track once used for sulky (harness) races, a grandstand, and two riding rings (eastern and western), with judging stands and temporary stables. These facilities may be rented for equestrian events. The track and grandstand may also be rented for various special events. For more information about the facilities in these complexes, call the Department of Parks and Recreation.

Ettrick Park

(25 Acres)

Also in the Matoaca District, on Laurel Road 1/2 mile north of River Road (one mile west of its intersection with Rt. 1) in the community of Ettrick.

An exceptionally large open play field is an attractive feature of Ettrick, which also includes the usual three lighted tennis courts, football and baseball fields, plus two lighted basketball courts.

Picnic tables with grills and a shelter are located conveniently close to the parking lot, with a shaded play area nearby. As in the other neighborhood parks, surrounding woods give the park a secluded aspect and shade, and a number of trees planted within the park create a landscaped effect as well.

Goyne Park

(Formerly Ecoff Park) (33 Acres)

> Located along the north side of Ecoff Avenue in the Bermuda District. From Chester take Route 10 west to Ecoff Avenue, turn north on Ecoff to the park., a total distance of about two miles.

Largest of the four neighborhood parks, Goyne was previously a part of the Hill and Dale Golf Course, which still adjoins the property. The park is nicely laid out with athletic facilities located in the old fairways, so that the surrounding wooded areas within the site could be preserved.

As in the other neighborhood parks, this one features lighted tennis courts, baseball fields, and a football field, and also two (unlighted) soccer fields. The nine-hole Hill and Dale Golf Course adjoining the park on the east is open to the public, a bonus for families with diverse recreational preferences.

Great Branch Creek flows along its northern and western borders, with a well placed picnic shelter overlooking it. The children's play area adjoins the tennis courts.

The park is named after Harold T. Goyne, a long time Bermuda District Supervisor and community minded citizen.

Harrowgate Park

(29 Acres)

> In the Matoaca District, just off Harrowgate Road four miles south of the town of Chester. To reach the park turn west on Harrow Drive.

Harrowgate's wooded surroundings and gently sloping topography add interest and shade to a park that is mainly devoted to neighborhood athletic facilities. These include three tennis courts, three baseball fields, and a football field, all lighted for night play, and one open play field for various other activities. Also on the site are an attractive picnic shelter, as well as outside tables, and a children's play area.

Huguenot Park

(56 Acres)

In the Bon Air section of the Midlothian District of northern Chesterfield County. Located behind Johnston Willis Hospital between Robious and Early Settlers Roads, with entrances from both.

Named for the French Protestants who settled the area in the 17th century, Huguenot is a modern community park, well designed to serve the rapidly growing residential area surrounding it. About half the park has been left in a natural wooded condition with trails, interpretive signs, and scattered picnic tables. An azalea garden has been planted in the woods, adding color in the spring.

The rest of the park is developed with athletic, playground, and convenience facilities and parking. A signed bicycle route provides access from the adjoining subdivisions on the northeast, an unusual amenity for a residential neighborhood in these days.

Athletic facilities include tennis and basketball courts and football, soccer, and baseball fields. Picnic areas, several with attractive shelters, are scattered throughout the park. A children's playground with those popular wooden structures is located adjacent to picnic shelter #1 just inside the Robious Road entrance, with restrooms equipped for handicapped visitors conveniently nearby. A second playground is near another shelter. (Park designers are making it easy to keep an eye on the children while setting out the food or lingering over a meal.) Still another shelter is in the plan.

An exceptional life course winds through the natural area and connects with other trails. All trails and walkways are suitable for just about any kind of perambulating - strolling, jogging, or wheelchair access. All in all, the park is well designed to meet a variety of needs without seeming congested, and will be an ever more valued amenity as the surrounding area becomes completely developed.

Huguenot Park

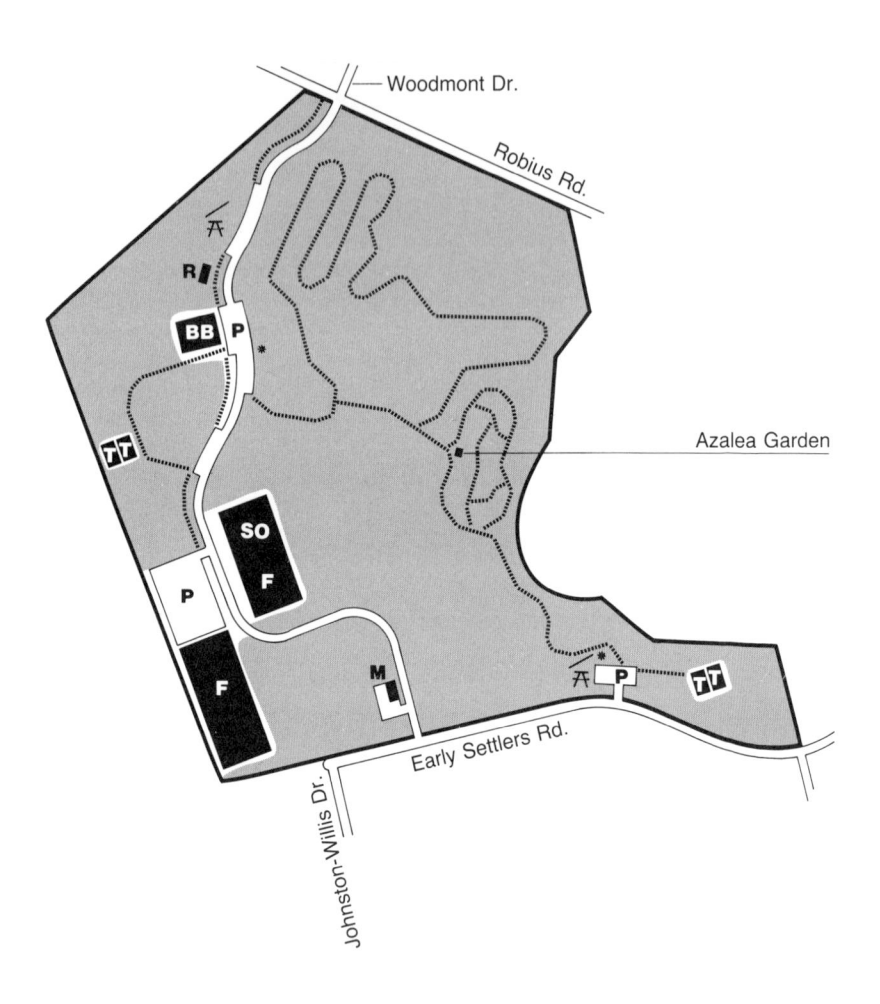

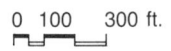

210

Matoaca Park

(30 Acres)

Located in the Matoaca District across from Matoaca High School on Halloway Avenue, 1-1/2 miles north of River Road.

Of the four neighborhood parks, Matoaca has the largest natural component. The northern half of the park, a pleasant mixed forest, has been left undisturbed, except for a small nature trail and picnic area on the edge, with the children's play area conveniently near. Athletic facilities include three lighted tennis courts, a basketball court, lighted football field, and three lighted baseball fields.

Not all visitors may know (though Chesterfield school children do) that the district and park are named for Pocahontas, who was raised in this area. (Pocahontas, we have learned, was the Indian princess's nickname. Her saving of Captain John Smith and later marriage to John Rolfe and move to England are well known to all.)

Huguenot Park

Developing Parks

Henrico City Park

(15 Acres)

On Farrar's Island in Chesterfield County, along the south bank of the James River just east (downstream) of Dutch Gap Landing. From Interstate 95 take Coxendale Road east to where it ends at the boat landing. Park in the landing parking lot and follow the trail markers to the park.

Few people today know that Farrar's Island in the great double oxbow formed by the James at Dutch Gap was the site of the first European community in the region and the second major English settlement in North America. Perhaps because the town, though ambitiously conceived, never took hold, and nothing remains of it today, history books* have largely passed it over; nevertheless, the Henrico City episode between 1611-1622 is a fascinating story that will soon be told.

One of the most intriguing parks in the region, Henrico City (in the planning stage at this writing) will take in a small section of the land that was once part of Henrico City (named after the English Prince Henry and variously known as Henricus, Henrico Town, and even Henricopolis), and by providing overlooks and interpretive signs make it possible to visualize the scene from the beginnings of the town until it was abandoned after an Indian massacre.

The 1-1/4 mile trail to the historic site will begin just east of the boat landing and follow the riverbank to a bluff some fifty feet above the river, where one of the farmhouses in the old town stood. Steps will lead up to the bluff, which is presently inaccessible (except for a service road through property owned by the Virginia Power Company.) Here and there where the trail crosses a marsh and swamp, an elevated board walkway will be constructed, and along the way, benches, an observation platform, and a gazebo will provide attractive places to stop and view the scene. The natural history of the floodplain environment the trail passes through is also interesting for its moisture loving plants. (See Section I - *Plant Communities*.) On the bluff an upland forest has taken over.

From an observation deck it will be possible to look across Dutch Gap to Hatcher Island and the north bank beyond, and to get some understanding of why and how Henrico City was built. The colonial period of the island began in 1611 when, at the request of the Virginia Company of London, Sir Thomas Dale took three hundred men from the Jamestown Settlement fifty miles up the James to what is now Farrar's Island to establish what was to be a "principall Towne," on a high ridge well removed from swamps and capable of being defended from attack by Indians or a Spanish naval attack. (The Spaniards never came, but an Indian massacre did finish off the town in 1622.) The town was to include, among other institutions, the first university in North America, for which 10,000 acres were ordered to be set aside -

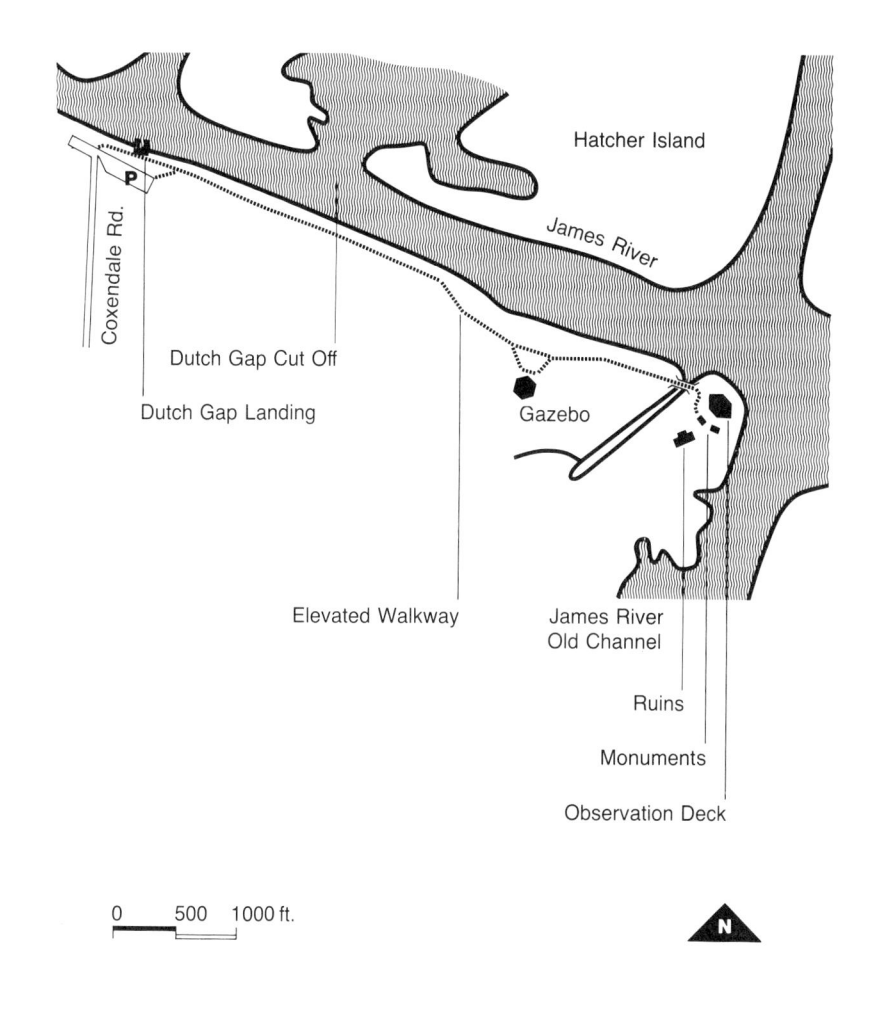

[Map with labels: Hatcher Island, James River, Coxendale Rd., P, Dutch Gap Cut Off, Dutch Gap Landing, Gazebo, Elevated Walkway, James River Old Channel, Ruins, Monuments, Observation Deck; scale 0–500–1000 ft.; N arrow]

ambitious plans for a handful of men in a country of hostile Indians!

In 1611 the James wound around Farrar's Island, which was then a peninsula connected to the north bank. Dutch Gap was cut through the narrow neck of the peninsula at the foot of the bluff by the Corps of Engineers during the Civil War, to circumvent the Confederate batteries along the wide loop of the James, and completed in its present dimensions in 1871, but the history of the Gap also goes back to the Henrico Town period. The first ditch along the route of the present cut was dug by Dale's men as a sort of dry moat ringed with a palisade to ward off attackers. It is said that because this was a technique Dale had learned in Holland, it was called a Dutch Gap, and the name stuck.

Interestingly, before the cut was made, the entire 5,000 acre peninsula extended from the north shore of the James and was part of Henrico County. After the cut

Henricus Hospital-1611-Dick Vranian (Commissioned by Henrico Doctor's Hospital)

became the main channel of the James, the land that lay to the south was designated part of Chesterfield, except for the small (about seven acres) site still occupied by the town in 1622.

The plan was to build a community of houses with vegetable gardens, storehouses, a hospital, and a brick church to begin with, followed by the university. The lowlands were to be used for growing crops. Accounts of what was actually accomplished vary, according to the authors of the time. The promoters described the town rather glowingly; however, some of the town's original settlers were more honest, describing it as a temporary affair of wooden houses with a wooden church in constant need of repair.

Even before the massacre things went wrong. Dale was a tyrant who treated his workers badly, to say the least, and the spirit of free enterprise made it seem more attractive to newcomers to settle in the outlying areas, so that by 1622 very little of the town was left to destroy. A hospital referred to as Mount Malada was built somewhere within the boundaries of the town, but its exact location is not known. (Henrico Doctors Hospital has taken an interest in the new park because of its relationship to the first hospital in North America, and has contributed the gazebo, as well as an artist's rendering of the hospital.)

All of the original structures in the old town have long since been destroyed. All that remains on the site today are the ruins of a lighthouse constructed in 1871 and two granite monuments standing strangely in the forest - an obelisk erected by the

Society of Colonial Dames in 1911 to commemorate the town and the university, and a shaft topped by a cross, contributed several years later by the Association for the Preservation of Virginia Antiquities in memory of the church. Both of these are visible on the bluff from the river, and are pointed out on the cruises sponsored by Richmond on the James.

Chesterfield's Henrico City Park will preserve the existing character of the site, adding only a railed observation deck and interpretive signage. The total walking distance of the round trip will be 2-1/2 miles. A small boat dock will eventually be constructed, at the foot of the bluff, with a short trail connected to the elevated walkway and steps, making the park accessible from the river as well.

*The historical information in this description is taken from Chesterfield County - Early Architecture and Historic Sites, by Jeffrey M. O'Dell, published by Chesterfield County, 1983.

Monument - Henrico City Historic Park

Iron Bridge Park

(362 Acres)

In the Dale District, east of Iron Bridge Road. The main entrance is off Iron Bridge directly across from that of the Chesterfield Airport. Another is planned from Kingsland Road.

Iron Bridge Park (originally called Dale), will be Chesterfield's largest multi-use park, with three active recreation areas, as well as lovely natural areas with trails and a nature center. It will also include some unusual features, such as a fitness trail for the handicapped, and an area designed for a therapeutic day camp. The park is scheduled to open in the summer of 1986 after the first development phase has been completed.

The topography of the park is fairly level in the east, rising to gently rolling land in the west. Much of the site was cut and reforested twenty-five years ago. Aside from the recreation complexes, the woods are being left in their natural condition. Reedy Branch Creek (a tributary of Kingsland Creek) flows along the northern boundary. A branch of Proctor's Creek and a small swamp associated with it touch the park to the south. The various habitats presently favor a diversity of wildlife, and it is hoped that this will continue after the park has been developed.

The first phase of development includes an attractive tree-lined main entrance and park road linking the three recreation areas. The therapeutic day camp, with a special playground and a 1/4 mile paved exercise trail for the handicapped, will be located nearest the entrance. Tennis courts, a pro shop, and an open play field will complete this smallest of the recreation areas. Another children's play area and a picnic shelter will be located nearby.

Beyond the first recreation area, a second will include a football and baseball field, two soccer fields, scattered picnic tables and grills, and a shelter. The natural area will be at the eastern end of the park, with trails, including a 1/2 mile fitness trail with exercise stations, more picnic tables and grills, and another shelter. One of the trails is linked with an old logging road running parallel to Reedy Branch and the main park road. Jogging should be good.

Trails have also been designed with handicapped access in mind. As for restrooms, to begin with, temporary facilities are expected to serve; in time regular restrooms equipped for handicapped visitors will be added.

Future plans include additional athletic and therapeutic facilities, a nature center, more trails, an amphitheater for outdoor performances, and possibly an olympic size swimming pool. In the meantime the considerable wooded area in which to roam and the initial facilities should provide a lot of enjoyable outdoor recreation for visitors for some time to come.

217

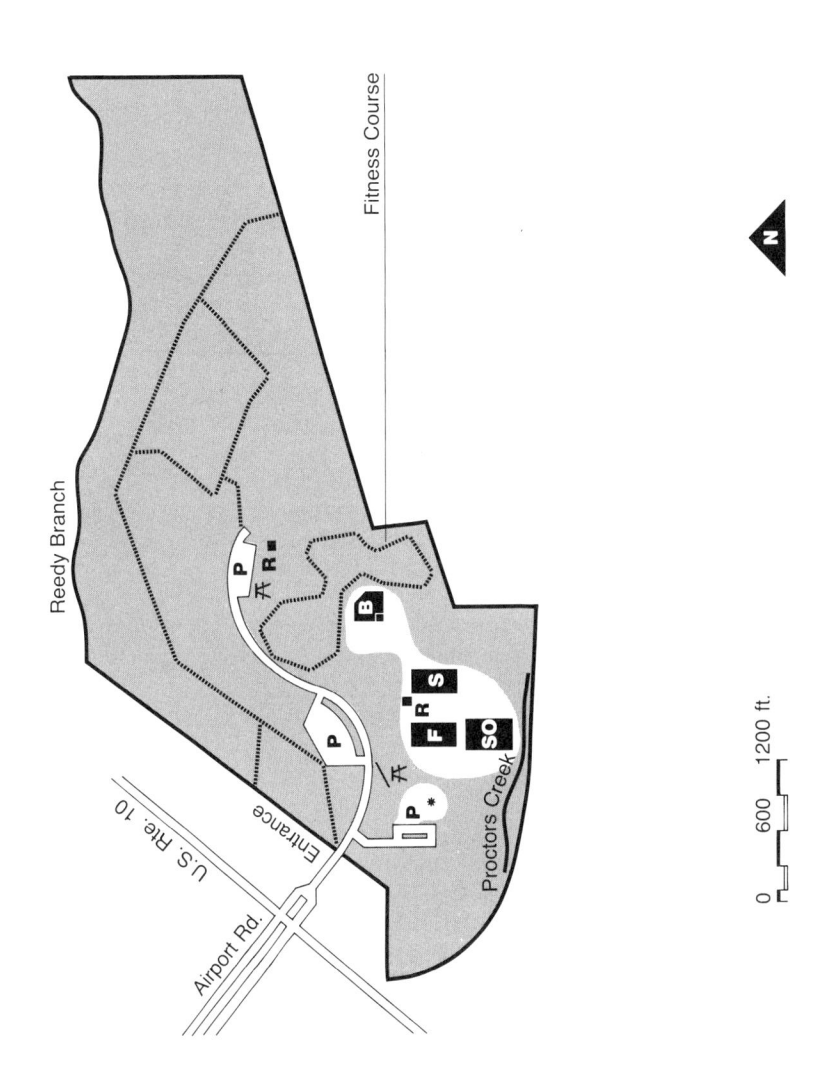

Henrico County Recreation and Parks

Recreation and leisure flourish in Henrico County through the efforts of the Division of Recreation and Parks and a growing system of parks, several of which attract visitors from all over the region. A successful park bond referendum, good planning, and good fortune (Crump Memorial Park/Meadow Farm was a gift to the county) have produced a variety of quality parks of unique character and appeal.

In addition to the county parks, three units of the Richmond National Battlefield Parks - Chickahominy Bluff, Malvern Hill, and Fort Harrison and its satelite forts - are located in Henrico. Also in the county is the lovely Bloemendaal Farm, now the beginning of the Lewis Ginter Botanical Garden, which is expected to take its place among the great botanical gardens of the world.

Although the Guide focuses on parks, it should be mentioned here that excellent athletic facilities and playgrounds are also distributed throughout the county, and that Belmont is the only public championship golf course in the region.

Among our favorite places is old-fashioned Meadow Farm in Crump Park. What makes it so irresistible is the way in which visitors are allowed to use the park (even to garden in it!) rather than being restricted to a sedate walk, as is required in so many other historic sites. Several of the other parks, including Dorey and Deep Run, also have historic significance, though not as clearly apparent as at Meadow Farm. Interpretive markers will soon be added to interpret the past in these.

The newly opened Vawter Street Natural Area (shown on the Alexandria maps as Horse Swamp Nature Trail Park) includes upland and lowland forests, marsh, and swamp habitats, all on one site, and already a favorite destination of naturalists throughout the area. A self-guided nature trail pamphlet and station posts are all that is needed to interpret this fascinating area. Four Mile Creek will be another interesting natural area when access has been completed. A small nature center will eventually be added there.

In addition to the parks described in this section, land has been acquired for another (to be called Three Lakes), and acreage is being added to Four Mile Creek Park and Deep Bottom Boat Landing on the lower James River. (See Section II - *Rivers*.)

Although each of the parks has its own special features, all have picnic tables and shelters for groups of various sizes. Grills are available, and - something new - picnic kits of various sorts may be rented. These include bats, balls, horseshoe or badminton equipment, volleyball nets, and even frisbees. Shelters and other group facilities must be rented; the picnic tables in the open are free.

As in all Capital area parks, certain common sense rules and regulations apply, among these, prohibitions against alcohol consumption, firearm use, and fires other than in designated grills.

Outdoor recreation programs add a great deal to the enjoyment of several of these parks. An extensive sports program conducted throughout the year includes classes and competitions in a full range of athletic skills and games for participants of all ages. The Division also offers special interest classes in topics as esoteric as archeology, programs in the arts, dance, music, and theater, and trips, including annual skiing excursions. For a day excursion, consider a wildflower or bird-watching walk, or one that interprets plant succession. These are well done and make successive visits to the sites even more interesting.

For children there are special summer day programs, two-week summer day camps at Crump and Dorey Parks, and other activities too numerous to list. As for older adults, senior citizen clubs and programs are available to residents at age 55 and are the envy of younger citizens! Many of these are held in the beautiful Belmont Recreation Center. (Seniors, of course, have the advantage of participating in other programs as well, and those with free time during the week can be of service as volunteers.)

Program brochures are inserted in the newspapers three times a year and are available at county libraries. Watch the calendars of events in the papers as well. For a brochure or answers to questions about parks, rentals, and recreation activities, call 804/649-0566.

Dorey Park

Belmont Park

(120 Acres)

Located in northern Henrico County along both sides of Hilliard Road, just west of Brook Road. (The address is 1600 Hilliard.)

Formerly the Hermitage Country Club and Golf Course, Belmont was acquired by the county in 1977, and is now one of the few public 18-hole championship courses in the region. The course is open to the public every day throughout the year, weather permitting. Greens fees are modest. Carts may be rented. Starting times are required on weekends and holidays, and can be scheduled by calling the pro-shop - 804/266-4949 - on the Saturday prior to the day of play. Lessons are available. Additional facilities include eight tennis courts.

Before it was purchased by the Hermitage Country Club, Belmont was a 19th century farm. The beautifully landscaped grounds slope down to the lowlands, through which flow North Branch Run and Upham Brook on their way to join the Chickahominy. The 80-year old main house, later the Club house and now the Belmont Park Recreation Center, is considered to be a local architectural landmark.

In its extensive renovations of the building, the county wisely preserved its distinguishing exterior features. The investment appears to have been most worthwhile. The Center today is both beautiful and functional, as well as extraordinarily roomy, with 14,000 square feet of space for recreation programs, meetings, classes, social functions, and special events, such as wedding receptions. Handicapped visitors have been considered in its redesign. Rooms may be rented as far as a year in advance. For information, call 804/262-4728.

Cheswick Park

(25 Acres)

>Located northwest of Forest Avenue where it makes a right angle turn at Koger Center (Office Park). Enter from the southbound lane of Forest Avenue.

Cheswick is a delightful neighborhood park serving the surrounding residential area and - to judge from the "brown baggers" at noon - the nearby Koger Center. The park designers have preserved much of its wooded setting and provided trails and rustic bridges over Upham Creek and Upham Branch Creek for access to the natural area.

Facilities include a large rustic picnic shelter with six tables (accommodating up to 50 people), additional tables with grills in the open, and restrooms accessible to handicapped visitors. The beautifully designed and shaded play area has wooden climbing, sliding, and balancing apparatus on a soft bark mulch surface, a large dirt hill, and sandbox. This is a very popular spot with children.

A 1/4 mile loop asphalt trail/exercise course (with stations) starts at the parking lot. An open play area across Upham Branch Creek is used for volleyball and badminton.

The attractive parking lot suffices most of the time, but on busy weekends overflow parking is available in Koger Center, an easy walk from the park.

Although a part of the old Franklin Farm, Cheswick derives its name from Cheswick Manor House, (circa 1796), which used to be located on the property. (The house has been moved 500 yards west to Three Chopt Road to allow construction of the Koger Center.) It is good to know that although much of the old heritage of the county must give way to modern development, some will always be preserved as landmarks and parks.

Cheswick Park

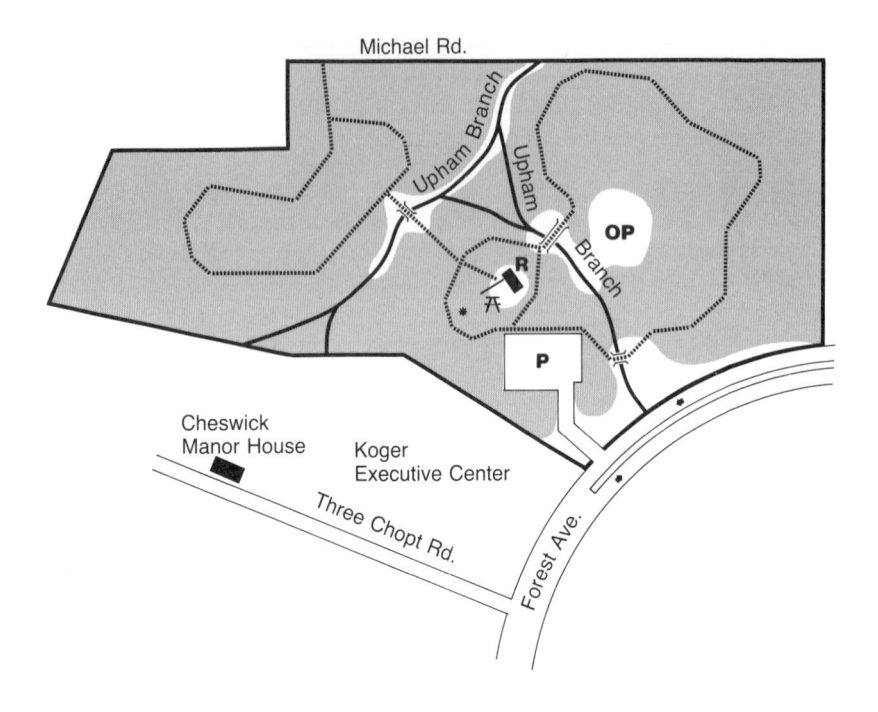

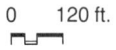

Michael Rd.

Upham Branch

Upham Branch

OP

R

P

Cheswick Manor House

Koger Executive Center

Three Chopt Rd.

Forest Ave.

0 120 ft.

N

General Sheppard Crump Memorial Park (Meadow Farm)

(150 Acres)

Located north of Mountain Road and east of Mill Road in Northern Henrico County. The entrance is at Mountain and Courtney Roads.

Meadow Farm (dedicated as the General Sheppard Crump Memorial Park in 1975) is one of the last remaining colonial land grant farms in Henrico County. It is listed on the National Register of Historic Places. (See also Cheswick and Dorey Parks.) Until 1960 it was the home of the late Adjutant General of Virginia, Sheppard Crump. His wife, Elizabeth, donated the farm to the county to be preserved as a park in memory of her husband. Today Meadow Farm/General Crump Memorial Park (the names are often used interchangeably) is truly an outstanding outdoor museum, with its 150 acres of pasture and woodlands. It preserves the history of two centuries of agrarian life, while providing a natural environment for a wide variety of wildlife and plants.

The simplicity of the sturdy old (1810) hilltop farmhouse and outbuildings, and the layout of the land in the patterns of the colonial period lend an extraordinary charm to the park environment. At the same time, unlike many historic landmarks, the park provides for many kinds of enjoyable experiences for visitors, including picnicking, nature walks, a summer day camp for children, and the use of garden plots throughout the growing season, as well as tours and living history events.

Meadow Farm Museum - Crump Park

The history of Meadow Farm runs deep. As early as 6,000 B.C. Indians camped along North Run Creek (a tributary of Upham Brook - See Belmont Park), which bisects the park. As the early colonial settlers moved in, the Indians moved out. Meadow Farm was part of a land grant made to an ancestor of General Crump in 1713. County historians and archeologists are researching the early history of the farm, including buildings that are no longer standing, and will no doubt from time to time come up with additional discoveries.

While the historic aspects of the park are mainly interesting as they portray the day-to-day life of a farm family in the 19th century, historic events did swirl around the farm and touch it from time to time. Interesting stories of these are part of the repertoire of park guides.

The farmhouse, with its authentic period country furniture and other artifacts, has become a museum designed for self-guided tours during which visitors can get some feeling for the everyday life of four generations of the Sheppard family. The museum is open Tuesday through Sunday from 12-4. (Handicapped individuals may drive up the service road to the house. The first floor is accessible, including doors, restroom, and water fountains, and a wheelchair lift is available.) The admission fee is $1 for adults, 50 cents for children under 12, and 50 cents for senior citizens on Tuesdays.

No admission fee is required to walk around the outside, where an old smokehouse, spring house (used to protect the spring and store perishables in the water cooled atmosphere), and the tiny doctor's house still stand nearby under stately old trees. The archeological sites of other early outbuildings - exterior kitchen, ice house, and brick kiln - have been exposed and are interpreted as a matter of interest. (These buildings may be restored in the future if funds become available.) The old ice pond is being resurrected, and the apple orchard near the house has been replanted with trees of the old varieties, which should be bearing soon.

The old barn is long since gone, but a few farm animals are kept in a shed and pens some little distance behind the farmhouse. Children especially enjoy looking in on these.

A visit to the farmhouse and its outbuildings is only one of the experiences to be enjoyed at the park; many other features make it worth returning to from time to time. Service roads and walkways are designed for easy strolling and handicapped access, and on pleasant days at any time of the year the two nature trails are fine for self-guided nature walks. (Interpretive pamphlets are available at the farmhouse.) The greening and wildflowers of spring, luxuriant plants of summer, the flaming leaves and berries of fall, and the glimpses of wildlife - you may even, on quiet days, see deer - are especially worth experiencing. In spring the meadow, with its old field grasses and wildflowers, is a sight to behold. In late July, if you like blackberries, bring a bucket to the North Run Creek Trail.

Henrico residents may rent a plot in a community garden area during the growing

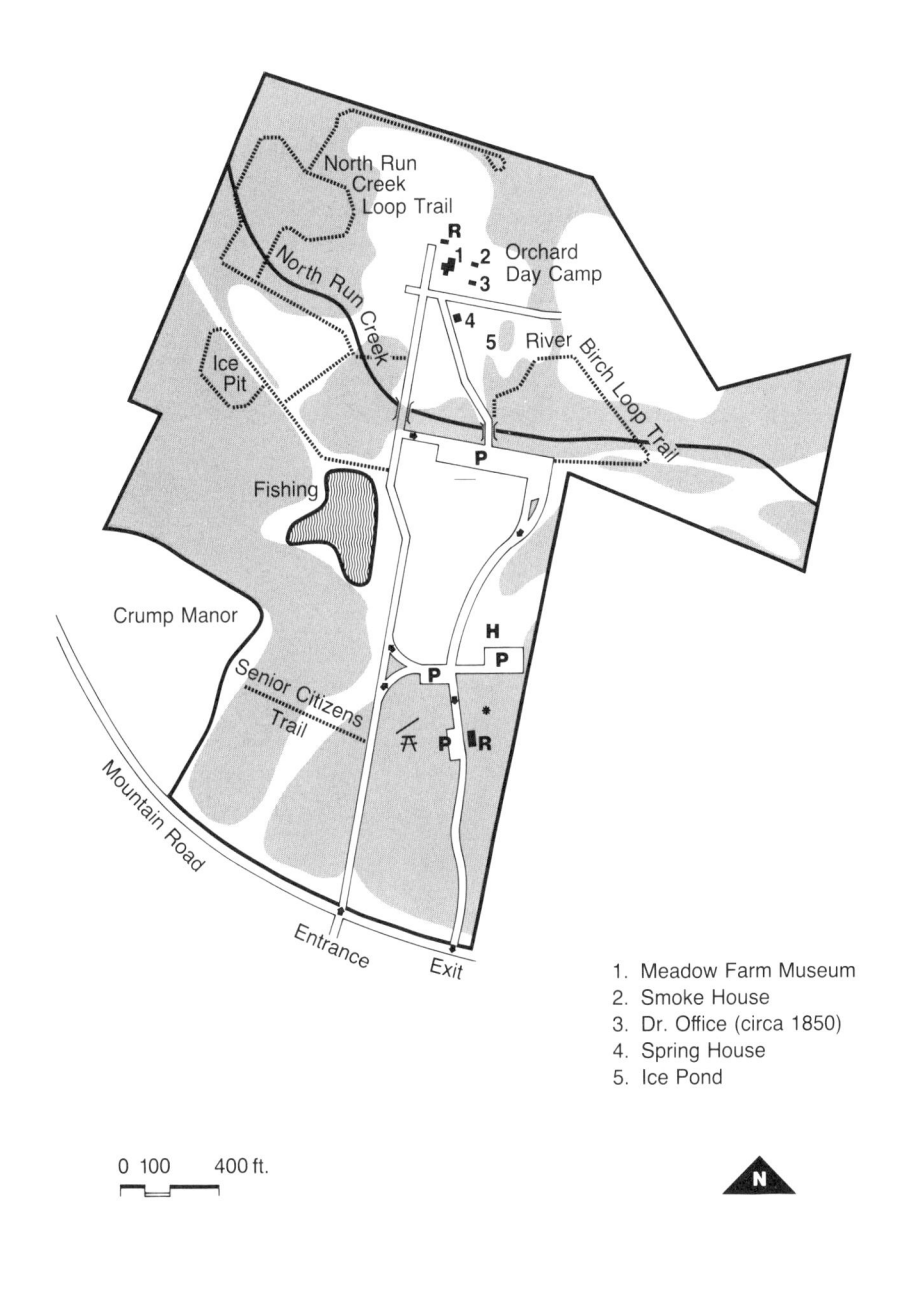

1. Meadow Farm Museum
2. Smoke House
3. Dr. Office (circa 1850)
4. Spring House
5. Ice Pond

season. Water is available on the site, and gardeners may drive their vehicles up the service road to their plots. For apartment dwellers with a yen to grow vegetables or flowers, this is a very popular feature.

Picnicking in this lovely environment is reason enough to visit the park. Beside tables, grills, and a shelter, several concessions have been made to visitors wishing some of the activities and conveniences traditionally associated with picnic areas - a well designed children's play area with wooden structures, horse shoe pit, and restrooms equipped for handicapped visitors. An easy fitness trail, designed for seniors and others wanting something less strenuous than a regular life course, is also located near the picnic area. Perhaps best of all, a pretty little 2-acre farm pond has been stocked with crappie, bluegill, and bass, and fishing will be allowed beginning in 1986.

Seasonal nature walks focusing on wildflowers and birds (birding is excellent) are conducted from time to time by the County and the Audubon Society, and several special events have become festive annual affairs.

Watch the calendars of events in the newspapers (or park schedules in the county libraries) for the dates of outings and the Yule-Tide Fest, Spring Bouquet of the Arts (a crafts fair), the old fashioned Fourth of July celebration, a Civil War skirmish re-enactment by uniformed volunteers in September, a Colonial muster in October, and the county-wide Harvest Festival, also in the fall.

A day camp area, available for use by organized groups, is operated in the summer by the County Division of Recreation. Organized groups (Scout troops, for instance) may also, with permission, use designated overnight camping areas. For group visits and other information call (804)-262-1327, or write Meadow Farm Museum, County of Henrico, P.O. Box 27032. Richmond, Virginia 23273.

Deep Run Park

(270 Acres)

>Located in western Henrico County west of Gaskins Road. The park will be accessible from the new Ridgefield Parkway, to be completed about the same time as the park (fall of 1986). From Gaskins Road take Ridgefield west for about one-half mile. The parks entrance will be on the right. Look for the sign. A planned interchange of Gaskins Road with Interstate 64 will add greater accessibility in the future. (Watch the newspapers or call the Division of Recreation for the park opening date.)

Deep Run, Henrico's newest park—scheduled to open in the fall of 1986—is a pleasant wooded area situated in the gently rolling piedmont of western Henrico County. The future park has been carefully designed to preserve many of its natural features—wooded sections, the bank of Deep Run Creek bordering the park on the east, and a small marsh—, while developing part of the property with active recreation facilities. "Mixed use," with something for everyone, is an approach that seems to be working well in many of the large new parks these days.

Although portions of the woods have been cut in the past, enough time has elapsed to allow some sizable trees to grow, and a lot of native understory plants cover the ground. At present the site supports a variety of wildlife, which is expected to continue after the park is opened, at least in the less densely developed areas. Footpaths will wind through the woods for visitors who enjoy strolling through a natural area. Birdwatching should be good.

The park is located in part of the Richmond Triassic Basin, which was mined for coal in the 18th century. (See Section I—*The Changing Landscape*.) Although no mining took place on the actual site of the park, the old Coal Pit Railroad trams ran through it, carrying coal to loading areas along the old James River and Kanawha Canal. A few remnants of the track route can still be seen in the park; these will be preserved and interpreted for their historic significance.

Phase I developments in the eastern section of the park call for an entrance and parking lot near two old ponds, which are being rehabilitated as part of the landscape. Water from the higher pond will fall through a spillway to the lower pond, and a picnic area overlooking them will make the most of the scenery. Scattered tables with grills, three shelters, restrooms (equipped for the handicapped), a children's play area with those popular wooden structures, and a basketball court are planned for this area, as well as a fitness trail with exercise stations.

An asphalt surfaced pedestrian/bike trail is planned to connect the eastern and western sections of the park. (Adding together the exercise, pedestrian, and nature trails, there should be enough jogging paths to go quite some distance.) The park road will continue on to the western section and another parking lot. Initially the

Deep Run Park

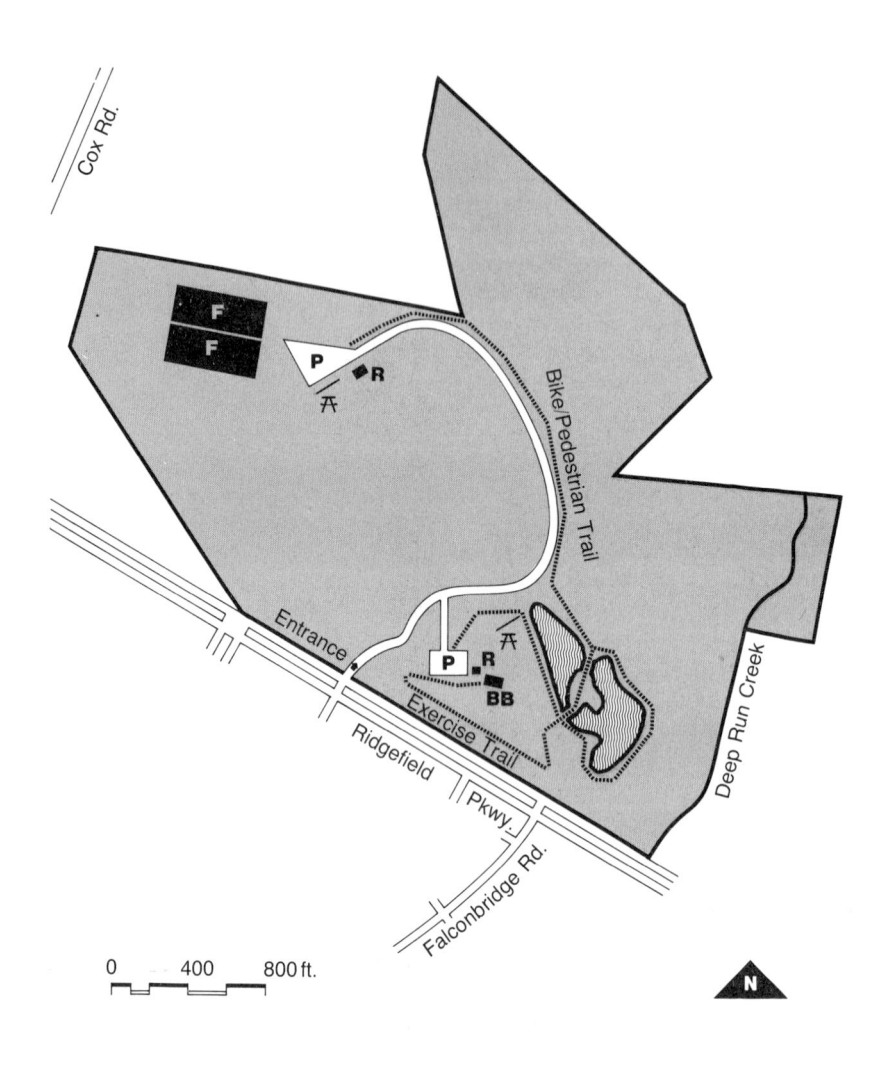

western section will be developed with additional picnic facilities, restrooms, and two soccer fields.

The ponds will be stocked with fish and, in time, opened to fishing. Future development plans (beyond phase I) include a small interpretive nature center, a wooden walkway and overlook along the bank of the creek, tennis courts, and an amphitheater for outdoor performances.

Dorey Park and Four Mile Creek Park

(400 Acres/380 Acres)

Located in the Varina District of (southeastern) Henrico County, extending south from Darbytown Road to New Market Road. Enter from Darbytown Road just west of Monahan Road.

Dorey is a rural county park, incorporating an old dairy farm reminiscent of the historic rural Varina heritage. The land was purchased from the estate of the late Fred O. Dorey, Sr., whose family operated the dairy farm for many years, and for whom the park is named.

Locally the area was known as Darbytown, one of the earliest settlement sites in the county. Archeologists have found an old pottery kiln on the site, dating back to the mid-nineteenth century; earlier finds are likely to turn up as they continue to explore the site.

Dorey is also located in an area where major Civil War engagements and skirmishes took place, both in the 1862 Peninsular Campaign and the 1864 Petersburg Campaign. (See Richmond Battlefield Parks, Malvern Hill and Fort Harrison.) Confederate earthworks skirting the northwest boundary of the park were part of Richmond's outer defenses.

Portions of the old farm are still under cultivation under a leased arrangement. Appropriately the first glimpse of the park is one of barn, silo, and farmhouse. While these structures are presently not open to the public, the county plans one day to run a model farm on the portion of the park that will remain as farmland in perpetuity, and at that time the entire operation will be a feature of the park.

Not far from the farm an "English ring" is available for group or individual equestrian activities, the only such public facility in the county.

The farm animals and visiting horses will have to co-exist with a nearby athletic complex being developed on this multi-use site; fortunately there is plenty of room for several activities to go on at the same time. Present facilities include an athletic area with a baseball field, lighted softball and soccer fields, and a concession building with restrooms (equipped for handicapped visitors). In time other facilities will be added. The parking lot is designed to accommodate a sizeable crowd.

As in several of the large new county parks, much of interest lies beyond the main athletic complex and other facilities nearest the entrance. The park is bounded on the east by Four Mile Creek (which empties into the James River at Deep Bottom), and on the south and west by branches of the creek. Along the creeks and in the southern section the land is rolling and wooded, providing habitats for a diverse population of wildlife.

The park road penetrates some distance into this area, ending in a second parking lot which serves a landscaped picnic area and associated facilities. A 3-acre lake reclaimed from a gravel pit adds to the scenery. (Swimming is not allowed, but the lake is currently being stocked with fish, and should be open for fishing at some time in the future.) Two attractive picnic shelters, one overlooking the lake, accommodate groups, and outside tables and grills are scattered about the area. A cluster of four picnic shelters located some distance from the lake is designed to handle large groups or small groups concurrently. Nearby facilities include three tennis courts, a fitness trail, open play field, a pleasantly shaded playground with new wooden equipment of various popular kinds, and more restrooms, also equipped for handicapped visitors.

An especially interesting feature here is a landscaped area in the form of a grassy amphitheater overlooking the lake. This was a spoil area left behind when a gravel operation was completed. The county has transformed it by grading, adding topsoil, and seeding grass. Loblolly pines planted during a less successful reclamation effort are finally establishing themselves, and the total effect is a testimony to successful reclamation for recreational purposes.

Anyone who wants to get away from it all can follow a trail leading south through a natural area along the creek that forms the eastern boundary of the park. This trail also provides the only access to the future Four Mile Creek Park, extending south from Dorey Park to New Market Road (Route 5).

The new linear park will run alongside the creek and will be left for the most part in its natural condition. Some clearcutting of the forest in the past has left open areas which are undergoing plant succession. In time they will return to forest; in the meanwhile the diverse habitats attract a variety of wildlife. This area was home to Indian tribes for thousands of years, a realization to stir the imagination in exploring it today.

Property for the park is being acquired from several landowners who wish to see Four Mile Creek and its environs preserved and protected. In the near future the county plans to extend the trail leading into it from Dorey Park, and add a bridle path, also accessible from the terminal Dorey parking lot. (Riders will have to bring their own horses.) A nature center has been proposed for the future.

Access for handicapped visitors will always be better in Dorey Park than Four Mile Creek because of the service roads and compacted paths. These can also be used for jogging and as bikeways (unless otherwise marked.) The model farm operation will have the added advantage of ensuring a continuing rural atmosphere for the park.

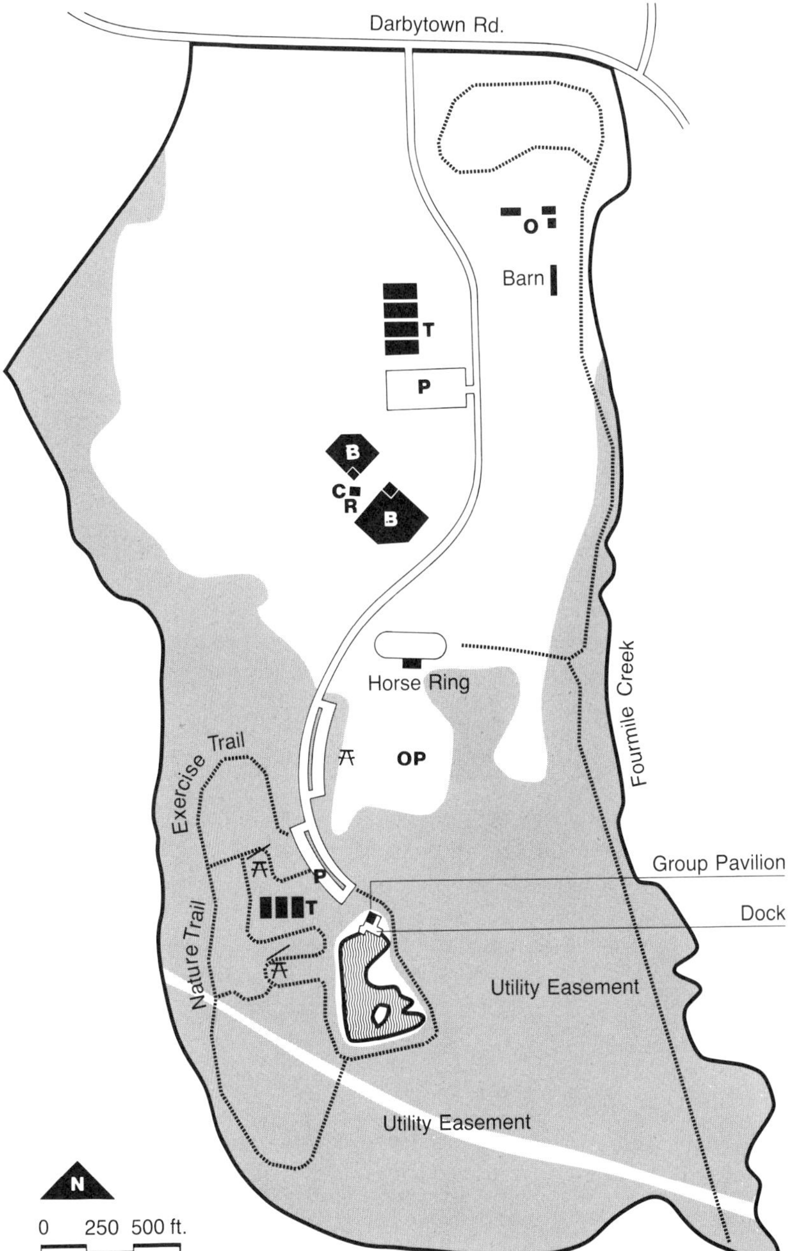

Darbytown Rd.
O
Barn
T
P
B
C
R
B
Horse Ring
Fourmile Creek
Exercise Trail
OP
P
T
Group Pavilion
Dock
Nature Trail
Utility Easement
Utility Easement
N
0
250
500 ft.

Echo Lake Park

(24 Acres)

Located along the south side of Springfield Road, west of Staples Mill Road in western Henrico County.

This little wooded park surrounds a ten acre lake, which occupies the center of the site and creates a pretty view of water no matter where you happen to be. Next to a small children's play area with wooden equipment, about the most popular activity here is picnicking. A number of picnic tables and grills are scattered about in the open, and a rustic group shelter accommodates eight tables. Restrooms are equipped for handicapped visitors.

The lake was created in the mid 1800s by the damming of Meridith Branch (a tributary of the Chickahominy) to supply power for a grist mill. The property was used as a private recreation area in the 1930s and '40s, but declined after a pavilion was destroyed by fire and the dam fell into disrepair. In 1981 the site was purchased by the County; the dam was repaired; the park was redesigned and opened in 1983.

One of its most attractive features is a rustic foot bridge crossing over the new dam, giving a good view of the falling water from above. Trails have been routed through the woods on both sides of the lake, but a swampy area at the far end of the lake prevents them from forming a loop. (A rustic bridge-connector is planned at some time in the future.) This is a likely place to see beaver, and in the spring, various frog species.

Swimming and boating are not allowed because the lake is deep in spots and supervision is impractical. The lake is being stocked, and it is hoped that by the fall of 1986 it will be open for fishing.

Springfield Rd.

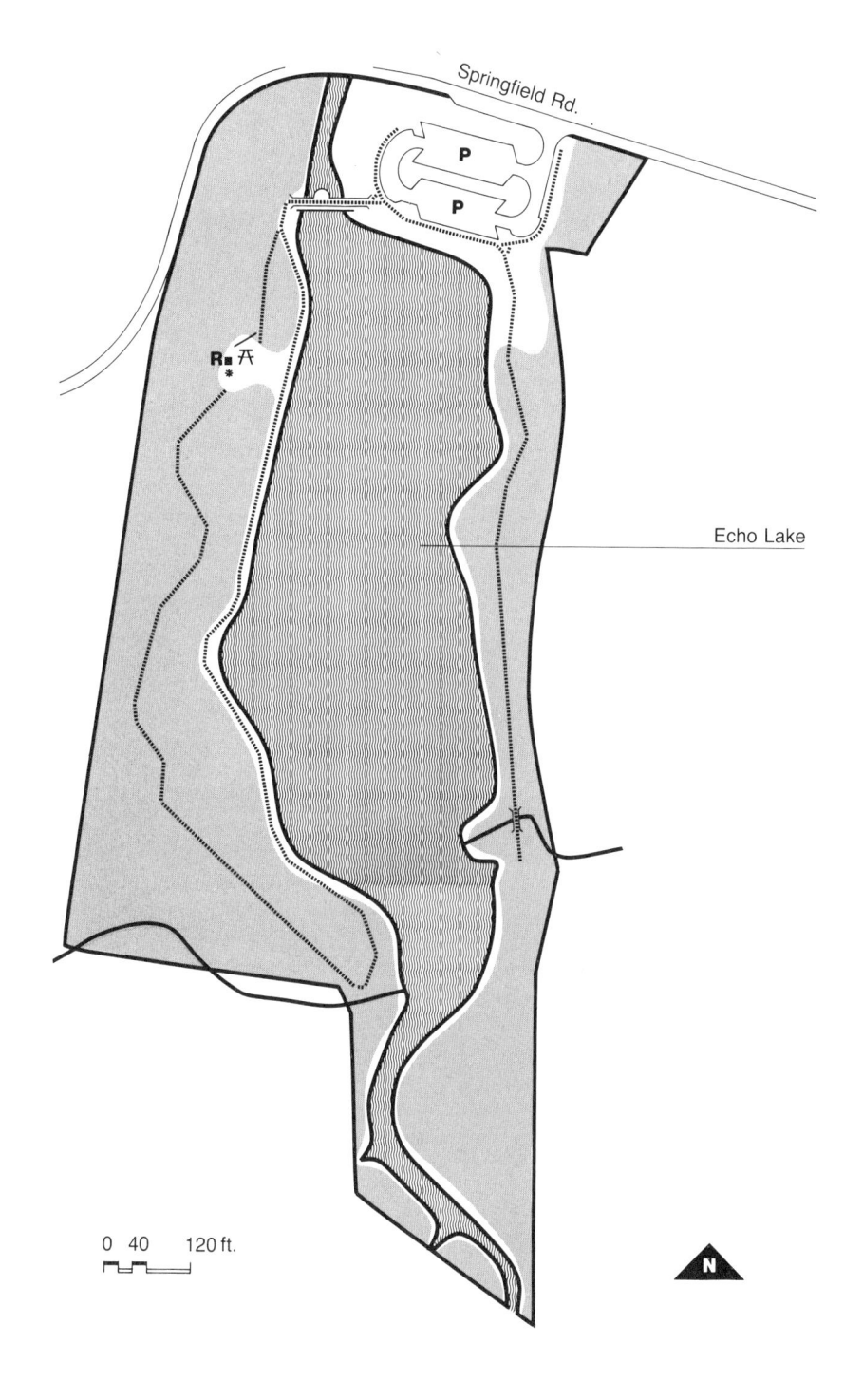

Echo Lake

0 40   120 ft.

N

Robinson Park

(9 Acres)

Located in northern Henrico County in the Bungalow City neighborhood, on Westover Avenue, just north of Nine Mile road.

Smallest of Henrico's neighborhood parks, tiny Robinson fits into the surrounding community like everyone's favorite backyard, and appears to be well used and tended. A well designed children's play area with wooden structures and other creative equipment adjoins an artistically painted picnic shelter and restrooms equipped for handicapped visitors. Nearby horseshoe pits and an open play area complete the needed amenities for a well-rounded communal picnic.

Athletic facilities include basketball courts and a small ballfield, parking is limited; most users walk in from the neighborhood. The western half of the park has been left in natural woods. Future plans call for trails and tennis courts.

The park is appropriately named for the late Matthew J. Robinson, Sr., who was instrumental in developing recreational programs in the community.

Vawter Street Park and Natural Area

(357 Acres)

Located along the Chickahominy Swamp about a mile east of the State Fairgrounds, where Horse Swamp Creek flows into the Chickahominy River. From Laburnum Avenue take Vawter Street north about one mile to the park entrance on the right.

Despite its citified name, most of Vawter Street Park encompasses a large natural area as close to being a wilderness as any in the region. As in many of the large new county parks, the natural area is situated well beyond the parking lot and separated from the athletic facilities, which in this instance occupy high ground, while marsh, woods, and swamp lie in the lowlands.

Within the park the Glen Lea Recreation Area is a small athletic complex including two lighted ballfields, a concession stand, and restrooms equipped for handicapped visitors. An attractive picnic area with one group shelter, scattered tables outside, and play equipment nearby is located at the edge of a wooded bluff known as Egypt's Hill (probably named for its steep slopes, resembling the sides of a pyramid.) A loop exercise trail leads from the area through the woods along the contours of the bluff and back.

Civil War earthworks - part of Richmond's outer defense fortifications - may be seen along the bluff. Do not walk on them, as this wears them down, causing erosion.

Access to the natural area is via a trail following the steep slope down Egypt's Hill to a marsh. (This area can also be reached from the end of Vawter Street, a short distance beyond the park entrance.) The marsh is apt to be wet, the grasses growing on spongy ground. If you plan to go exploring, wear appropriate shoes or boots. A causeway of sorts crosses the marsh on slightly higher and firmer ground, which makes the going easier than it would be otherwise (though none of it is suitable for handicapped access).

From the end of the causeway a primitive trail leads into the wooded area, past a couple of bogs and patches of sphagnum moss. Plank bridges cross the small creeks and other wet places. (These may overflow in wet weather.) The trail through the woods follows a narrow canal of unknown origin. Interestingly, an upland forest with fine old beech trees is only a few feet higher than the lowland forest on the other side of the canal.

Although the natural area is quite large, the trail ends at the edge of the Chickahominy Swamp, about a mile in, and you have to double back to return. In time, a more extensive trail system may be developed, allowing hikers to see more of the area. This area is habitat for many wildlife species. Bird watching is excellent. The swamp is a great blue heron rookery; look for their stick nests in the tallest trees.

Vawter Street Park and Natural Area

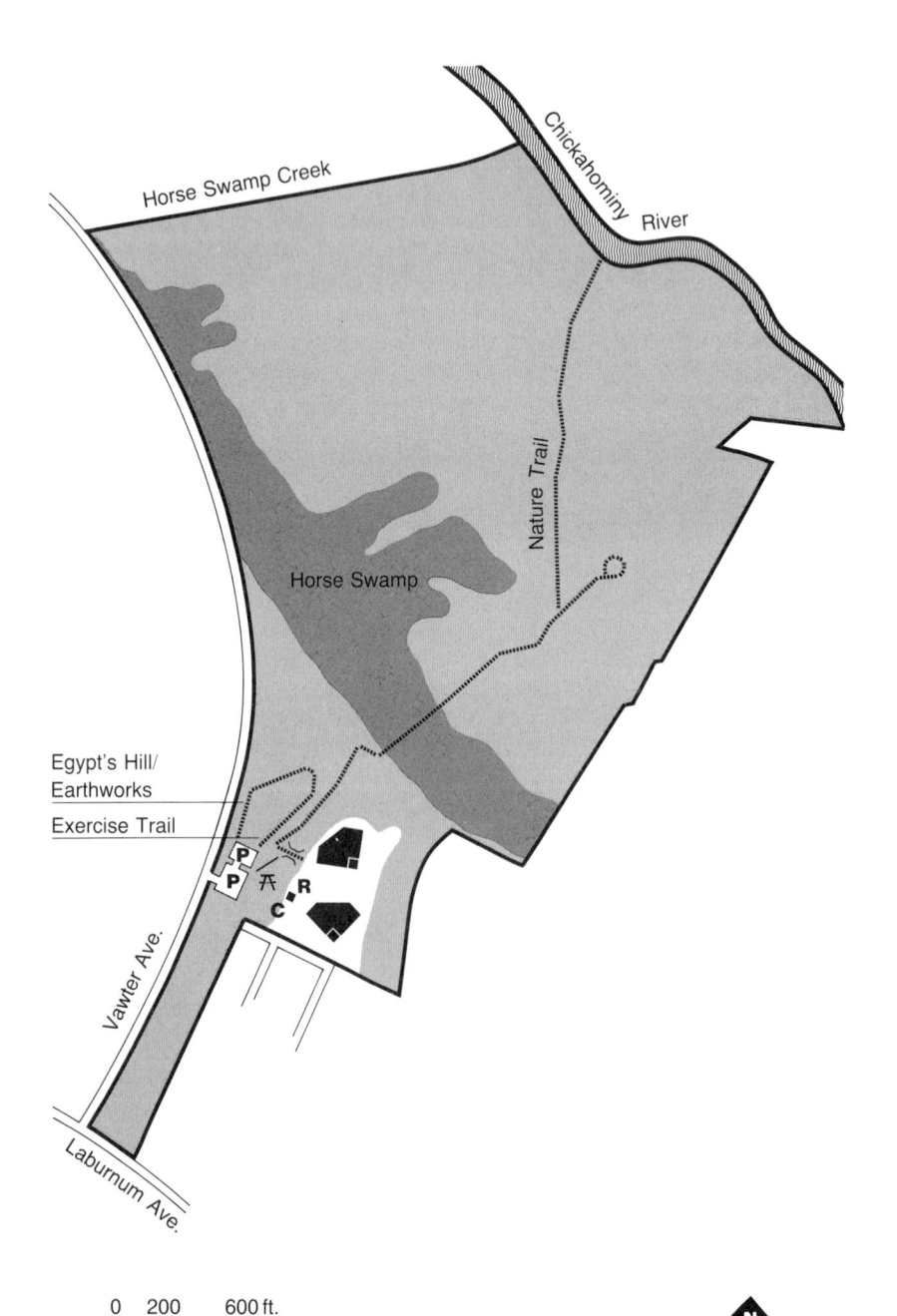

Chickahominy River

Horse Swamp Creek

Nature Trail

Horse Swamp

Egypt's Hill/ Earthworks

Exercise Trail

Vawter Ave.

Laburnum Ave.

0   200   600 ft.

N

Petersburg

(See also the *Petersburg National Battlefield*.)

Appomattox Riverside Park

(130 Acres)

(Shown on old maps as Ferndale Park.) Although this is a Petersburg Park, it is located in Dinwiddie County, along the Appomattox River just west of the city. From Petersburg take US Route 460 west to State Route 600 (Ferndale Road, which becomes River Road). Follow Route 600 to the park entrance on the west side of the road, just south of the Matoaca Bridge. From State Route 36 in southern Chesterfield County, take Route 600 south across the Matoaca Bridge to the entrance.

One of the most delightful park discoveries in the region is a walk along the towpath of the old Upper Appomattox River Canal, between the historic canal and the falls of the Appomattox Scenic River far below. The presence of the old canal with water still flowing through it, the granite outcroppings rising above it on the far side, and the wildness of the wooded stream valley, with glimpses of the tumbling river below, all combine to create a beautiful historic and natural environment unique in this region.

This superb area is located in Petersburg's Appomattox Riverside Park a short distance beyond the developed section. To reach the towpath, follow a trail behind the park house, skirting a small fishing pond, and cross over the canal on a rustic footbridge.

The Upper Appomattox River Canal, built between 1795 and 1816, afforded boats safe passage around 5-1/2 miles of falls along the Appomattox, to the Petersburg Basin. (The James River and Kanawha Canal was a contemporary project. For a brief description of that canal, See *Great Shiplock Park* in Richmond.)

These were times when roads were difficult to build and maintain; rivers were the chief transportation routes. Where falls and other obstacles made navigation difficult, canals were built to carry boats around these areas. This segment was part of the Upper Appomattox Navigation System consisting of several canals that left and re-entered the river as needed.

Most of these old canals have disappeared as they fell into disuse and were covered over before the importance of historic preservation became a movement. Fortunately this segment was found to be useful in furnishing water power to a Virginia Power substation, and has been taken over and maintained by the power company, along with its towpath for access purposes. By a special arrangement with the power company, the property has become part of the park.

The two-mile long path leads from the active section of the park westward to the

Rte. 601

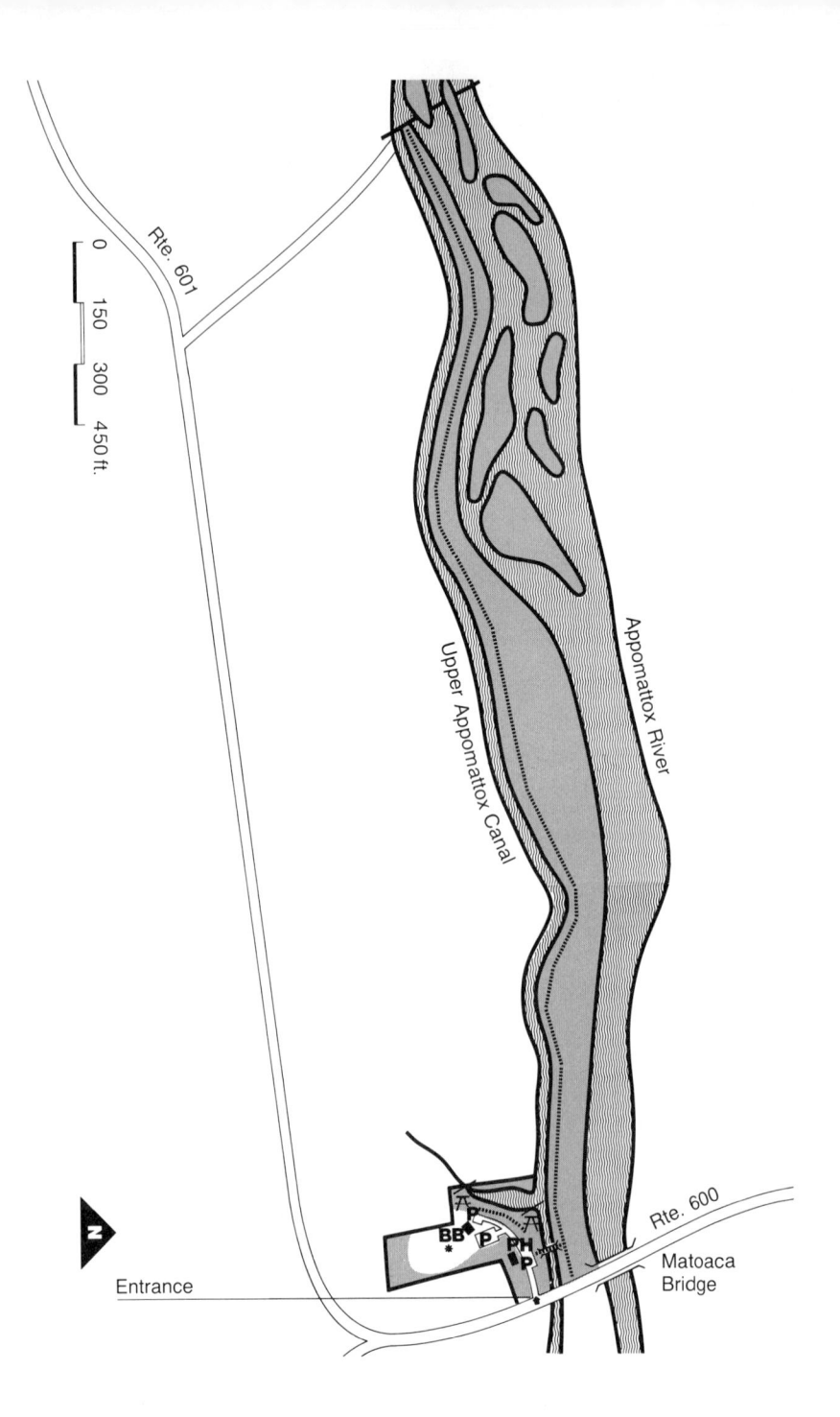

0
150
300
450 ft.

Appomattox River

Upper Appomattox Canal

N

Entrance

BB
P
PH
P

Rte. 600

Matoaca Bridge

238

Granite Bank - Upper Appomattox River Canal - Appomattox Riverside Park

sluice gates diverting water from the river into the canal. Here one can see the Appomattox River approaching the sluice gates and an abutment dam. The water flows through the gate into the canal on one side, and over the dam to the rapids below on the other side. The river drops steeply - about 125 feet - through this area, while the canal follows a gentle gradient almost to the end, where it flows back into the river below the park.

About two miles downstream the canal crossed Rohoic Creek on a structure that must have been an engineering marvel of its time. Water in the canal was carried high over the creek on a stone arch supported by two forty-two-foot-high gravity stone walls. The arch collapsed during the civil war and was replaced by a rickety wooden aquaduct until the canal fell into disuse as a transportation route. The aquaduct is no longer in existence; however, the mighty ruins of the buttressed stone walls are still standing in an old forest - a virtual wilderness - that now belongs to Virginia Power. The property is not open to the public, but interested groups may obtain permission to visit the site by calling the Manager of the Petersburg District - 804/733-9222. A note of caution - the trail is very rough, steep in places and almost non-existent in others. Persons with disabilities should not attempt it.

The canal was hewn from the granite slope of the stream valley, waterproofed with a clay mixture, and bolstered along its lower side by timbers, many of which are still in place. The towpath was used for controlling the speed and direction of boats floating downstream, and for towing them upstream by mule power.

Today the towpath is a simple dirt road, wide enough for three or four to walk sociably abreast. The surface is firm enough for service vehicles, which also makes it suitable for bicycling and handicapped access. At this writing very few people seem to have discovered the area. In time as it becomes known, it should become a favorite destination for hikers, naturalists, and history buffs.

Whitewater canoeists run this section of the Appomattox, putting in above the park at Chesterfield's Appomattox Canoe Launch, and taking out either under the Matoaca Bridge just east of the park, or downstream at Campbell's Bridge. (See Section II - *Along the Waterways*.) It is also possible to put in under the bridge for the downstream run to Battersea Beach or Campbell's Bridge, leaving cars in the park's parking lot.

Fishing is said to be excellent along this stretch of the river, but access is pretty much limited to the area under the bridge east of the park and the abutment dam area two miles up the towpath, as the steep river bank in between is a virtual wilderness with only the most rudimentary paths leading down from the towpath to the river.

As to the other features of the park, at this writing they include two parking lots, a park house with restrooms accessible to handicapped visitors, a basketball court, a large picnic shelter accommodating up to 125, several family size shelters, and a small fishing pond. An Appomattox River Map showing the rapids and providing other information important to canoeists is posted near the park house.

The park house has two meeting rooms which are available for use by small community groups (12-15). For information regarding rental of these and shelters, call the Department of Recreation - 804/861-1261.

Ferndale Park, as this developed section was originally called, was once a turn-of-the-century amusement park at the end of a trolley line that ran from Petersburg on a half hour schedule. Like the other trolley parks of the period, it featured a merry-go-round, shooting gallery, ice cream parlor, dance hall, silent movie theater, and other attractions intended to lure customers to the trolleys. (See also Forest Hill

Ruins of Stone Arch over Rohoic Creek - Photo by Lyn Woodlief

Park in Richmond.) Also like the other "trolley parks", Ferndale lost business to the automobile and the lure of the road and closed at the end of the 1920s.

In 1972 the city of Petersburg purchased the property for a new park. The first attempts at development were not very successful, owing to problems with maintenance and supervision; however, improvements are now being made, and with the addition of the towpath extension and opportunities for canoe launching and fishing in the river, the park is seeing a new day.

Fleet Street Peninsula

(Approximately 8 Acres)

> Along the south bank of the Appomattox River just west of Campbell's Bridge and Fleet Street in Petersburg. Park nearby.

About two miles downstream from the Appomattox Riverside Park, the Fleet Street peninsula is a small strip of riverbank owned by the City of Petersburg and under consideration for future development as a natural park. In the meantime the area is open to the public, without any particular status. An ideal site for a park, the peninsula was formed by an old canal that now opens into the river, cutting the area off from the rest of the riverbank to the west. This area is one of very few publicly owned places where one can have access to the Appomattox Scenic River rapids without walking some distance or canoeing the falls.

A dirt road used as a trail extends for about 1/3 mile westward to the tip of the peninsula, running closely parallel to the shore, with the river more or less continuously in sight. A park on this site will offer spectacular scenery and access to excellent fishing. Naturalists will also appreciate the exceptionally diverse floodplain plant community, including not only the typical trees and shrubs of a lowland forest, but also many wildflowers, ferns, mosses, and other kinds of plants, including horsetails (Equisetum), some of which are not often seen in this region.

Battersea Beach, a tiny area at the upstream end of the peninsula, is used by canoeists as a portage and take-out during high water periods, when the rapids become too dangerous to continue downstream past the bridge. (See Section II - *The Appomattox River*.)

A small beach just downstream from the bridge, also on the south bank, is a popular fishing spot and is also used by canoeists as the last take-out of the downstream run through the rapids, when the river level is low. This area is also owned by the city and may at some time in the future become a small park or an extension of the one upstream.

As tempting as this stretch of the river may be, as seen from the shore, it is important to realize that *swimming can be very dangerous and is not recommended,* because of the strong current, depth, and whirlpools, especially during high water level periods.

Other good views of the river may be had from Campbell's Bridge. From this vantage point it is also possible to get a good look at the ruins of old stone mills along the banks.

Still another parcel of the riverbank upstream is being considered for development as a park. Already shown on the Alexandria maps as McKenzie Park, this area is less accessible and less used than the Fleet Street peninsula, with the result that its development is probably further off in the future.

242

Lee Park

(326 Acres)

Located in south central Petersburg along Lieutenant's Run (creek), south of Defense Road. Enter the natural area from the north at the intersection of Defense Road and Baylor's Lane. The entrance to the athletic facilities area is at South Boulevard and Johnson Road. The Lee/Walnut Hill bus stops at the corner. To reach the natural area on foot from the bus stop, follow the path around the park to the field office and boat dock on the northeastern edge of the park, where Defense Road turns south.

Petersburg's largest park surrounds 20-acre Wilcox Lake, an impoundment in a deep stream valley on Lieutenant's Run. The steep western slopes above the lake are covered with a mature upland forest, which should be especially interesting to naturalists because of the many young chestnut trees - a rare species today - growing there. (See Section I - *Plant Communities*.) Granite outcroppings add to the interest and beauty of the scene.

Two rough trails (not suitable for the handicapped) traverse the slopes, one starting at the boat dock on the east, and the other from the picnic shelter on the west. The views over the lake from on high are beautiful. Beside the chestnut trees, many other interesting plant species can be seen along the way, at least one with edible fruits; blueberries grow and bear profusely on the slope, ripening in August. Birdwatching should be very good. Fishing from boats is permitted and said to be excellent, but bank fishing is not allowed. The lake has been stocked with largemouth and smallmouth bass, trout, catfish, bream, northern pike, and crappie. State fishing licenses are required. Row boats may be rented for a small fee.

Although the park is mainly passive, a few facilities have been developed in the level area above the eastern slope of the valley, and more are planned. At this writing, facilities include a large picnic pavilion seating up to 125, scattered picnic tables, restrooms (soon to be equipped for the handicapped), a large free play area, and a lighted basketball court, baseball field, and tennis courts. Parking is ample. For information about rental of the pavilion and equipment, call the Department of Recreation - 804/861-1261.

The park was the scene of Civil War action in 1864, when Union troops attempting to destroy the Petersburg Railroad moved through the ravine now occupied by Wilcox Lake, only to be repulsed by Confederates. Traces of an earthwork fortification may still be seen in the park.

Part of the internal road has been closed to all but service vehicles, creating a good place to walk or jog, and pick blackberries in season. Take the Guide along for the map, because it is difficult to find one's way around. Signs were needed at this writing, but may have already been installed.

Lee Park

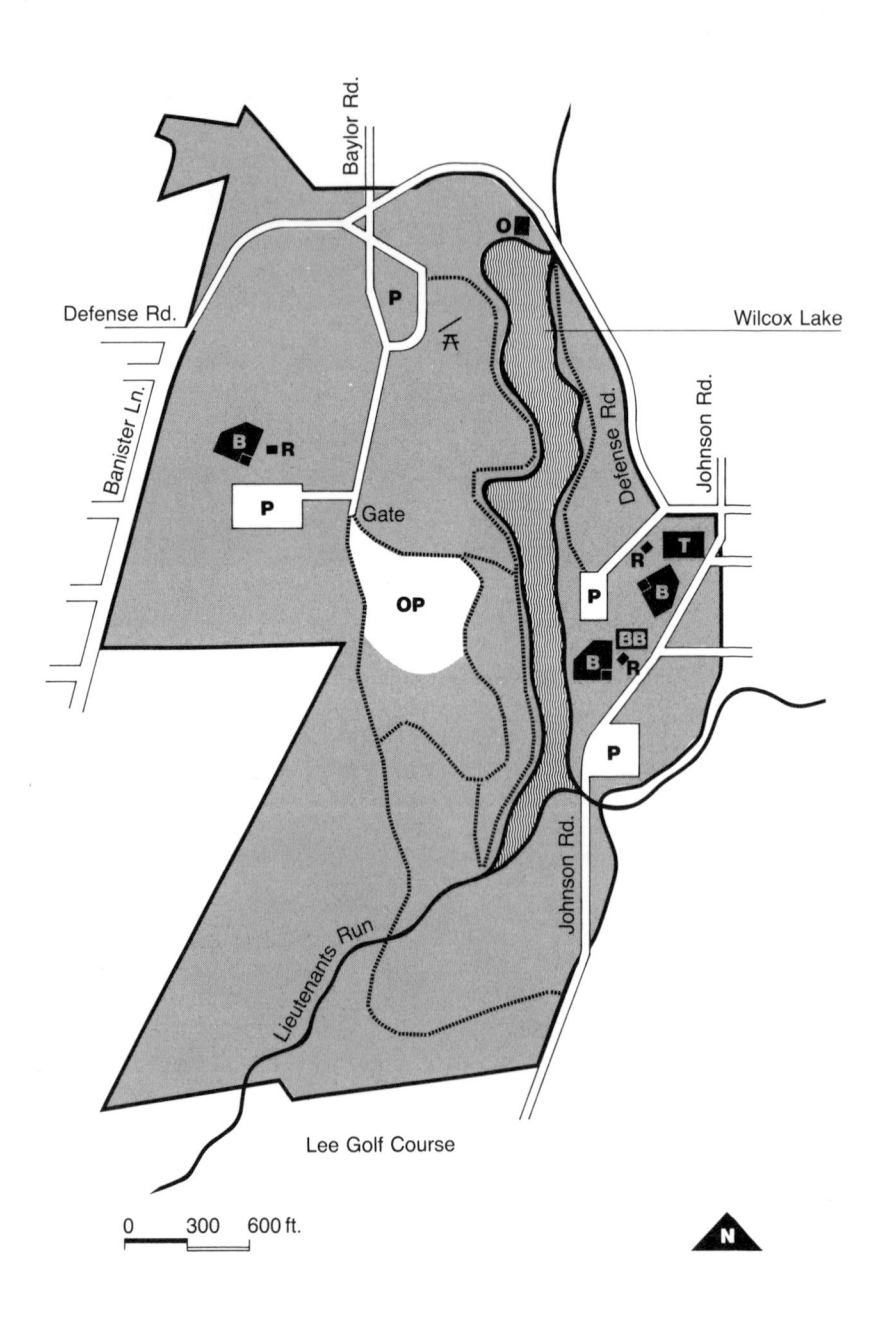

244

Poplar Lawn Park

(12 Acres)

>In northeast Petersburg, along the east side of Sycamore Street (US Alternate 301), north of Fillmore Street. The Mall Plaza bus goes right by the park.

One of historic Petersburg's featured sites and its oldest park, Poplar Lawn was established as the town square in 1846. Even before its official designation, the square enjoyed an illustrious history. Petersburg volunteers trained here during the war of 1812; the elderly Lafayette held a reception for a large group of schoolchildren on the grounds in 1824; and a Confederate field hospital was operated on the site during the Siege of Petersburg.

In the early 1880s the square was developed and landscaped as Central Park. In 1934 the City Council restored the name Poplar Lawn. As seen today, the old fashioned park design has been faithfully preserved, its handsome old trees, lawns, walkways, and central fountain conveying a peaceful sense of the past. A curious stone basin in the southwest corner, moved from an island in the river, is said to have been used for bathing the infant Pocahontas, but this has never been verified.

In recent years the old fashioned tradition of the ante-bellum fourth of July celebrations has been revived, with colorful contemporary additions. This has become a gala affair, worth attending for the music, exhibits, and fun filled events. Watch the papers for announcements.

Colonial Heights

Berberich Park/Fort Clifton

(24 Acres)

Along the west bank of the Appomattox River 1/2 mile upstream (south) of its confluence with Swift Creek. Berberich Park is a short distance east of White Bank, across the little peninsula formed where creek and river flow together. To reach the park, take Conduit Road north in Colonial Heights to Brockwell Lane and turn right on Brockwell past Tussing Elementary School to the entrance. From Interstate 95, take Exit 4 east to Conduit Road and proceed as above.

Fort Clifton is one of the few Civil War forts in the region to be incorporated in local parks. Interpretive signs add an interesting dimension to its otherwise contemporary aspects.

Like White Bank, this park also features a fishing pier and a canoe take-out area (no ramp, just a place to pull out), the last on the Appomattox before it flows into the James River. Launching is also possible here, but except for the short trip to the James, good downstream paddling is limited to exploring in the vicinity; the only other way to go is up the river or up Swift Creek against the current. (See Section II - *Along the Waterways*.) Be careful in the vicinity of the river; eastern cottonmouth snakes are known to inhabit the lower reaches of Swift Creek and might also be found here.

The park itself is wooded, except for a marsh at the edge of the river. To reach the river, one crosses the marsh on a small footbridge with an observation deck that gives an excellent view of the plants growing in it.

Several small picnic tables with grills are scattered throughout the park. Restrooms are available and accessible to handicapped visitors, as are most of the paths.

The topography lends itself well to a small amphitheater with a bandshell for performances, used during an annual arts and crafts festival in May, and on other special occasions.

The park is the site of a Confederate Battery with cannon emplacements built for the defense of Petersburg during the Civil War. Shelled by five Union ships on June 11, 1864, the cannon drove off the attackers, and the fort remained in Confederate hands. Many earthworks criss-cross the park. They should not be walked on, as this accelerates their erosion.

While in the vicinity, first-time visitors should also take the short drive across the peninsula to White Bank, to see the panoramic view over Swift Creek and the extensive marsh spread out below.

White Bank Park

(22 Acres)

Along the east bank of Swift Creek about 1/2 mile upstream (south) of its confluence with the Appomattox River. To reach the park, take Conduit Road in Colonial Heights north to White Bank Road across from Tussing Elementary School. Turn west (left) to the end of the road. From Interstate 95 take Exit 4 east to Conduit Road and proceed as above.

Ninety feet high on a bluff overlooking Swift Creek and acres of tidal marsh, White Bank is a perfect spot for a park. In combination with a boat ramp/canoe launch and fishing piers at the foot of the bank, the park has a lot to offer as a staging area as well. Canoeists and fishermen can park cars after unloading, use the restroom facilities, and picnic in an attractive wooded setting on the breezy bluff.

Two large picnic pavilions with fireplaces and electrical hookups accommodate as many as 200 and 300. (For reservations call the Colonial Heights Department of Recreation - 804/526-3388.) Several smaller shelters for 15, with grills, are scattered about the site, some at the edge of the bluff for a beautiful view, but children must be watched; the dropoff is steep! Youngsters should enjoy the most elaborate wooden play equipment we have seen, including the skeleton of a Viking ship, complete with rigging to climb, and a bridge to cross, and a fort to defend.

Gravel paths connect the use areas. Well maintained restrooms are also equipped for handicapped visitors. Other little trails (beaten paths) make the most of this limited site. An attractive foot bridge affords another view over a natural ravine. Park designers have surely made the best possible use of this site.

Naturalists, including bird watchers, will appreciate the view over creek and marsh. (Bring binoculars.) Unfortunately, however tantalizing the prospect for exploring more, the shore is too watery to do it on foot. A canoe trip is the only way to get close to the marsh. Fortunately, the canoe launch makes this possible. For information about sponsored canoe trips, call the Chesterfield County Department of Parks and Recreation - 804/748-1623.

A word of warning to venturers along the creek - keep an eye out; this is a habitat for eastern cottonmouth snakes. (For more information on these and other snakes, see Section I - *Wildlife.*)

Visitors interested in Civil War sites should consider taking the short drive to Fort Clifton Park across the peninsula, to see the earthworks from a battery that defended Petersburg from Union attack in 1864. From this park it is also possible to get a look at the Appomattox River above its confluence with Swift Creek.

Hopewell

(See also *City Point Unit of the Petersburg National Battlefield*.)

Atwater Park

(18 Acres)

Located in the north west section of Hopewell at the intersection of River and Atwater Roads, across from Fort Lee Military Reservation. To reach the park from Hopewell, take River Road west to its intersection with Atwater; from Fort Lee, drive east on River Road to the park just outside the Reservation line.

In the past few years the Hopewell Department of Recreation has concentrated its resources on a fine new indoor recreation center with a gymnasium, swimming pool, and related facilities. In the future the city will be turning its attention to refurbishing an old park and improving a new one, as well as working with the National Park Service in featuring City Point and surrounding historic sites.

Atwater is a small new neighborhood park gradually being developed in a pleasantly wooded area. A one-mile exercise/fitness trail winds through the woods, doubling as a path for strolling. Other facilities include a picnic shelter with four tables and a grill, and a small tot lot with play equipment. At this writing restroom facilities had not been added.

The park is level, and generally accessible to the handicapped.

Riverside Park

(20 Acres)

Located across from the Hopewell Yacht Club on Riverside Avenue just off Route 10 in Hopewell. The park extends south to Division Street at 12th Street, and may be entered from either direction, although the main entrance is at Division and 12th. Limited parking is available at either end.

Riverside is a narrow community park secluded between two old cemeteries. The northern half of the property slopes steeply down to Riverside Drive, and has been left in a natural condition, with fine old trees and a thick understory. The site has good possibilities for developing a passive park in the natural area, but not much has been done with it yet. The Hopewell Jaycees helped the city acquire the property as a park and presumably will continue to take an interest in it.

The level upper section is developed with athletic facilities - tennis courts, a basketball court, and softball field, all lighted for night use. The park is scheduled for improvements throughout, and could be a real asset to the community.

Visitors should note a that a curious landmark separates the park from the adjoining Appomattox Cemetery. The old stone wall around the cemetery was built with rocks taken from the great outcropping that gave Point of Rocks (now a Chesterfield County park) its name. The Point of Rocks is no more; it has been moved to this location.

Fort Abbott

(3 Acres)

> A square block along the east side of Cedar Lane just south of the City Point Unit of the Petersburg National Battlefield (on the way to City Point.)

This site was used for a gun emplacement protecting City Point during the Civil War. The earthen fort and circular trail around it are still visible, although a great deal of erosion has taken place, (unfortunately much of it due to misuse by dirt bikes). Today is is mostly used as a simple picnic area, with one table in a shady spot. (This is a good stop for visitors to City Point, where picnicking is discouraged.)

The area is also interesting for the great trees that have stood undisturbed on the site for many years, perhaps for over a century. Visitors with an interest in trees should also look for a historic pecan, believed to be one of the world's largest, growing across from the City Point Unit up the road. Several old paper mulberry trees grown for the silk industry also still stand in this area.

We are told that the orginal Fort Abbott was two miles away, and lost to development. The name of this fort was not known, so it was named after the other, and the historical marker will continue to designate it as such.

Hanover County

Poor Farm Park

(270 Acres)

Located 3½ miles west of Ashland off Route 54 behind Patrick Henry High School and Liberty Junior High. From Route 54 turn south next to the entrance to Liberty Junior High. Park visitors may use the school parking lot. Vehicular access to the park is restricted by a gate; if needed, the key may be obtained from the Hanover Department of Recreation. (Call 804/798-6081.)

Another of the "best kept secrets" of the region, Poor Farm Park features a working farm and trails through a beautiful old forest sloping down to little Stagg Creek. On the slimmest of budgets the county Department of Recreation and Parks has blazed primitive trails, crossed ravines with rustic bridges, and maintained a simple old picnic area (without water or shelter) in a grassy clearing near the entrance.

The park is a wildlife sanctuary, and its diverse habitats—field, creeks, upland and lowland forest, and edges—attract a variety of birds and other wildlife. During our morning on the trail we saw deer and turkey, among other animals, and undoubtedly missed seeing others.

The history of the park is unusual for a recreation area, for at one time it really was a poor farm, established for paupers in 1755 by St. Paul's Parish, and later taken over by the county. Residents were charged with working on the farm for their room and board. After the institution was abolished, the buildings were removed, and the fields were cultivated by local farmers, but the woods belonging to the property were mostly left alone and have developed into mature stands of trees, except for a fire trail cut through them. In 1977 when the Board of Supervisors recognized the recreational value of the property, the farm became Poor Farm Park.

The park is still in the early development stage, with improvements to be made as funds become available—water to be brought into the picnic area, new tables, perhaps a shelter or two, conversion of an old field for free play, restrooms, and signs along the trails. In the meantime, visitors who are mainly looking for a beautiful place to hike, bird-watch, or otherwise commune with nature can enjoy the use of the trails.

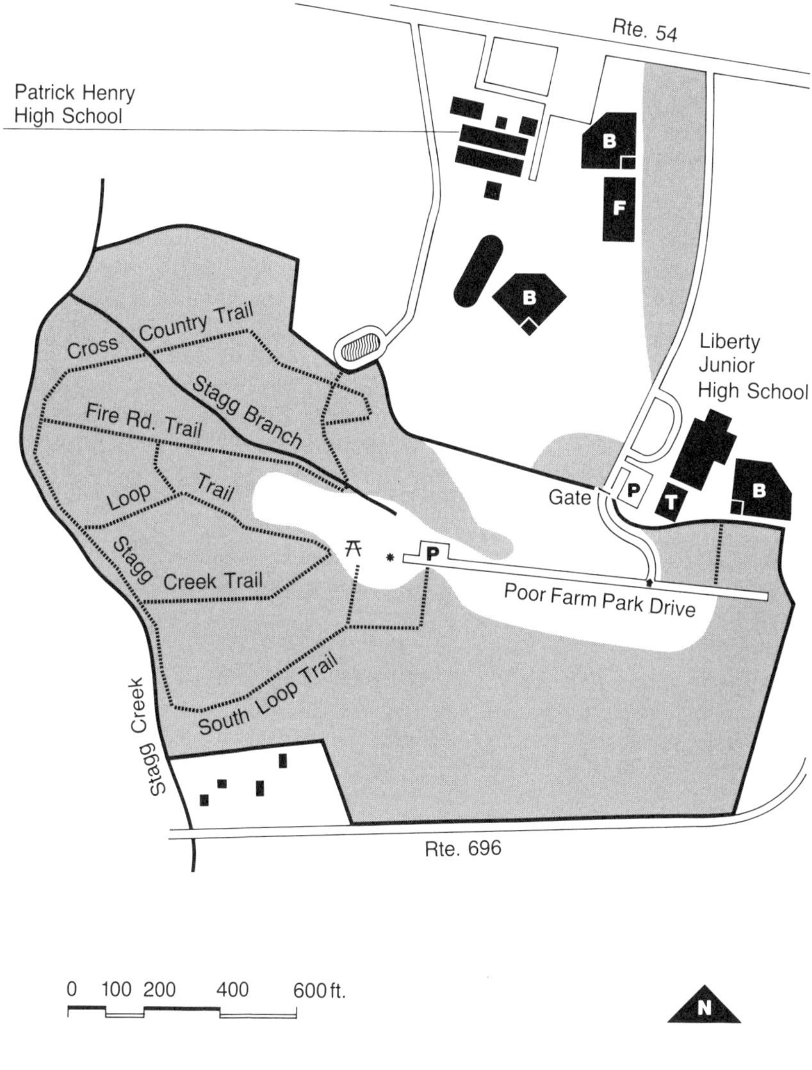

Rte. 54
Patrick Henry
High School
B
F
B
Liberty
Junior
High School
Cross Country Trail
Stagg Branch
Fire Rd. Trail
Loop Trail
Gate
P
T
B
Stagg Creek Trail
P
Poor Farm Park Drive
South Loop Trail
Stagg Creek
Rte. 696
0 100 200 400 600 ft.
N

Wayside Park

(32 Acres)

> East side of Route 301, approximately three miles south of Hanover Court House in Hanover County.

This pretty, wooded park was formerly a wayside used by passing motorists for picnicking in a shady spot. When the Virginia Department of Highways and Transportation disposed of it, Hanover County purchased the property as a park because the site was unusually large for a wayside, and included a seven-acre mill pond, suitable for fishing.

The park today still emphasizes picnicking as a favored activity, with tables and grills scattered throughout the site, some with a view of the pond, all convenient to the circular drive. A large shelter accommodates eight tables for groups as large as 60–75. The space enclosed by the drive can be used as an open playfield. Nearby restrooms are equipped for the handicapped.

The pond has been stocked with smallmouth bass, bluegill, crappie, and catfish, and is open for fishing the year round. Conceivably you could cook and eat your catch on the spot.

A ¼ mile trail follows along one side of the pond and the creek that flows from the lower end. This makes a pleasant little walk, especially on a hot summer day. The slope down to the water is steep, however; not everyone will find the going easy.

For shelter reservations, call the Hanover Department of Recreation—804/798-6081.

Prince George County

Prince George County Park

(14 Acres)

Adjacent to the Prince George County Courthouse and Beazley Elementary School on State Route 106, about one mile west of its intersection with Route 156 (Prince George Drive).

Prince George has recently dedicated its first community park, a combination athletic complex and open space picnic area. The first facilities include a softball field with grandstand, a large picnic shelter with grills and tables, playground, and fitness trail.

Wooded areas are being preserved and considered in the over-all plan, for a natural setting and shade.

Eastern Chipmunk

Charles City County

Hillside Park

(2 Acres)

  Located adjacent to the historic Charles City Courthouse at the intersection of State Scenic Route 5 and Route 155.

Hillside is a wayside-type picnic spot in a wooded area serving also as part of the courthouse grounds. The property slopes down to little Courthouse Creek, a tributary of the James River, which, surprisingly, is a herring run in the spring. Local residents enjoy catching the herring with nets right in the park.

Several picnic tables with grills are located in shady spots throughout the site. These seem to be especially appreciated by county workers at noon and motorists passing by in search of a wayside. Restroom facilities accessible to handicapped visitors are available from 8-5 in the Neighborhood Facility Building next to the park. The gravel paths in the level area on high ground are also accessible to the handicapped.

Harrison Park

(19 Acres)

  Located on Route 607 three miles east of State Scenic Route 5.

Mainly a community athletic complex, Harrison Park also features a short bike and jogging trail around its circumference, plus a picnic pavilion, four small picnic shelters, and a children's play area.

Athletic facilities include two tennis courts and baseball, softball, and combination football and soccer fields. Two concession stands also house restrooms accessible to handicapped visitors. Parking is ample.

Charles City Recreation Center

(10 Acres)

>Located on Route 615 about three miles north of its intersection with State Scenic Route 5.

This park is also primarily a community athletic complex, with a recently refurbished gymnasium and swimming pool on the grounds. Two tennis courts and three ballfields (one lighted) make up the outside facilities, along with a simple picnic area and children's pool and playground. Restrooms accessible to handicapped visitors are located inside the gymnasium.

Eastern Bluebird

The National Battlefield Parks of the Region

Introduction

That the Capital Region is rich in Civil War history is well known. Less known is the fact that many of the battlefields and related sites have been preserved as historic parks of great interest. Because time has healed the scars of war and the sites have returned to their pre-war condition of fields and woods and because they have been carefully tended, these parks are also beautiful and poignant places to visit.

The Richmond National Battlefield Park consists of a series of fortifications and battlefields scattered throughout Chesterfield, Henrico, and Hanover Counties, with a Visitor Center located in Chimborazo Park in Richmond. The Petersburg National Battlefield includes a large park in Petersburg and a smaller unit at City Point in Hopewell. With careful planning you should be able to see them all in two days.

Historians point out how geography - the lay of the land, so to speak - had much to do with Civil War strategy and the results of the various actions that took place. In visiting these sites it is very interesting to see how the landscape determined the location of fortifications, for instance, and how one side or the other was affected by the positions taken up or forced by circumstances to assume.

For the best understanding of the history of Richmond Battlefield Park, take the

Civil War Cannon

automobile tour mapped out by the National Park Service, starting at the Visitor Center in Chimborazo Park at East Broad and 33rd Streets in Richmond. An orientation film and exhibits will give you an excellent perpective of the sequence of events, including the strategies, troop movements, and battles. The tour guide pamphlets provide a map showing the stops, a brief history of the 1862 and 1864 campaigns, and interpretations of every site along the way. Allow one day for the complete tour, including several short walks. If you plan a picnic, it is a good idea to schedule a lunch stop at Cold Harbor or Fort Harrison where tables and other facilities are provided.

The tour guide map may be used to chart a shorter tour of selected battlesites if you have limited time to visit. A self-guiding auto casette tour is available for sale or rent at the Chimborazo Visitor Center for visitors who would like a detailed historical narration of the 1862 Seven Days Battle sites.

Notice that Drewry's Bluff (Fort Darling) is located west of the James River and just off Interstate 95 between Richmond and Petersburg. If you are planning to visit the Petersburg Battlefield via I-95 from Richmond, this would be a good time to take in Drewry's Bluff along the way.

In the historical sequence of events, the Petersburg National Battlefield, including the City Point Unit in Hopewell, takes up where Richmond National Battlefield Park leaves off. Another day will take you through the events of 1864-1865, by automobile and afoot. Start at the Visitor Center in the Petersburg Battlefield for another excellent orientation and tour guide pamphlets. Tour the park by automobile, with walking side trips. (Bicycling is also allowed.) Picnic facilities are provided at this site. Visit the Siege Museum in Petersburg for an insight into the besieged city, then go on to City Point in Hopewell to see Grant's headquarters and logistical center for the Siege.

The Park Service is very protective of the Battlefield Parks and its visitors. Rules and regulations prohibit the possession or use of firearms and metal detecting devices, taking any natural, cultural, or archeological resources, bothering wildlife, and the use of alcohol in the parks. It should also be noted that walking on the earthworks is prohibited, for this wears them down and subjects them to erosion.

Not all Civil War sites are located in the National Battlefield Parks. Some old forts and earthworks are on private property. A few may be found in other parks and preserves. Where we are aware of these, we have mentioned them; an example is Fort Clifton in Berberich Park, Colonial Heights. The same kinds of rules relating to the natural and archeological resources apply in these.

Chickahominy Bluff

(39 Acres)

Located on the Chickahominy Bluff in Henrico County on the east side of Route 360 (Mechanicsville Turnpike), about one mile south of Mechanicsville. Turn east up the park drive at the sign.

Part of the outer Confederate line defending Richmond, the bluff commands a fine view over the Chickahominy Swamp north to Mechanicsville. It was from this vantage point that General Lee observed Union troop movements prior to the beginning of the Seven Days Battle in June, 1862.

An interpretive overlook (with a panoramic painting and an audio program) explains the situation of the Confederate army on the eve of Lee's efforts to seize the offensive against the Union forces, and relates the subsequent events. Visitors can appreciate the strategic military advantage the Confederates enjoyed for a time in holding the heights and understand why the Union forces would not attack through the rain-swollen Chickahominy Swamp.

The site is attractively landscaped with lawns and paths. The earthworks surrounding the bluff have been carefully preserved and are covered with vegetation. The Park Service asks that visitors not walk on them, as this wears them down and accelerates their erosion.

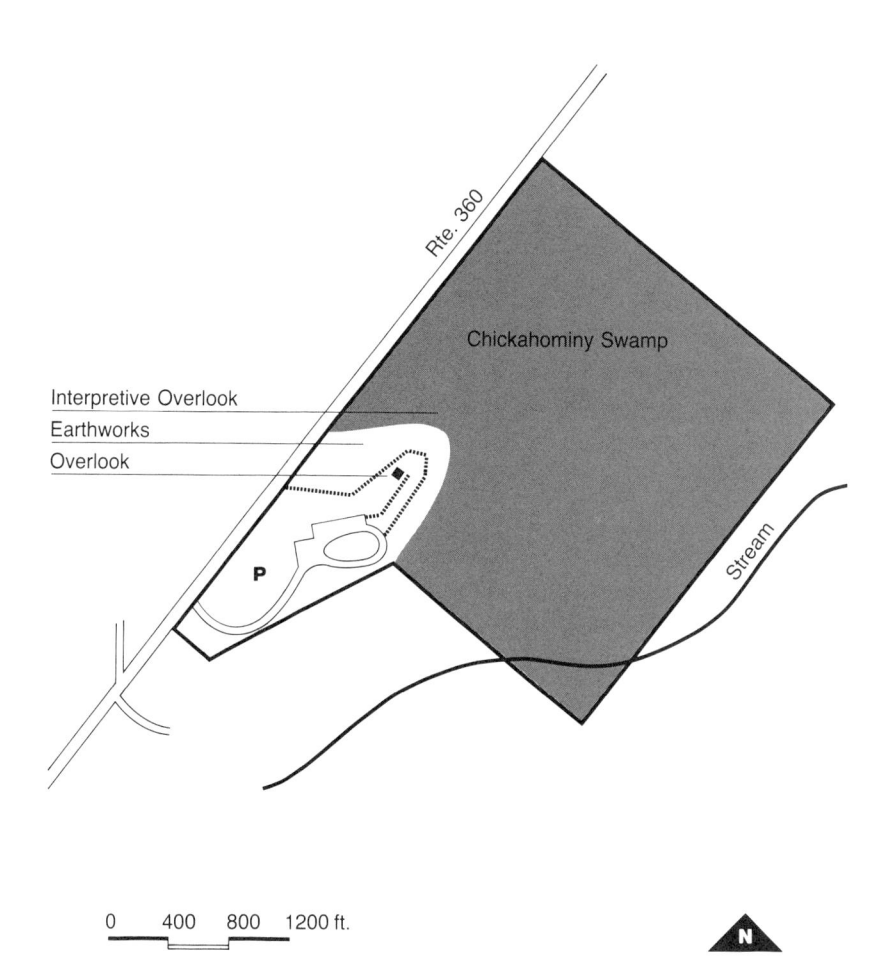

Interpretive Overlook
Earthworks
Overlook

Rte. 360

Chickahominy Swamp

Stream

P

0   400   800   1200 ft.

N

Beaver Dam Creek

(14 Acres)

Located in Hanover County along the south side of Route 156 just east of its intersection with Route 360 (Mechanicsville Turnpike.) Look for the Richmond National Battlefield Park sign at the entrance.

Here in this pleasant little creek valley in June, 1862 the first battle of the Battle of Seven Days was fought, when Confederate troops under General Lee attempted unsuccessfully to break Union lines by fording the creek and a millrace, waist deep in water, and under fire from Union troops on higher ground to the west.

The topography today is much the same as it was then, though the millrace is gone, and the interpretive overlook displaying a map of the battle lines and movements can easily be understood. It has been said that natural features often dictate the location, strategies, and outcomes of military campaigns. The significance of these factors can be readily observed at Beaver Creek Dam.

Aside from its military importance, the park today is a pleasant spot for a stop and an impromptu picnic. Most of it is still in a natural condition of floodplain, creek, swamp, and lowland forest. Interestingly, the swamp is becoming a marsh; notice the drowned trees and the grasses taking over. (See Section I - *Plant Communities*.) A high and dry grassy area is being maintained for resting and taking in the scene.

Rte. 156

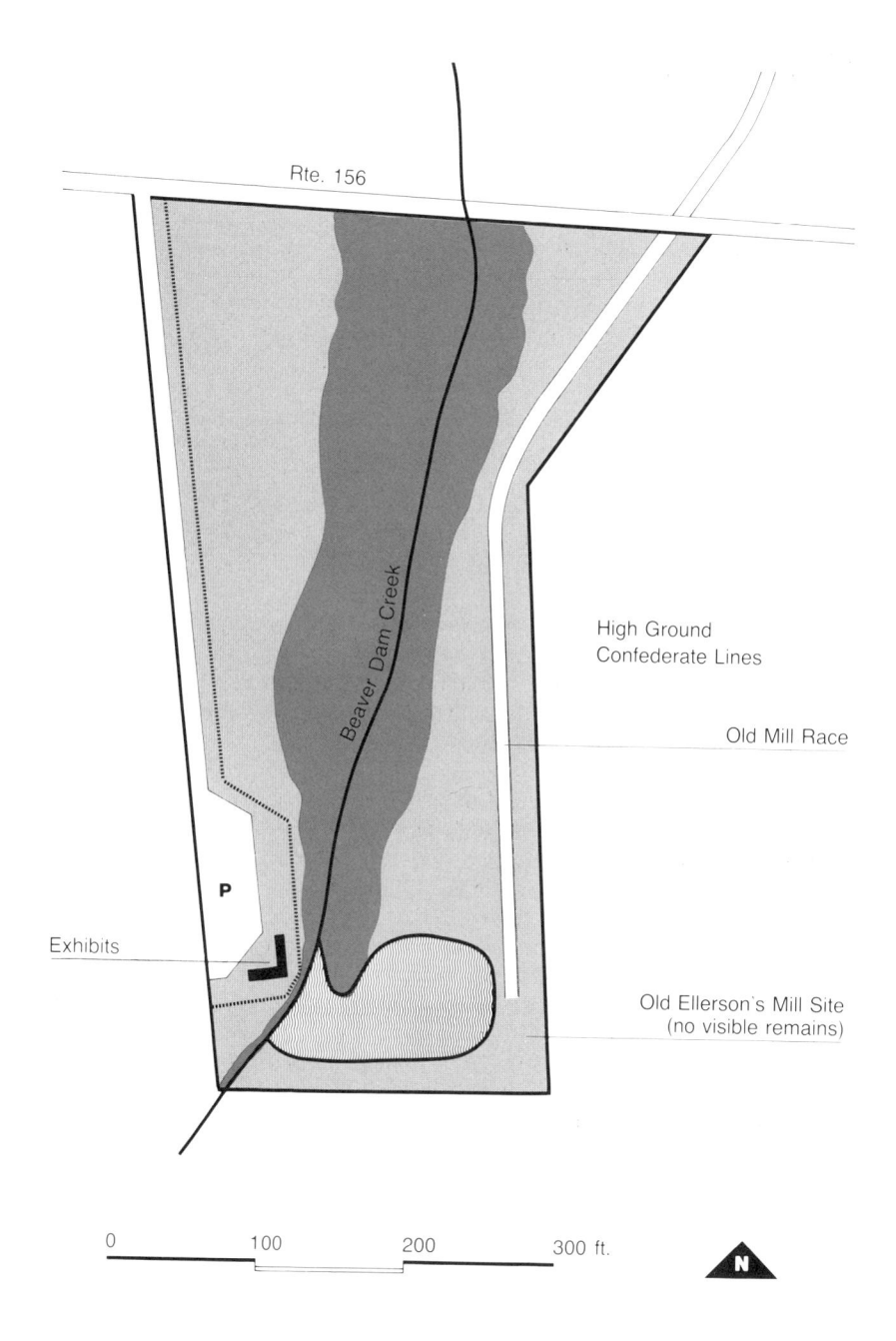

Beaver Dam Creek

High Ground
Confederate Lines

Old Mill Race

Exhibits

P

Old Ellerson's Mill Site
(no visible remains)

0   100   200   300 ft.

N

261

Gaines Mill Battlefield

(Watt House) (60 Acres)

> In Hanover County south of Route 156, 1-1/2 miles east of its intersection with Route 615. Look for the Watt House sign at the intersection of Routes 718 and 156.

Beside the historical significance of the Watt House and its grounds, this battlefield site is worth visiting for the unique history/nature trail that winds through a very old forest on the property.

An antebellum farmhouse (circa 1835), Watt House was occupied by Union General Fitz-John Porter as a headquarters and hospital during the Battle of Gaines Mill, second of the Seven Days Battle on June 27, 1862. The Union battleline occupied fields on both sides of the house. Here Georgia and Texas troops broke the Union line within a few hundred feet of the house. A wayside exhibit near the parking lot interprets the history of the site.

The farm environment has been preserved much as it was in 1862, helping one to visualize the scene at the time. The house has been restored, but is occupied by Park Service staff and not open to the public. A carriage house and barn add to the interest of the scene. Horses still graze in the pasture, which is leased to a farmer, and the fields are planted in soybeans and corn.

Visitors are encouraged to walk the ¼ mile loop history/nature trail, which follows part of the Seven Days Battle line through the forest where the Confederate troops broke down to Boatswain Creek (a tributary of the Chickahominy River). Observant visitors may identify traces of Union earthworks along the trail.

Whenever battles had to be fought in forests, if there was time the soldiers cut them down for visibility. The returning forests on most battlefield sites are relatively young. Many of the trees on this wooded slope are, however, ancient, to judge from their great size, and are remnants of the original forest of the area. (See Section I - *The Changing Landscape* and *Plant Communities*.) These tremendous oaks must have been very old even in 1862 when the battle was fought. Many large hollies also grow in the forest, adding a touch of green during the winter season. Anyone interested in old forests should visit this site, if only to see these magnificent trees.

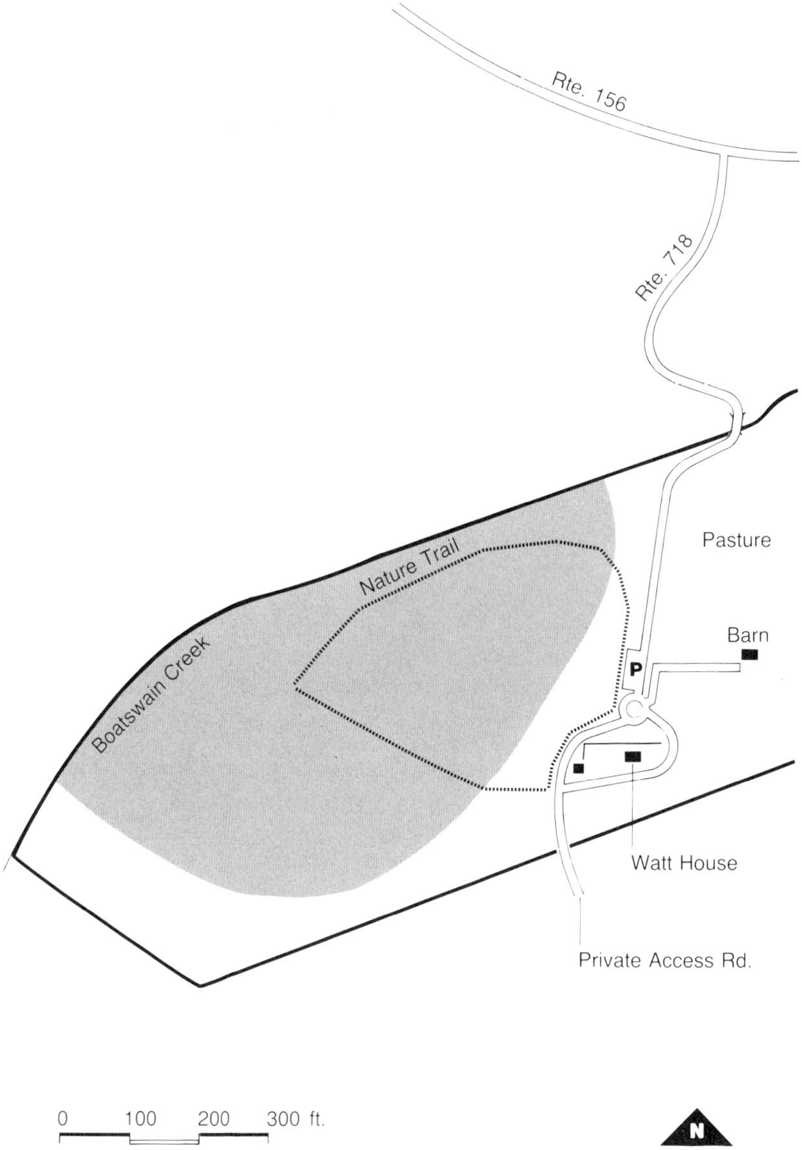
Rte. 156
Rte. 718
Pasture
Nature Trail
Barn
P
Boatswain Creek
Watt House
Private Access Rd.
0
100
200
300 ft.
N

Malvern Hill

(130 Acres)

In Henrico County. Along both sides of Route 156, just south of its intersection with Route 600, (Carter's Mill Road), and one mile north of its intersection with State Scenic Route 5, (New Market Road).

This beautiful open Virginia farmland appears much as it did on July 1, 1862, when the last of the Seven Days Battles was fought. Union troops under McClellan were retreating to Harrison's Landing after the Battle of Gaines Mill, with the Confederates in pursuit, when they stopped to make a stand from a superior position on high ground.

"The Federals, on the defensive, dug no trenches. Instead they stood at bay in parade-ground, line-of-battle formation across the gently sloping fields, their massed artillery and infantry fire shattering the ranks of the attacking Confederates. The steep slopes of Malvern Hill on the Union left and the swampy bottoms on the right forced the southerners to advance across open ground. According to one Confederate officer: 'It was not war - it was murder.'" (From the National Park Service Richmond National Battlefield Park brochure.)

A small interpretive center features excellent wall maps and an audio-visual program explaining the battle. Civil war cannon pointed in the direction of the battle lend authenticity. The surrounding fields are under cultivation, leased to local farmers for hay. The small wooded areas within the park are open to the public; however, no trails run through them, and boundaries are indistinct. If you walk in them, be careful not to trespass on neighboring properties, and in summer be on the lookout for poison ivy and ticks.

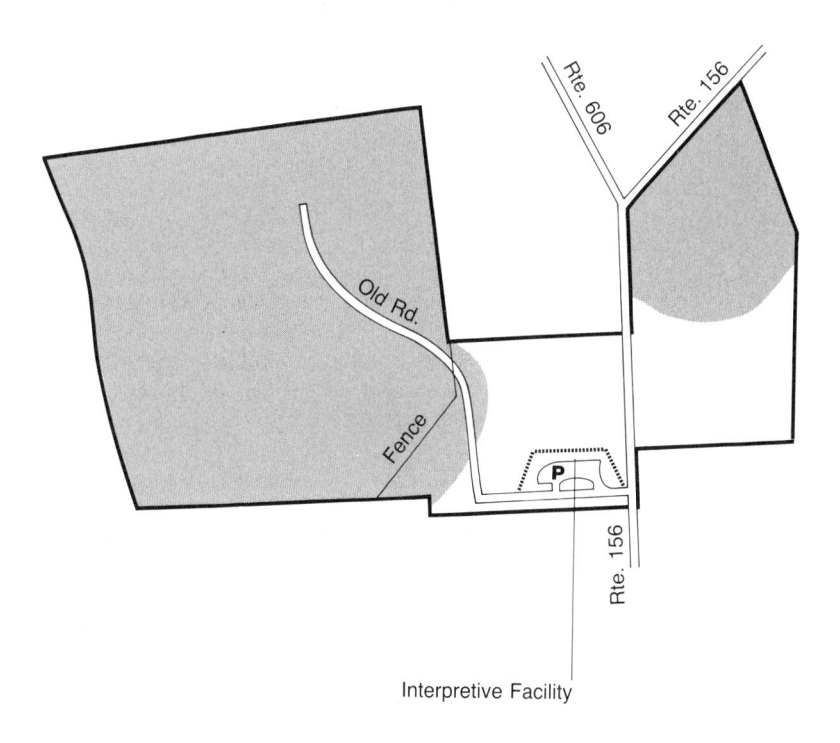

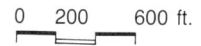

Rte. 606

Rte. 156

Old Rd.

Fence

P

Rte. 156

Interpretive Facility

0 200 600 ft.

N

Cold Harbor Battlefield

(149 Acres)

In Hanover County, along the north side of Route 156, one mile west of its intersection with Routes 619, 632, and 633.

Only a short distance north of Watt House and the Battle of Gaines Mill in 1862, Cold Harbor was the scene of another battle in June, 1864, in which a terrible toll of lives was taken, after which the Union Army moved south to cross the James, attack Confederate forces defending Petersburg, and ultimately lay siege to the city.

Although it is a bit confusing to shift to another period in trying to follow the sequence of historic events, do visit Cold Harbor while you are in the vicinity, before continuing on to Malvern Hill, site of the last of the Seven Days Battles in 1862.

In 1864 much of Cold Harbor was an open field. Today it is a wooded park, on undulating ground that clearly shows the patterns of trenches and earthworks dug by the Confederates, the hastily dug trenches of the attacking Union forces, and the pathetic no man's land that lay between them. Here for several days the dead and wounded soldiers lay unattended until a truce could be arranged, during which both sides could attend to their fallen. Even in these lovely surroundings, there is a poignancy about the scene that is unforgettable.

The battles fought at Cold Harbor emphasized the deadly strategy of trench warfare. Confederate troops had dug in, awaiting attacks from Union troops under Grant. When the attacks came, they were among the most intense of the war. During one frontal assault along a section of the line Union troops suffered over 7,000 casualties in 30 minutes. The battle was a Confederate victory at great cost to both sides. Richmond was saved for the time being, though it fell a year later.

A small visitor center here features an outstanding audio-visual presentation of the battle, with excellent maps and color coded representations of moving armies. On summer weekends living history programs feature soldiers in Confederate uniforms showing how they prepared for the battle.

Adjacent to the visitor center is a picnic area with scattered tables. Restrooms and water are available except in winter. The entire area is treated as a park, with a two mile park road looping through it. Pull-over parking lots and observation bridges allow visitors to view the earthworks from both battle lines - Union on the east, and Confederate on the west - without walking on the eroding earthworks.

Visitors can jog or bike along the park road and walk over a mile of internal trails criss-crossing the park.

On leaving the park, take note of the Garthright House (circa 1720), located just to the east of the park road exit onto Route 156. The house served as a field hospital, first for Union and then Confederate troops after the battle. Now occupied by a Park ranger, the house is an exterior exhibit only, and is not open to the public.

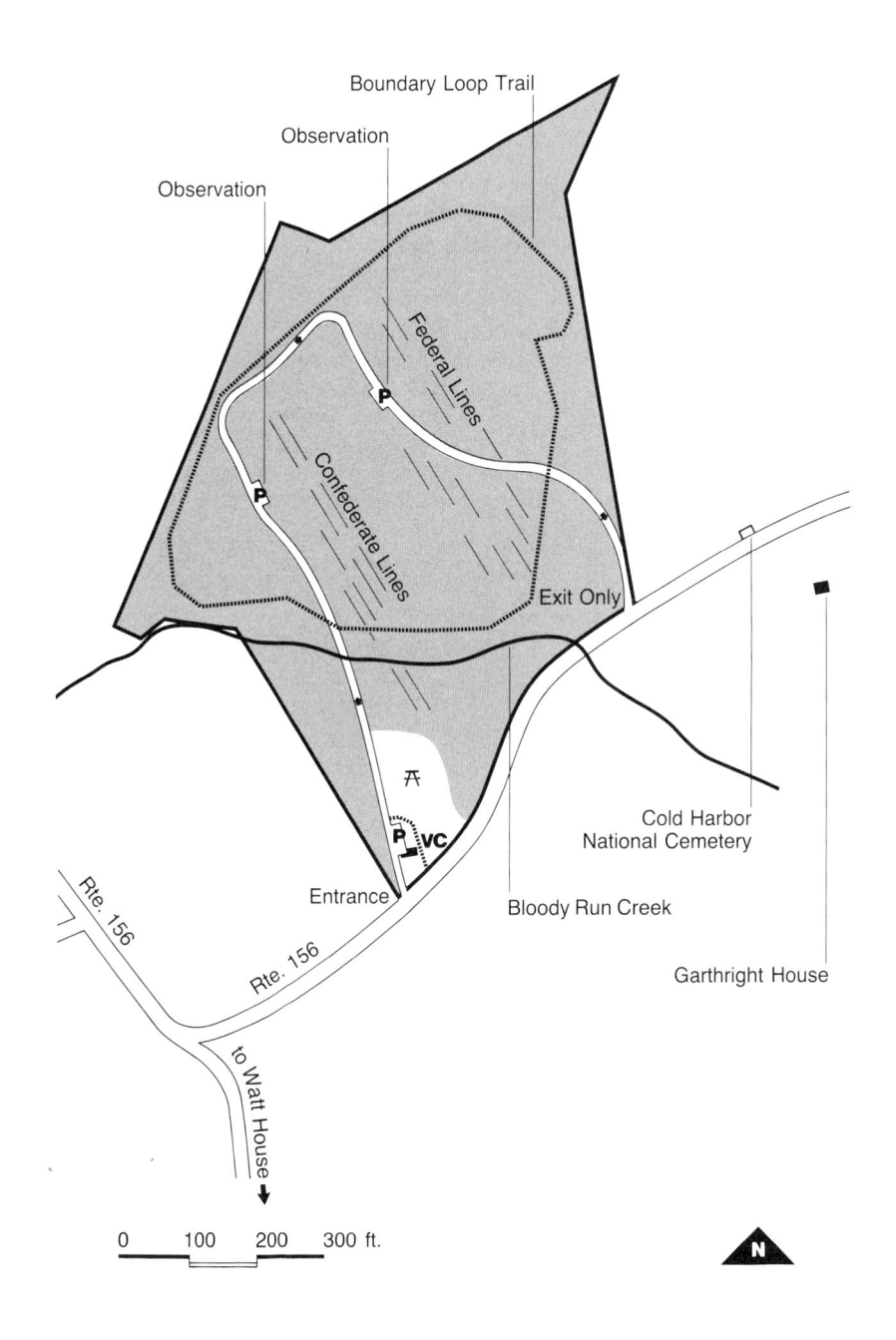

Fort Harrison

(315 Acres)

In eastern Henrico County, west of Scenic Route 5 (New Market Road), one mile south of its intersection with Laburnum Avenue. Turn west off Route 5 onto Battlefield Park Road and follow it and Hoke-Brady Road past several small forts to Fort Harrison and Fort Brady.

Originally part of the ring of outer defenses around Richmond, Fort Harrison and several other Confederate fortifications have been preserved along a pleasant seven mile park road paralleled by the grass-covered earthworks that were built to link them. Major fortifications along the road include Forts Gilmer, Gregg, Johnson, Harrison, and Hoke. Of these the largest was Fort Harrison.

Each of the fortifications is marked with signs and wayside maps, with pull-outs for stopping to look at these. Fort Harrison and, to a lesser extent, Fort Brady at the end of the road are the only substantial park land holdings with exhibits, trails, and other features.

One of the intriguing aspects of the Civil War fortifications is the way some of them changed hands and were later used by the other side. Until Grant captured Fort Harrison on September 29, 1864 it had been a Confederate fortification. After this date Union troops occupied and enlarged it, adding earthworks around the western end as a defense against Confederate lines, for the other forts along the line had not been captured. At the same time, they constructed Fort Brady overlooking the James to neutralize Fort Darling across the river on Drewry's Bluff, and to anchor the Federal line from Fort Harrison. For several months Union and Confederate troops occupied forts within shouting distance of one another. It is said that enemy pickets sometimes conversed.

Fort Harrison today is a pleasant wooded park, with a wide loop path (designed for handicapped visitors) leading past old earthworks, cannon, gun emplacements, and other interesting relics of the war. In summer and on special occasions living history exhibits demonstrate how soldiers lived in the fort. Soldiers dressed in Union uniforms work and rest near tents and other installations, creating a sense of how it was at the time.

Be sure to visit the interpretive visitor center near the parking lot. The exhibits are well worth seeing, and a staff member is usually on hand in summer to answer questions about the history of the forts. The building also houses restrooms. (A new facility is equipped for handicapped visitors.) A picnic area with quite a few scattered tables is located near the parking lot.

Fort Brady, four miles down the road. is nestled in a wooded area overlooking the river and Hatcher and Farrar's Islands, site of Henrico City, the first English settlement in Henrico County. (See *Henrico City Park* under Chesterfield County.)

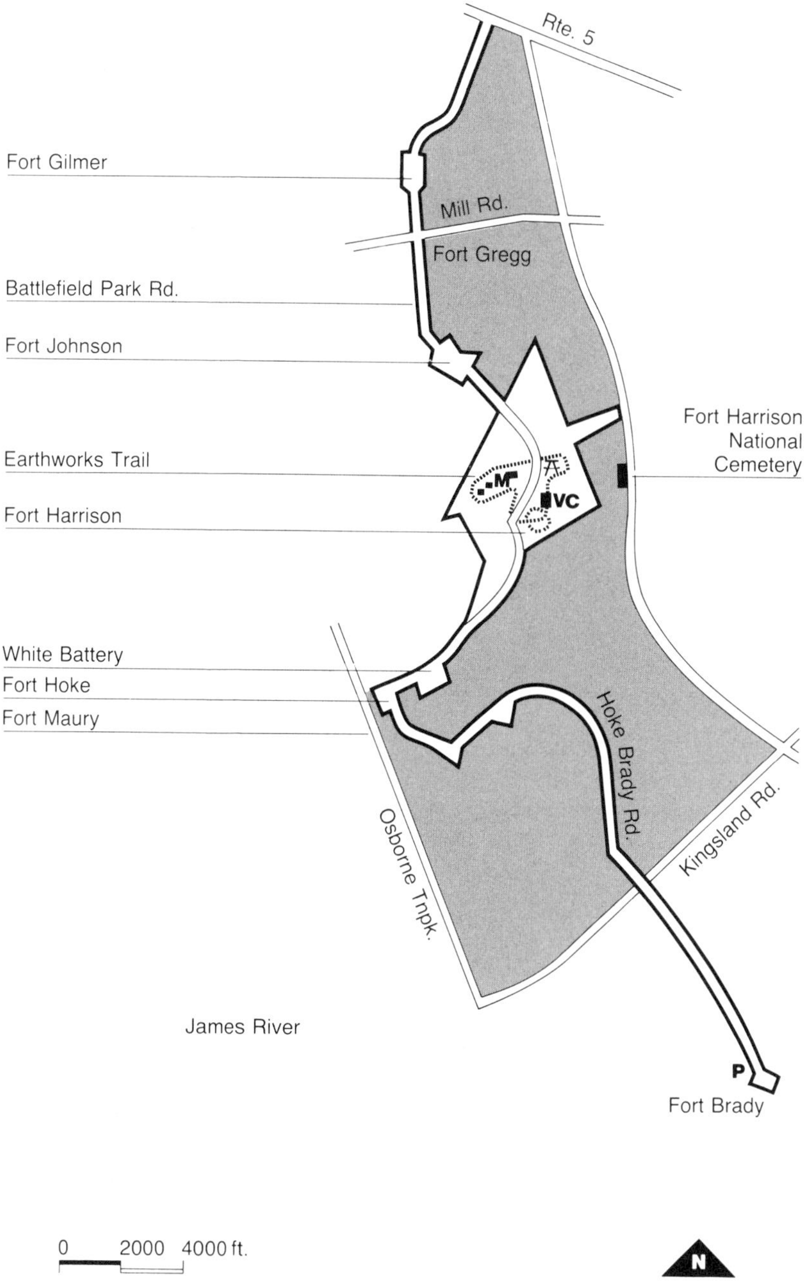

Rte. 5
Fort Gilmer
Mill Rd.
Fort Gregg
Battlefield Park Rd.
Fort Johnson
Fort Harrison
National
Cemetery
Earthworks Trail
M
VC
Fort Harrison
White Battery
Fort Hoke
Fort Maury
Hoke Brady Rd.
Kingsland Rd.
Osborne Tnpk.
James River
P
Fort Brady
0
2000
4000 ft.
N

The visitor center is closed during the winter, open weekends in the spring and fall, and every day from Memorial Day to Labor Day. Hours are 9:30 - 5:30. The park road itself, or any part of it, is a wonderful place to jog, and one of the few places in the region where it is possible to ride a bike for any distance in relative space and safety.

Breastworks - Fort Harrison

Drewry's Bluff

Drewry's Bluff/Fort Darling

(42 Acres)

On the south bank of the James River, roughly east of the Defense General Supply Center in Chesterfield County. From U.S. Route 301 (Jefferson Davis Highway) turn east on Bellwood Road (at the first light south of the Supply Center). Immediately after passing under Interstate 95, make a sharp left turn on Fort Darling Road and proceed to the end. (Bear right at the Park Service sign.) From I-95, exit on Willis Road, turn north on U.S. 301 and proceed as above.

One of the loveliest parks in the region, Drewry's Bluff was a Confederate fortification overlooking the James River eight miles south of Richmond. As a fortification in the 1860s, surrounded by raw earthworks, scarred land, gun emplacements, tents, and temporary buildings, it was anything but beautiful, to judge from early photographs and drawings, but time has been kind to the site. The forest has returned, and today it is a pleasant grove, with a fine view over the James River ninety feet below. Paths wind through the historic fort, and a well constructed nature trail descends through a verdant ravine to the shore below.

Before the Civil War the site was part of Drewry's Farm, and was selected for a major artillery fortification because of its strategic location. The guns of the fort could fire down on any craft coming up the James, and no guns below could get a shell trajectory high enough to inflict damage on the fort. Twice the garrison at Drewry's Bluff saved Richmond from attack by Union forces, once by driving off the Monitor, along with several gunboats attempting to come up the river. Drewry's Bluff was also the location of the Confederate Naval Academy and Marine Corps Camp of Instruction.

The Federals called Drewry's Bluff by a code name, Fort Darling, which seems to have stuck, although the Confederates never used it. The fort was never captured during the war, but it was occupied by Union troops for a period afterward.

The paths are firm, but steep in places. Handicapped visitors may require help to get about even at the upper levels. We recommend taking the 1/2 mile historic loop trail, which provides a fascinating self-guided interpretive walk through the fort. As in the other Battlefield Parks, it is important to stay on the trails to avoid causing erosion on the earthworks.

A river overlook platform affords a fine view up and down the James, with a diorama and audio program that help to explain its strategic importance. On summer weekends living history exhibits include uniformed soldiers acting the parts of Confederate troops guarding the fort, adding color and atmosphere.

The 1/4 mile nature trail (1/2 mile round trip) through a little glade down to the river is very steep and stepped in places. The going may be a little difficult, but for

Drewry's Bluff/Fort Darling

visitors who don't mind, the scenery is worth it. The trail ends at a little beach, where troops and supplies were once brought to the fort. Local fishermen use it today.

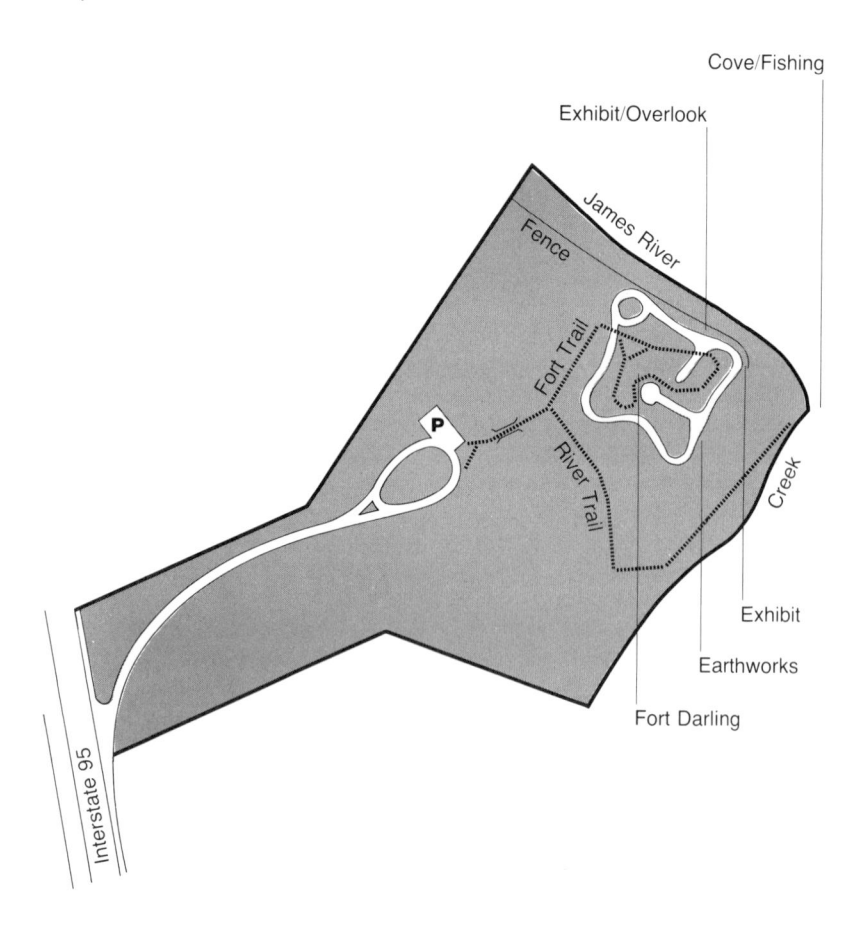

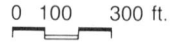

Petersburg National Battlefield

(1,531 Acres)

Located in northeast Petersburg on the west side of Fort Lee. Access is from East Washington Street (State Route 36); look for the entrance sign. From Interstate 95, take Exit 3 to Route 36 and travel east.

Established in 1926, this beautiful and fascinating park preserves a major portion of the Civil War Battlefield where Grant's army relentlessly sought to lay siege to Petersburg and capture the city. The series of battles associated with these attacks is known as the Campaign for Petersburg, which lasted 9-1/2 months and cost 70,000 lives—42,000 on the Union side, and 28,000 to the Confederate Army.

After abandoning at least temporarily his plan to capture Richmond in 1864, (see Cold Harbor/Fort Harrison Battlefield Parks), Grant moved his army south of the James River to capture Petersburg first. Poor timing on Grant's part, however, allowed Lee's army to shift troops south and reinforce the Dimmock Line (fortifications built around Petersburg between 1862-63).

Unable to penetrate Confederate lines, Grant was faced with a deadlock and shifted strategies, attempting to cut rail lines into the city, and thereby strangle Confederate supply lines. Because all rail lines leading into Petersburg from the south, east, and west converged into one railroad serving as Richmond's main supply artery, the capture of Petersburg was necessary to accomplish the fall of Richmond.

Soldiers' Quarters Reconstruction - Petersburg National Battlefield

Although he was successful in cutting two rail lines in 1864, the city did not fall, and the lengthy and bloody campaign consisting of a series of battles primarily to the south and west of the city began. This period is also known as the Siege of Petersburg. After 9-1/2 months Lee was forced to retreat westward on April 3, 1865, and Petersburg was captured.

The park preserves many of the forts and historic sites associated with the siege operations, both within the park proper and along a sixteen mile self-guided auto tour which interprets a number of smaller forts, batteries, and battlefields south and west of Petersburg.

Time and attention have been kind to the land, once so torn. The open rolling terrain, now in grass, is important from a historical perspective, representing the farm fields where soldiers lived and fought over the months. The woods that were cut during the siege have been restored, along with several pretty creeks that meander through the property.

Be sure to stop at the attractive Visitor Center located a short distance from the entrance. A 17-minute orientation map program is very helpful to an understanding of the history of the park, and courteous Park Service personnel are on hand to answer questions and offer suggestions about the self-guided (drive-and-park) historical tour.

Tour pamphlets with maps amplify the information on markers and give a good over-all perpective, relating the sites to one another. Be careful to take in everything you wish to see the first time, as the 4-mile road only goes one way, and you must exit on U.S. Route 301 (Crater Road) and drive back to the entrance on East Washington if you decide to return to any point along the way.

Park tour stops offer fascinating glimpses into a tragic episode in American history. A short walk from the Visitor Center is the Battery 5 Trail, where "the Dictator," a 13 inch seacoast mortar, lobbed 200 pound shells into Petersburg, only 2.5 miles away. (To see a battered iron church pillar, among other beautifully presented exhibits on life during the siege, visit the Siege Museum in Petersburg.)

Most of the stops along the tour feature audio-visual interpretations of the ruins and reconstructions. Union Camp, stop 3, features an authentically restored trench line with dugout shelters, a wooden fraise or obstacle (made of pointed pickets), and, from mid-June to mid-August, a sutler store displaying the items sold to soldiers - tin cups, Bibles, tobacco, and the like. You can buy a cup of cool apple cider here, just as the soldiers did on steaming summer days during the siege.

Living history programs held during the summer season, with young soldiers in authentic wool uniforms going about their daily life in the camp, make it easier to imagine how it was in those days, and to sympathize with the people caught up in the war, on both sides. Fort Stedman (stop 5) was the target of Lee's final and unsuccessful effort to relieve the encircling siege lines just prior to his retreat to Appomattox. Summer programs here include a cannon and mortar demonstration.

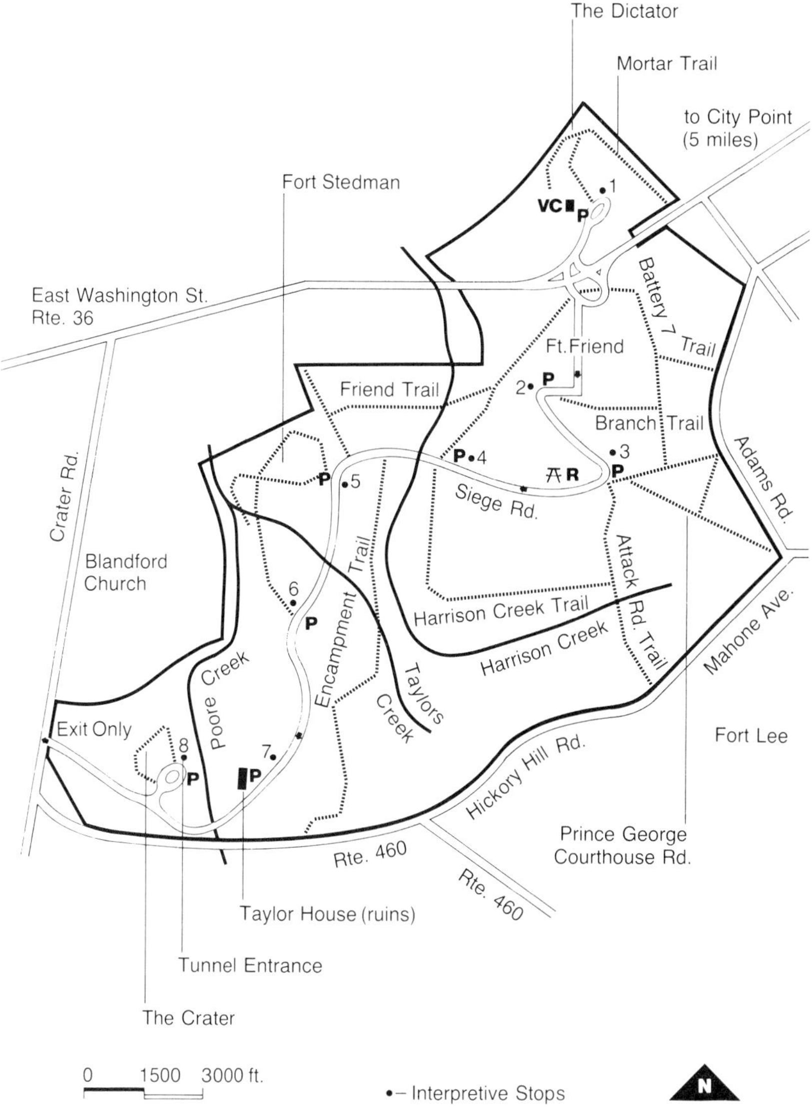
The Dictator
Mortar Trail
to City Point
(5 miles)
Fort Stedman
1
VC
P
East Washington St.
Rte. 36
Battery 7 Trail
Ft. Friend
Friend Trail
2
P
Branch Trail
Crater Rd.
P
4
3
P
5
Siege Rd.
R
P
Adams Rd.
Blandford
Church
Attack Rd. Trail
Encampment Trail
6
Harrison Creek Trail
P
Mahone Ave.
Harrison Creek
Poore Creek
Taylors
Creek
Creek
Exit Only
Fort Lee
8
7
P
P
Hickory Hill Rd.
Prince George
Courthouse Rd.
Rte. 460
Rte. 460
Taylor House (ruins)
Tunnel Entrance
The Crater
0
1500
3000 ft.
•– Interpretive Stops
N

Perhaps the most fascinating stop is the site of the Battle of the Crater, so much more understandable when seen. The siege had just begun when troops of the 48th Pennsylvania Regiment, coal miners by trade, conceived a plan to dig a tunnel under a Confederate fort known as Elliott's Salient, and blow it up with four tons of gun powder. After the explosion, Union troops were to rush through the gap and hold it for the main body of General Burnside's IX Corps to pass through and capture the city.

A black division of infantry was selected and trained to lead the assault, but the Union high command decided against using them for fear that if anything went wrong, they would be criticized for sacrificing black troops. General Burnside was forced to select an unprepared white division to lead the assault. The result was a series of blunders and a Union defeat. Union soldiers were trapped in the Crater and subjected to a heavy Confederate bombardment. Union casualties totalled 4,000, Confederate casualties, 1,500. The Confederate defenses were restored, and siege operations would grind on for another eight months. Today the tunnel and crater remains can still be seen.

Aside from its historic importance, the park includes several miles of nature trails and a pleasant picnic area with tables, grills, and restrooms, all well maintained. Jogging and biking are allowed along the main road and nature trails, but not on the historic paths. Paved paths and restrooms have been designed with handicapped visitors in mind.

While you are in the vicinity, visit old Blandford Church (circa 1735) and Interpretation Center adjacent to the Battlefield Park. The church was used as a field hospital during the war and later restored as a Confederate shrine honoring the 30,000 soldiers buried in the churchyard. Fifteen stained glass windows designed by Louis Tiffany are dedicated to the fallen from each of the Confederate States.

If time permits, before leaving the area, plan to also visit the City Point Unit in Hopewell. City Point was Grant's headquarters and logistical center during the Campaign for Petersburg. This small unit of the Petersburg National Battlefield, acquired in 1979, is another beautiful and fascinating area, which can easily be seen in an hour.

Living History Re-enactment - Petersburg National Battlefield

City Point Unit of the Petersburg National Battlefield

(13.5 Acres)

From Route 10 in Hopewell take West Main Street, at the second light south of the bridge, east to Cedar Lane. (West Main becomes Appomattox Road along the way.) Turn left on Cedar, and drive to the end of the road.

Situated high on a promontory overlooking the confluence of the Appomattox and James Rivers, peaceful Appomattox Manor, ancestral home of the Eppes family, was thrust into the Civil War in 1864, when it became the logistical center of the Campaign for Petersburg. General Grant also established his headquarters on the Manor property, from which he directed the strategy of all Union armies, between June, 1864 and the fall of Petersburg in April, 1865.

Before the Civil War began, City Point, a little hamlet founded in 1613, was mainly important for its port on the James where the river was wide enough and deep enough for sailing vessels to maneuver. The City Point Railroad, one of the nation's first, built in 1838, extended from Petersburg to the City Point Wharf at the foot of the bluff, and although the roadbed had deteriorated, the facilities, coupled with its strategic location, made the area a perfect choice for a military logistical center. Food and supplies could be delivered by ships and carried to troops by rail and wagon roads, and soldiers and civilian workers could arrive and leave by water without risk of Confederate raids.

Under Grant's direction, City Point quickly became the site of the largest supply depot of the Civil War. The Construction Corps repaired the line, extended the railroad, and renamed it the City Point and Army Line, adding several sidings. 280 structures were built, including eight wharves (some of great size), a number of warehouses and barracks, bakeries, chapels, a post office, prison, hospital facilities for 10,000, and a telegraph communication center linking all segments of the Union Army with telegraph lines.

The record shows that for a few months City Point was one of the busiest seaports in the world; on an average day there were forty steamships, seventy-five sailing vessels, and one hundred barges tied up along the mile-long waterfront. Soldiers and civilian workers lived in tents and temporary huts, many of them crowded into the grounds of the Manor (the family having moved away for the duration).

General Grant moved his headquarters from Washington to City Point and took up residence in a small log cabin on the front lawn of the Manor, directing the Campaign of Petersburg from this location until it fell. (That he chose to live in an army built log cabin instead of the Manor shows his democratic character.) From these headquarters he was able to travel back and forth, as were many important visitors to City Point, including President Lincoln and members of his cabinet and

City Point 1864 - Courtesy of the National Park Service

Congress. After the capture of Petersburg he moved to the front for the final actions of the war. Less than two weeks later General Lee surrendered his army at Appomattox Court House.

Time has brought tremendous changes to City Point. After the war most of the structures built on the post were demolished and taken away by the federal government. Those that remained on the Manor grounds were removed by the Eppes family at their own expense. Only the Confederate earthworks remained. (Grant's log cabin was removed to Fairmont Park in Philadelphia and returned to its orginal site in 1981.)

The railroad and the piers are gone. Today the tree-lined shore at the foot of the bluff, where these structures used to be, has eroded so much that it is almost inundated at high tide. The small wharf area at the end of Pecan Avenue continued to be used for many years (during World War I this was an embarkation point for troops departing for France); however it too is gone today. Only a few tugboats tie up to the pilings that remain, and fishermen are its only visitors.

The City Point Unit of the Battlefield was purchased from the Eppes family in 1979, and includes Appomattox Manor and its grounds, which occupy the promontory and the narrow beach directly below it, about one-fourth the area of the Union post. (See the map.)

Today in this beautiful and tranquil setting it is almost impossible to imagine the concentrations of structures and people and the intense activities that took place here between 1864-1865. Thanks to the Eppes family, which owned the property for 344 years until its purchase by the Park Service, the Manor, grounds, and outbuildings have been preserved and look much as they did before the Union occupation.

Grant's Cabin - City Point

Park Service visitor facilities include a large parking lot, restrooms equipped for handicapped access, and gravelled paths. The Manor, built around 1763 with additions over the years, is now a Visitor Center - open daily from 8:30 - 4:30 - and headquarters for the Park Service staff. Three exhibit rooms contain family furnishings predating 1860.

Start with a visit to the Center; be sure to pick up the pamphlets interpreting the history of City Point from the time of its founding through the Civil War. Then walk about the grounds, take in the magnificent view of the Appomattox and James Rivers coming together, and imagine what City Point was like from colonial times through its fascinating Civil War history.

If time permits, consider taking the City Point Historic District Walking Tour, keyed to a pamphlet available at the Center. This takes in the rest of the area occupied by the post, and includes several 19th century historic sites and a pecan tree believed to be one of the largest and oldest in the country (circa 1675).

At low tide you can walk along the narrow beach below the bluff and see where the Appomattox River is cutting through the plain as it makes a right angle turn to join the James. The scarp or bluff is the result of this erosion over millions of years. Geological forces have created the landscape, which in turn has influenced history.

Index

Parks and Preserves
Abner Clay, 183
Appomattox Riverside, 237
Atwater, 248
Battery, 184
Battlefield Parks, National, 256
Beaver Dam, 260
Belle Isle, 152
Belmont, 220
Berberich/Fort Clifton, 246
Bryan, 127
Byrd, 130
Cannon Creek, 186
Capitol Square, 174
Carter Jones, 189
Charles City, 255
Chesapeake Nature Trail, 120
Cheswick, 221
Chickahominy Bluff, 258
Chickahominy Wildlife
  Management Area, 107
Chimborazo, 164
City Point, 278
Cold Harbor, 266
Crump, General/Meadow Farm, 223
Deep Run, 227
Dorey/Four Mile Creek, 229
Drewry's Bluff, 271
Echo Lake, 232
Ettrick, 207
Fleet Street Peninsula, 242
Forest Hill, 134
Fort Abbott, 249
Fort Brady, 268
Fort Clifton (See Berberich)
Fort Harrison, 268
Four Mile Creek, 229
Gaines Mill/Watt House, 262
Gamble's Hill, 176
Glen Lea (See Vawter Street)
Goyne, 208
Great Ship Lock, 166
Harrison, 252
Harrison Lake Fish Hatchery, 101
Harrowgate, 208
Henrico City, 212
Highland Park Plaza, 186
Hillside, 252
Hollywood Cemetery, 180

Huguenot, 209
Huguenot Woods, 159
Iron Bridge, 216
James River, 146
Jefferson, 169
Kanawha Plaza, 175
Lee, 243
Lewis Ginter Botanical Garden, 122
Libbie Hill, 170
Lombardy Triangle, 179
Malvern Hill, 264
Matoaca, 211
Maymont, 138
Meadow Farm (See Crump)
Meadow Triangle, 179
Monroe, 181
Monument Median, 179
North Bank, 154
Patrick Henry, 171
Petersburg National Battlefield, 273
Pine Camp, 187
Pocahontas State Forest, 111
Pocahontas State Park, 111
Pocosham, 190
Point of Rocks, 200
Pollard, 188
Pony Pasture, 155
Poor Farm, 250
Poplar Lawn, 245
Powhatan Hill, 172
Powhatan Wildlife Management Area, 117
Powhite, 192
Presquile National Wildlife Refuge, 104
Prince George, 253
Richmond National Battlefield Park, 256
Riverside (Hopewell), 248
Riverside (Richmond), 182
Robinson, 234
Rockwood, 204
Taylor's Hill, 173
Texas Avenue (See North Bank), 154
Vawter Street, 235
Virginia War Memorial, 177
Wayside, 252
Wayside Spring, 195
White Bank, 247
Williams Island, 162

282

Rivers. Lakes, Public Boat Landings and Canoe Launch Areas

Ancarrow Boat Landing, 77
Appomattox River, 78
Appomattox River Boat Launch, 78, 198
Beaver Lake, 111
Beaumont/Maidens Landing, 70
Berberich Park Boat Landing, 246
Bryan Park Lakes, 128
Byrd Park Lakes, 133
Cartersville Landing, 68
Chesdin, Lake, 93
Chickahominy Lake, 84
Chickahominy River, 83
Columbia Landing, 68
Crump Park Pond, 226
Deep Bottom Boat Landing, 77
Diascund Reservoir, 94
Dorey Park Lake, 230
Dutch Gap Boat Landing, 77
Echo Lake, 232
Harrison Lake, 102
Huguenot Canoe Launch Area, 72
Intermediate Terminal, 76
James River, 68, 143
James River Park Main Section Canoe Launch Area, 74
Lester Manor Landing, 90
Little River, 88
Morris Creek, 84, 110
Morris Creek Landing, 84, 110
North Anna River, 86
Pamunkey River, 88
Pony Pasture Canoe Launch Area, 72
Powhatan Lakes, 118
South Anna River, 88
Swift Creek, 81
Swift Creek Lake, 114
Watkins Landing, 70
Wayside Pond, 252
Westview Landing, 69
White Bank Landing, 81, 247
Wilcox Lake, 243
Williams Island Portage, 72
York River, 86

About the Authors

Louise Burke is a widely known conservationist and writer, a graduate of the University of California, and a former instructor at the University of Oregon. She has long been active in civic and governmental affairs in Richmond. As Chairman of the Richmond City Planning Commission, she also represented the City on the Richmond Regional Planning District Commission for several years. A former Girl Scout leader, she is presently Secretary of the Commonwealth Girl Scout Council, and also serves on the Board of Directors of the Maymont (Park) Foundation.

Dr. Keith F. Ready, Associate Professor, Department of Recreation, Virginia Commonwealth University, teaches park planning and development and is a consultant to a number of park and recreation departments in the region. A graduate of Massachusetts State College, Salem, he received his master's degree from Miami University, Oxford, Ohio, and his doctorate from Michigan State University. His initial inventory of the region's parks and preserves was the forerunner of this Guide.